Murderers and Life Imprisonment

CONTAINMENT, TREATMENT, SAFETY AND RISK

Eric Cullen and Tim Newell

With a Foreword by Stephen Shaw

Contributions by David Wilson and Roland Woodward

WATERSIDE PRESS
WINCHESTER

Murderers and Life Imprisonment
CONTAINMENT, TREATMENT, SAFETY AND RISK

CONTENTS   Page

Murderers
and
Life Imprisonment

CC   SK

Eric (years
exper   senior
prison   :torate
resea   le has
been   nality
disor(ies in
prison   ity of
Birmi   iunity
prison   igton,
Staffc   d has
publis   ogical
theme

Tim   with
youn   e was
educa   after
gradu   f HM
Prisor   with
long-t   :m to
exerci   their
comm   had a
partic   :cts of
the in   lifers
for hi   nal.

Murderers and Life Imprisonment
CONTAINMENT, TREATMENT, SAFETY AND RISK

First published 1999 by
WATERSIDE PRESS
Domum Road
Winchester SO23 9NN
Telephone 01962 855567
Fax 01962 855567
email enquiries@watersidepress.co.uk
Web-site www.watersidepress.co.uk

Reprinted 2003

ISBN Paperback 1 872 870 56 2

Cataloguing-in-Publication Data A catalogue record for this book can be obtained from the British Library.

Printing and binding Antony Rowe Ltd, Eastbourne.

Cover design John Good Holbrook Ltd, Coventry. From an original painting by Eric Hood, former long-term prisoner, entitled 'Supressed Feelings' and accompanied by the following inscription:

> Suppressed feelings (headache)
> Anger with the damaged person, in my mind,
> My arms aglow with my needs, which show me . . .
> Security, of what love there is within me . . .
>
> A flame inside
> Holding my anger in,
> My hands portray the pressure . . .
> Of my mixed emotions . . .

Foreword

Stephen Shaw*

The life sentence is an Anglo-American enthusiasm. While this country may not begin to rival the United States either in its murder rate or in the size of its lifer population, we outstrip all of Western Europe in our use of life imprisonment. Indeed, to repeat a statistic which continues to amaze: Britain has more prisoners serving life sentences than the rest of Western Europe put together.

On present trends, the number of lifers—which has already passed 4,000—seems set to reach 6,000 or 7,000 by the middle years of the next decade.

Life sentence prisoners are now serving half as long again on average as they did in the 1970s. The number of lifers beginning their sentence exceeds the number released by a ratio of 3:1. And use of the life sentence has been extended under the Crime (Sentences) Act 1997 to include those convicted of a second, serious violent or sexual offence.

This book is, therefore, an extremely timely addition to Waterside's remarkable series or criminal justice texts. Eric Cullen and Tim Newell deserve the highest praise for the way in which they combine an authoritative account of the lifer system with a clear campaigning agenda, all illustrated with sensitive case-histories of individual lifers they have known.

There are two key elements to that campaigning agenda. First, we should follow the example of our European partners and establish the life sentence as the *maximum* not the mandatory penalty for murder. Second, the depoliticised system of tariff-setting and release procedures which apply to discretionary lifers (and to 'two strikes' lifers) should be extended to all those upon whom a sentence of life imprisonment is imposed. It is an outrage that the Home Secretary (or his junior Minister) should play any part in determining how long an individual prisoner should spend in prison. The case for a separation of powers between judiciary and executive is overwhelming.

My own feeling is that a third issue also merits attention: the very definition of murder. Public sentiment may be more sympathetic here. The conviction for murder—and subsequent life sentence—for those guilty of so-called mercy-killings is not something people at large regard as just. Similarly, the conviction of women who are driven to kill husbands or partners who have abused them for years. Likewise, the convictions of young soldiers placed in positions of extreme danger and stress in Northern Ireland. It is true that such convictions are sometimes reduced from murder to manslaughter, but the achievement of such an outcome is all too often a lottery.

Within the prison system, life sentence prisoners present a contradictory picture. Frequently older than the mainstream population, and with much less custodial experience, lifers are seen by many prison governors as a stabilising force. Their disciplinary records are certainly much better than those of the prison population as a whole. On the other hand, it seems around half of all life sentence prisoners suffer from some form of psychiatric vulnerability, many having been abused or brought up in dysfunctional family settings.

What most distinguishes lifers is the degree to which their sentences are planned, with the aim of reducing risk of re-offending on release. Recent research by the Prison Reform Trust,[1] and the thematic review conducted jointly by the Chief Inspectors of Prisons and Probation, has shown that, in practice, the process of managing a life sentence can be very hit and miss. And I share the view of this book that to expect all lifers to follow a similar 'career' through the prison system, no matter what their individual circumstances, is neither necessary nor desirable. However, judged by outcomes, there is a happier story to tell. The level of reconviction of released life sentence prisoners is low and declining. Reconvictions for further grave offences are statistically tiny, albeit even one such case can occasion public alarm and anger.

Most murderers kill someone they know (although am I alone in finding repellent the phrase 'domestic murderer'?). After serving their 'tariff' (another word with which we could sensibly dispense), they pose little or no continuing risk to the public. The horror of their crimes can never be undone. But as Cullen and Newell remind us, treated with dignity, courtesy and respect, almost all lifers can lead a reasonably responsible life in custody—and throughout what is usually a much longer period subsequent to their release on licence.

* **Stephen Shaw** is Director of the Prison Reform Trust

---

[1] Clare Sparks, *Lifers' Views of the Lifer System: Policy Versus Practice*, Prison Reform Trust, 1998

Preface

In the criminal justice system of the United Kingdom, there are no more serious or emotive issues than those of murder and life imprisonment. Given that we imprison more people for life than the rest of Western Europe combined, there would presumably be a sense of disquiet and concern over this aspect of modern British life. Do the general public know that the rate of imprisonment for life is growing faster than for any other group of offenders, and that it has doubled in ten years? Some of the most momentous legislative and executive decisions and informed debates regarding procedures for dealing with murderers and discretionary lifers have occurred in the past 15 years, yet the public remain largely oblivious. This book is intended to address these concerns—the combination of record increases in the levels of lifer imprisonment and of the response of successive governments to these events—and to give focus to the implications for the UK if, as is possible, patterns emulate the growth witnessed in America over the same period.

Chapter 1 summarises the scale of the problem in view of record rates of murder and life imprisonment in England and Wales and contrasts this with Western Europe and America. *Chapter 2* reviews past efforts to organize murderers into types, some of the authors' experience of murderers and discretionary lifers, and gives sample accounts of individual lifer's lives and crimes. *Chapter 3* is contributed by Dr David Wilson of the University of Central England and addresses the contentious, but compelling arguments surrounding those prisoners who continue to protest their innocence well into their life sentences even at the risk of prolonging that imprisonment indefinitely, and of the ethical issues this occasions for all concerned.

Chapter 4 explores a wide range of effects of life imprisonment for both mandatory and discretionary lifers, the stages of a sentence, how HM Prison Service uses lifers within its regimes, and gives an overview of the skills and competencies staff require to be, or to become, effective in helping and managing this population. *Chapter 5* summarises the most extensive research available on the introduction of Discretionary Lifer Panels for considering the release of such prisoners following the Criminal Justice Act 1991. *Chapter 6* by Roland Woodward addresses the abiding difficulties in assessing risk on release and degrees of dangerousness for lifers, reviewing the research on previous efforts and reflecting on the practical and ethical issues involved.

Chapter 7 looks beyond the current dynamics to the wider questions of the ethics of life imprisonment as punishment, the political nature of executive decision-making, and current proposals to extend life imprisonment to violent and sexual repeat offenders.

Finally, in *Chapter 8,* we provide a summary of our main findings and offer some practical recommendations for improvements in the effective management of this uniquely challenging group of criminals.

Throughout the text we have tried to illustrate our comments with first-hand accounts: those which stem from our work as practitioners in prisons during which we have been in constant daily contact with murderers and other serious offenders; and those of the lifers themselves whose views, perspectives and explanations we have relied on extensively in certain parts of the book, particularly *Chapter 2* and *Appendix A.* We hope that the result will be of help to all people who come into contact with prisons and life sentence prisoners and to a wide range of people who wish to understand the nature of much serious offending, the kind of people involved and the methods which we believe are most likely to lead to justifiable periods of containment, the best corrective treatment strategies, the highest levels of public safety and the lowest levels of risk when life sentence prisoners are released—as virtually all of them will be, sooner or later.

Acknowledgements

Our thanks go to the many lifers, and the staff who look after them, with whom we've worked and who have informed and enlightened us along the way. Particular thanks also to our wives Margaret and Ann who have endured far too many hours of book widowhood over the past two years and to whom we promise not to re-offend! Thanks also to Stephen Shaw, Clare Sparks and colleagues at the Prison Reform Trust for access to their library and references, and to the Prison Service Lifer Section for their support and information. We acknowledges the rewarding and challenging stimulus of working with Dr Roger Sapsford of the Open University and Professor Philip Bean of Loughborough University during our doctorate research. We are indebted to Bryan Gibson at Waterside Press for his publishing expertise and firm shaping of the manuscript into something resembling commercial viability.

A particular thanks to Alex Alexandrowicz and other, unnamed, lifers who contributed their own stories—an especially powerful aspect. Our final debt of thanks is to Grendon Underwood Therapeutic Community Prison, a uniquely positive place which has probably had the single most influential effect on causing this book to be written. It was at Grendon that we both became most painfully aware of the devastation wrought by those who take lives and are imprisoned indefinitely for it. It was there where we both did our doctorate work. It is there, with uniquely abiding power, where murderers and other lifers really can learn to live 'good and useful lives'.

Eric Cullen and **Tim Newell**, January 1999

CHAPTER 1

The Scale and Nature of the Problem

This chapter plots the progress of national policy towards people who kill or are otherwise determined to require a life sentence. The origins of the current levels of lifer numbers and concomitant issues of policy spring from the abolition of the death penalty. While of the two groups of lifers, mandatory and discretionary, it was those for whom a life sentence was made compulsory who obviously benefited most, the irony is that the numbers of discretionary lifers, and the average time in prison they served, went up and up without there being any appreciable change in the type of crimes they were committing. What is the scale of the problem in terms of numbers of offenders? How many are imprisoned for life? What do exceptional cases tell us and how long do lifers actually stay inside?

How many people commit murder in England and Wales? How often does it happen? How high is the risk of someone being killed in this way? What sort of person does it and who is most likely to be a victim? How do we compare to European and American figures? There can be no starker introduction to the questions of murder than to offer a few comparisons between the figures for the United Kingdom and those for the undisputed murder capital of the western world, the United States.

I. MURDER

HOW OFTEN DOES IT HAPPEN?

Stone (1997) tells us that 3,294 people were indicted for murder in England and Wales in the five years from 1989-1993 inclusive, of whom 2,376 were subsequently convicted of homicide (72%), with another 984 (30%) convicted of manslaughter.

In 1991, in England and Wales, *250 murders* were prosecuted for which a guilty verdict was delivered. It is reasonable to assume that this represents the overwhelming majority of murders which actually occurred as murder is the crime with the highest detection and conviction rates (although we must allow for a small number of offences where no-one was found guilty and a presumably even smaller number which remained either undetected or unprosecuted). The total population of the United Kingdom in 1991 was approximately 55 million, with England and Wales accounting for over 90% of the total, i.e. nearly 50 million people. This means a risk of being a murder victim of roughly *one in 200,000*.

In America in 1991, there were *more* than 250 murders in *each* of 25 of the 50 states and a total of *23,674 murders in total.* Given a total population of approximately 270 million, this works out at a risk rate of being a murder victim, again roughly, of *one in 10,000.* In other words, an American is 20 times more likely to be murdered than an Englishman (or Welshman).

Another comparison which may shock but which serves to illustrate the point is that there were more murders in New York City *in one day* in 1991 (17) than in any two weeks in the whole of the UK. More recently, Currie (1998) in *Crime and Punishment in America,* calculated that 'by the mid-1990s, a young American male was 37 times as likely to die by deliberate violence as his English counterpart' and 26 times as likely as a young Frenchman and 60 times as likely as a young Japanese.

Why such remarkable differences? Are Americans simply a far more violent people by nature? Does the American lifestyle lend itself in some complex way to the resolution of differences by lethal force or are there other explanations of varying degrees of clarity? Certainly most of us would immediately mention guns as a major contributing factor and we could well be right. Over a third of all homicides (a term used interchangeably with *murder* in the USA) involved the use of some form of firearm. In Britain, fewer than 10% of all murders are committed by shooting. Of the total population of murderers imprisoned in England and Wales at the end of 1990 (2,685), only 239 (9%) used firearms. The most common method in the UK was 'a sharp instrument', which accounted for over 1,000 (38%) of the total number of offences. The difference in lethality of method is obvious and this must be a major factor. Other factors which appear to contribute to the higher rates include race, the prevalence of alcohol and drugs and societal attitudes to self-defence.

WHO ARE THE MURDERERS?

In Britain, the most common defining characteristics of murderers (i.e. what they are most likely to be) are: unmarried; white; male; in their twenties or thirties. He (as indicated most murderers are men) is less likely to have been in prison than other offenders but still significantly more likely than the general male population. He will probably—by odds of over three to one—have killed someone he knows, in a situation of jealousy, revenge, anger or all three. These profile figures are extracted from a submission from S2 Division of the Home Office to the House of Lords Select Committee on Murder and Life Imprisonment, 1989.

Relationship to the victim and other recurring features

Most murderers have killed someone they know, usually a wife, girlfriend or close family member. The great majority, over 90%, have only taken one life and that was determined as much by the circumstances as by the personality of the offender. Most murderers have less criminal lifestyles than other offenders—as measured by the total number of crimes for which they have been convicted and the age at the onset of their criminal activity. A significantly higher percentage of lifers than non-lifers had never been to prison prior to their current sentence.

If we look at a representative sample of lifers (73) serving sentences in 1992 the distribution by offence looks like this:

- **Murder** = 61 (83%)
- **Attempted murder/manslaughter** = 10 (14%)
- **Sex Offence** = 0
- **Arson** = 1
- **Other** = 1

These 73 lifers had a total of 80 victims. *Table 2* indicates the relationship of the victims to the offenders.

Table 1: Relationship between Murderers and Victims (N = 80)

Relationship	Number of Cases (%)
Friend/acquaintance	21 (26%)
Wife/cohabitee	17 (21%)
Child (own or cohabitee's)	13 (16%)
Girlfriend/lover	11 (14%)
Sexual rival	6 (8%)
Other relation	4 (5%)
Boyfriend	3 (4%)
Stranger	5 (6%)
Total:	80 (100%)

A sample of 66 lifers from the three Main Centre prisons dealing with lifers in England and Wales in 1991 were given a questionnaire about:

(a) their attitudes to their crimes;
(b) their families;
(c) their friends, various institutions (e.g. school);
(d) the extent to which they felt integrated into society or alienated from it; and
(e) their attitudes to imprisonment.

Over 90% (60) of the sample had been convicted of murder. The same questionnaire was given to a sample of non-lifer prisoners (N = 44) and where relevant, the contrasts between the groups will be included in this summary of the findings.

Most of the murderers were 16 years of age or older when they first committed a crime, contrasted with an average age of just over 14 for the non-murderers. Fewer than one in three thought of themselves as a criminal, regardless of the nature of their crimes, although the overwhelming majority expressed regret for their offending. Only half of the murderers recalled happy family backgrounds and there were frequent accounts of violence and/or serious arguing in almost a third of the lifer cases. This question evoked many extensive and frequently moving accounts of childhoods marred by the death of one or both parents, divorce, alcoholism (almost always on the part of the fathers), related aggression or abuse, and of having been placed in the care of a local authority. Only just over a third (38%) of the lifers said their parents were still together.

When asked about their relationships with friends and with their school, the murderers' friends were less likely to have committed crimes than the friends of the non-murderers. They were more likely to say that they had done things (apart from their crimes) which they felt were wrong (42% compared to 29% for non-lifers), but were less likely to have been put into the care of local authorities. Although a high proportion (62% of both samples) said they felt alienated from society, the majority of lifers made positive comments about the need for society to have rules and regulations (63% compared to only 33% of the non-lifers). It should be noted that the questionnaires were completed anonymously and that all those invited to participate were free to decline.

The Home Office Statistics Department, S2, provided the most detailed analyses of the entire lifer population for the first named author's doctorate research. *Table 2* opposite gives a complete analysis of the 2,900 lifers in England and Wales as of 31 December 1990 in terms of the circumstances and method used for murder and manslaughter.

The information revealed in the table is very far removed from the popular perception of who murderers are, of how they commit their crimes. 'True life' crime programmes such as Crimewatch UK, or Crime Stoppers, inevitably concentrate on murders which involve atypical—classically stronger—murders, whereby the offender and victim have never previously met, and where the crime itself is committed in a public as opposed to a private place. These scenarios obviously make for better TV, but also create a 'Crimewatch' mentality in the minds of the viewers which is frankly at odds with the reality of murder in the UK. That reality is that the people most at risk of murder are children under the age of 12 months.

Table 2: Lifer Population—Murder and Manslaughter:
Circumstances and Methods of Offence.

CIRCUMSTANCES	Murder	Manslaughter	METHOD	Murder	Manslaughter
Rage or quarrel	813	70	Sharp instrument	1027	7
During theft	553	25	Strangulation	481	46
Jealousy	318	22	Blunt instrument	418	47
Sexual-Pathological	258	32	Kick or kill	317	18
Family stress	70	4	Shooting	239	6
Provocation	67	5	Suffocation	55	2
For other gain	57	3	Drowning	33	5
Baby battering	56	4	Arson causing death	30	11
Contract conspiracy	38	0	Burning-Scalding	16	0
Motiveless	29	0	Explosion	12	0
Informant	27	4	Struck by motor	10	1
Witness	19	0	Poisoning	9	1
Terrorist—IRA, NI	16	0	Exhaust fumes	7	2
Arson	15	6	Causing to kill	7	1
Resisting Arrest	15	0			
Reckless Act			Others		
Motor, drugs, other	14	0	Arson after killing	4	
Family feud	10	0	Negligence	3	
			Various	7	
Others			Not known	10	
Political		9			
Ritual killing		8			
Mercy killing		4			
Punishment of child		6			
Self-preservation		5			
Various		36			
Not known		180			

HOMICIDE IN AMERICA

There have been many books and articles on American murder and life imprisonment. An extensive compilation of both theories and patterns of homicides was provided by Wilson (Ed.) in *Homicide: The Victim/Offender Connection* (1993). Many current academic theoreticians combine three explanations:

(a) the interaction itself, seen as a series of escalatory moves or transactions;

(b) a culture or subculture that encourages the use of force in interpersonal relations; and/or

(c) structural or societal forces such as a lack of opportunity, poverty and institutional racism which create frustrations and limit alternatives to violence.

Luckenbill and Doyle (1989) combined these factors to develop a 'cultural model' of violence, labelling the three perspectives as 'naming, blaming and claiming' (whatever that means). They summarised criminal homicides in America as a progression where:

> It follows that . . . individuals who occupy positions featuring high rates of violence would be more disputatious and aggressive than individuals who occupy other positions when a negative outcome involves an equal's attack on the self in a public setting than when it does not.

> Further, young adults, males, blacks, lower-income persons, and urban and Southern residents are more likely than their respective counterparts to be disputatious and aggressive when a negative outcome bears on a personal attribute, stems from a harm-doer who shares the victim's status, and occurs in public than when it does not.

As far as can be guessed, this mind-numbingly tautological excerpt translates as:

> . . . poor southern city-dwelling young adult black males are most likely to be aggressive and to be so towards other poor Southern city-dwelling young adult black males.

Another delightfully objective chapter, by Wilson, asserts that

> . . . deaths are wrongful only when they are dangerous to the stability of the social system.

This appears in a passage about the patriarchal dominance of women in American society being part of a current trend towards the wider criminalisation of abortion (which she considers a form of homicide).

Saltzman and Mercy summarise research relating to 27 fatal and 150 non-fatal incidents—and come to support Finkelhor's cluster of commonalties:

- abuse gravitates toward relationships of greatest power differential, i.e. is more likely when one partner's power is far in excess of the other.
- abuse is often a response to a perceived powerlessness on the part of the abuser.
- victims tend to respond in similar ways, often blaming themselves
- abuse appears to be more prevalent in lower socio-economic strata; and
- ambiguity about the boundary between acceptable behaviour and abuse, 'normative boundaries', is common to different forms of abuse.

As with the data in the UK, a review of national American homicide figures between 1966 and 1988 (Rojek and Williams), found that homicides between intimates or acquaintances were most often triggered by sudden violent arguments over relatively trivial matters or 'romantic entanglements', while homicides between strangers tended to be more property-oriented and rational.

Riedel and Przybylski, reviewing the field concerning stranger murderers found that:

... while most murders are intraracial, stranger murders involve black offenders and white victims more than others, regardless if the motive is exploitative or confrontational.

Again, with a racial theme, Jenkins found that: 'Among those arrested for murder or manslaughter, blacks usually comprise between 40 and 50 per cent while representing only approximately 15% of the population nationally'.

It seems clear that the frequency of violent crimes in general, and homicides in particular in the USA are far higher than in the UK. Equally clear is that there are significant societal, cultural, racial and attitudinal differences to the phenomenon as well as an approach to the possession of firearms which seems to account for the greatest single proportion of violent deaths, a fact which we in Britain must heed. It seems equally clear that public misperceptions of the nature of murder and other violent crimes in the United Kingdom are influencing political executive decisions about the imprisonment and release of murderers in a highly punitive and ultimately unjust manner.

II. LIFE IMPRISONMENT IN THE UK

The Homicide Act 1957 created a mandatory life sentence for certain types of murder and the Murder (Abolition of the Death Penalty) Act 1965 changed the nature and significance of life imprisonment, ensuring that the number of those so imprisoned would rise significantly in each ensuing year. The history of prison policy for lifers must therefore be divided into pre and post-abolition phases.

During the prolonged debate concerning whether or not to repeal the death penalty,[1] one of the key issues was the argument that letting murderers live was unsafe as their behaviour inside prison would be particularly troublesome. Koestler and Rolph (1961) quoted the Royal Commission of 1959:

---

[1] For a comprehensive review, see Brian P Block and John Hostettler, *Hanging in the Balance: A History of the Abolition of Capital Punishment in Britain*, Waterside Press, 1997.

There is a popular belief that prisoners serving a life sentence after conviction of murder form a specifically troublesome and dangerous class. This is not so.

The Commission referred to evidence by a former Governor and Chair of the Panel of prison governors:

> Taking murderers as a class, there are a considerable number who are first offenders and who are not people of criminal tendencies . . . Previous to that they were law-abiding citizens and their general tenor of life is still law-abiding . . .

The authors provided considerable evidence to support the impression that murderers were at a very low risk of subsequent violent offending, predicting that:

> . . . the cessation of the Death Penalty would simply mean that on an average five persons per year would be added to the British prison population.

Unfortunately, their predictions were gross underestimates. In 1997, nearly 300 people were sentenced to life imprisonment, pushing the total so imprisoned near to the 4,000 mark, another all-time record. A Home Office report in 1965—*Home Office: Study Group on Life Imprisonment* (unpublished, 1965)—on the likely consequences of the Homicide Act 1957 and of the abolition of capital punishment, attempted to project the likely increase over the then total of 300 lifers, concluding:

> It is certain that there will be some increase until the discharge of prisoners begins to balance reception . . . an estimate of 600 . . . may be excessive.

This actuarial aberration was further compounded by the assertion that:

> . . . there was a need to make an early decision about the probable length of sentence so that proper diagnoses would lead to abandoning the pretence that "all their charges will be released at a time which is reasonably close to the average of nine years".

In a refreshing—and rare—display of candour they opined:

> . . . after a period of nine years imprisonment, the only purposes which can be served by further imprisonment are the protection of the public or the avoidance of a further expression of public indignation concerning the particular offender.

This group, composed of senior prison administrators and Governors, the Director of Prison Medical Services and Regional Psychologists, reserved perhaps their most critical comments for the then current treatment of under-aged lifers:

> The present situation for dealing with adolescent prisoners subject to life imprisonment can only be described as crippling. The fact that some of them survive in order to lead normal and useful lives suggest that they had a basic resilience which sustains them in spite of the attacks made upon it by the present form of incarceration.

By 1969, the Prison Service had become conscious of the pressures being exerted by the growing life sentence population (then standing at 700) and determined that a review of long-term policy for the management of this (lifer) population must be included among Prison Department priorities. At a conference in 1973, senior administrators enumerated seven principles to inform official policy, which formed the basis of the official authority, called Home Office Circular Instruction 39 of 1974, for the next 15 years. This was replaced by another instruction in 1989 and, finally (to date) by the latest lifer policy statement, the *Lifer Manual* of 1995. Two useful and up-to-date publications about lifers are the Prisoners' Information Book, Life Sentenced Prisoners 'LIFERS' (1998) produced cooperatively by HM Prison Service and the Prison Reform Trust, and Prisoners' Views of the Lifer System—Policy Vs Reality (1998) by Clare Sparks, again published by the Prison Reform Trust as part of its Prisoners' Advice Service. The former answers questions commonly asked by lifers about their status within the system and the latter reports results of two studies, the first summarising interviews with 89 lifers currently serving sentences, the second a Prisoners' Advice questionnaire-base study of 116 male lifers.

NUMBERS AND PLACES

An independent survey by the Quaker Council for European Affairs, entitled *A Fair Deal for Lifers* (1990) found that the number of lifers in England, Wales and Scotland—3,054 at that time—exceeded the combined figure for all other Western European countries (excluding Switzerland, Malta, San Marino and Liechtenstein!). If we add the figures for Northern Ireland, the total of 3,503 compared at that time with 2,688 for *all* other countries of Western Europe (whose combined populations are roughly six times that of the UK). Life imprisonment is

- the *mandatory* sentence for murder committed by someone aged 21 or over;
- a *discretionary* maximum sentence for a number of other serious offences including manslaughter, robbery, arson, rape, kidnapping

and causing an explosion. The discretionary life sentence is described in *Chapter 5*.

It is also, and under relatively novel provisions:

- the *mandatory* sentence for certain offences under the 'two strikes' provisions of the Crime (Sentences) Act 1997: see *Two Strikes and You're In* at the end of this chapter.

If an offender is aged between 10 and 17 at the time of the offence, he or she may be ordered to be detained 'during Her Majesty's Pleasure' under section 53(1) Children and Young Persons Act 1933. Detention for life is also available to the courts for people under 18 convicted of offences other than murder which, in the case of an adult, attract a discretionary life sentence (Section 53(2)). Finally, for offenders between 18 and 21, life sentences may be imposed under section 8(1) and (2) Criminal Justice Act 1982.

The political nature of mandatory life sentences

Ever since the abolition of the death penalty when in 1965 the mandatory sentence of life for murder was first introduced there has been a close political involvement in the determination about the nature of the detention and the length of sentence for those so sentenced. There has been much discussion and concern that the judge has no discretion in cases of murder. The differences between the many cases of murder which are tried cannot be reflected by the judge in the sentence, so that the mercy killing of a loved one cannot be differentiated from a shooting carried out in the process of a robbery. There has thus been a considerable movement towards the abolition of the mandatory nature of the sentence for murder both from independent review bodies who have looked closely at the issue as well as the Home Affairs Committee. Resistance to this change however has always come from Governments (of different political persuasions) who have insisted that the unique nature of the offence justifies the severest sentence available.

As well as challenging the mandatory nature of the sentence there has been great concern about the continuing involvement of the executive in the determination about the length of sentence the lifer should serve. The Home Secretary may order the release of a life sentenced prisoner after he has been recommended by the Parole Board, which can be seen, in this context, as a judicial tribunal. The Home Secretary has already had a considerable say in the tariff—the minimum punitive element of the sentence which has to be served before the element of risk comes into play for consideration for release. It is only when this has been exhausted that the case is considered by the Parole Board. The Home Secretary does not have to accept the recommendation of the Parole Board that the lifer is ready for release. There are regular numbers each year which the Home Secretary does not accept for release.

The basis of these decisions is very controversial. There are three concerns which can effect the decision—the length of time necessary for retribution and deterrence—whether it is considered safe to release the lifer and—'the public acceptability of early release'.

'The system confers on a politician decisions that are by their very nature sentencing decisions. This means that considerations of politics rather than justice may determine the length of offenders' detention. Politics often means vote catching'. These words of Lord Lane, Lord Chief Justice, who chaired a committee reviewing the mandatory sentence reflect the concern about politicians taking such decisions. The movement towards considering the release of all lifers through the system of judicial tribunals as reflected in the Discretionary Lifer Panels (*Chapter 5*) is gathering pace with each judicial review tending to move the balance from the executive to the judicial.

PROFILE OF THE LIFER POPULATION

On 28 February 1998, there were 3,873 people serving life sentences in England and Wales, an increase of nearly 35% from December 1995 and more than double the total for 1987. By the time this book is published, the figure will exceed 4,000. Every year, roughly 2.5 times as many lifers are received into prison as are released. Over 90% of all lifers are *adult men*, with almost 5% being young males and most of the rest adult women. The young male population of lifers is growing at the fastest rate.

Almost 90% of all lifers were found guilty of murder or manslaughter, with the next highest life sentence category being rape. The length of time served by released lifers is increasing and has done so regularly for most of the past 20 years. The average time served in 1979 was 9.1 years; by 1989 had gone up to 12 years and in 1997 was just over 14 years, an increase of 55%. Stone (1997) found that sentence lengths have been increasing for some time. In 1975, *only 9.5%* of the then lifer population had been inside for ten years or more, compared with *32.3% in 1995*. Further, he noted that 405 (12%) of all lifers in 1995 had been imprisoned already for over 15 years and, critically, that a *higher percentage of discretionary lifers serve longer sentences than of mandatory lifers*, with 17.4% of the former group serving over 15 years compared to only 11% of the latter! It is interesting to contrast this with Government assertions to the effect that the mandatory sentence must be retained to signal that the crimes involved are the most heinous. Apparently, the worst crimes do not necessarily occasion the longest sentences.

There are lifers in 64 prison establishments in England and Wales: five 'Main Centres' for lifers—Brixton, Gartree, Wakefield, Wormwood Scrubs and Durham (female); three Dispersals (holding Category A prisoners)—Frankland, Full Sutton and Long Lartin (Brixton and Wakefield are both Dispersal and Main Centre); 12 other Category B prisons; 21 Category C; ten Category D; two Resettlement prisons; seven female prisons and four Young Offender establishments.

All lifers in England and Wales now have something called a Life Sentence Plan (LSP). These were introduced as formal policy in 1993 to replace career plans prepared by the Lifer Section of the Prison Service. An ambitious, very labour intensive and thoroughly laudable initiative, LSPs are intended to ensure that all lifers will have:

- a detailed risk assessment (see, especially, *Chapter 6*);
- a record of offending behaviour to be addressed;
- details of the arrangements for addressing offending behaviour;
- annual reviews and progress reports.

and to ensure also that each lifer has a 'continuous record of . . . personal growth and progress, and to what extent behavioural problems, negative attitudes and other areas of concern have been identified and are being addressed'.

This systematic, integrated approach to the lifers' time in prison is a huge improvement, as are the right to disclosure of information and the Discretionary Lifer Panels discussed in *Chapter 5*.

'MYRA SYNDROME'

We have already mentioned the way in which successive Governments have clung to the political stake inherent in being able to control the actual period served by mandatory life sentence prisoners (see page 20). This applies for even stronger reasons where the decision is whether or not to set the tariff at 'natural life'.

Natural life
There is a small group of lifers (currently 26) who have been told that their tariff is considered to be a full life one. Their cases will be reviewed every five years after they have served 25 years. The management of this group pose unique problems for the Prison Service which has based its strategy for the management of lifers on encouraging the prospect within staff and prisoners of the eventual possibility of release (see, generally, *Chapter 4*).

Locking away lifers for so many years shows imprisonment at its most extreme. The problem of managing old age is a concern which the service is coming to terms with. Some prisons will become old people's homes, dealing with geriatric problems such as the loss of mobility and senile dementia. Kingston Prison (Portsmouth) has developed such a unit for elderly lifers. Although these problems may be in the process of being tackled those posed by younger lifers facing all their life in custody are new and will call for extremes of skill and perseverance. There will be responses varying from acceptance of the tariff and a consequential numbing of the senses to those who fight all of it. There are special close supervision units in prisons which will provide a temporary place for those who seek to fight the system. There are also other units which have in the past provided some constructive approach towards the long sentenced prisoner such as the special unit in Barlinnie and the therapeutic community approach of Grendon. But these locations were and are concerned with the installation and sustenance of hope about the future. There is no experience yet in how to handle making prison the ultimate horizon. This will have to be learned quickly as the numbers grow and as the appeals to the European Court are exhausted. The experience of other countries such as the USA does not provide much to go on, as the atmosphere and staff relationships in contact with such prisoners are very different from those of most English prisons. There would be a general reluctance to pursue some of the policies of distancing and segregation which enable the situation to be managed in the USA. The ultimate impact of the full life sentence has still to be worked through.

How political involvement works

The instructions regarding the particular responsibilities of the Home Secretary in relation to mandatory lifers seek to embrace this questionable political element. Once the lifer:

- has served the 'tariff' (that time deemed necessary to satisfy retribution and deterrence); *and*
- has satisfactorily addressed offending behaviour; *and*
- moved through the full sequence of prison security types until h e or she is proven capable of living in 'open' conditions; *and*
- has satisfied any other questions of risk of reoffending; *and*
- has been recommended for release by the Parole Board (who have also consulted the trial judge who has expressed no substantive objections or concerns)

it is the entire prerogative of an elected politician to decide whether or not the release of the particular individual would undermine 'public confidence in the life sentence system', i.e. how the public would be likely to respond to the mandatory lifer being released at that juncture. This curious arrangement cannot fail to raise questions including:

- Can a politician (who may or may not have experience of the criminal justice system) genuinely transcend the popular clamour for a particular decision to be made, so as to ensure that lifers are treated with equanimity and justice?
- Why is it appropriate for this power to be applied to *mandatory* lifers and not *discretionary* lifers?
- If someone has satisfied the needs for retribution (i.e. *revenge*), for deterrence (i.e. *punishment*) and for the maximum reduction of *risk*, what is the purpose of this additional constraint?

And, irrespective of who makes the release decision:

- Why is it that, unique amongst Western European countries, a life sentence is mandatory for *all* murderers regardless of the circumstances in England and Wales?

It is difficult not to conclude that this recent additional act of punitive retribution is an entirely political expedient, aimed at enhancing voter popularity, premised on a presumption regarding the general need for imprisonment for natural life for some of the most *notorious* offenders (or at least those who have received the most vituperative and sustained adverse media attention). This is at best a 'back-door' argument for re-introducing the death penalty and at worst a form of capitulation to 'mob rule'. Would it not be better, more honest, to say that the Home Secretary reserves the right to detain some lifers indefinitely on the grounds of the severity of their crimes? This is what happens in practice now and has done ever since the abolition of the death penalty. Every year, some lifers die in custody from natural causes or protracted illnesses having spent their entire adult lives in prison. They are not even released during their final days or weeks on compassionate grounds even though the discretionary power to do this exists. Their cases attract no media attention or public outrage *because* they were murderers or other terrible criminals. Also, the evidence in *Chapter 3* suggests that the numbers of prisoners who are innocent of their crimes but imprisoned for life may be larger than we imagine. Could there actually be people who are innocent who are destined to die having spent most of their lives wrongfully imprisoned?

It is obvious that the media attention given to the case of Myra Hindley over the past 30 years has had a telling impact on deliberating Home Secretaries, perhaps none more so that the former Conservative Home Secretary, Michael Howard. A determination to identify a small number of lifers whose crimes were so extreme and heinous as to pre-empt any consideration of imprisonment other than 'Natural Life' has meant that inmates are now so designated (i.e. as 'natural lifers'), with no recourse to law in England and Wales. This was neither a judicial nor a legislative decision, rather it was taken by an individual politician now voted out of office. Is this really how we wish our society to determine our penal policy?

The last—decidedly polemical—paragraph aside, the changes made by the Prison Service in life sentence offender policy in recent years is on the whole commendable, bringing as it does far greater regularity, accountability and access to the process and, most particularly, because it states that 'It is essential that the lifer is involved in the sentence planning process'.

STRUCTURE OF A LIFE SENTENCE

The *Lifer Manual* goes through the stages of a typical life sentence:

1. *Local Prison:* Following conviction, a lifer serves a period of months in a local prison where:
   (a) the tariff setting procedure begins; and
   (b) he or she is allocated a Main Centre by the HQ Allocation Unit.

2. *Main Centre:* This phase starts the longer-term clock in earnest. Lifers can expect to spend between three and four years at one of the three Main Centres, when they will learn the rules, ropes and survival skills as well as having their initial assessment and Life Sentence Plan drafted. At the end of this period, the first progress reports (called F75s) will be requested.

3. *Category B Trainer or Dispersal Prison:* By this stage, the lifer usually feels himself a 'veteran of the system'. If he has been put 'on the book', i.e. categorised as a serious risk, a 'Cat A man', then he definitely goes to one of the dispersal prisons which have both special procedures for secure supervision and the highest physical security extant. Most lifers experience more than one Cat B and some experience many, depending upon their behaviour. The more compliant, the fewer the moves. It is also at this stage that lifers are expected to have addressed their offending behaviour, especially if they are a 'sex offender', i.e. someone who has committed a sexual offence *or* someone who is determined as having had a sexual element to their crime, even if the crime was primarily a violent one. There are an appreciable number of lifers, particularly those with (a) mental

instability labels, (b) records of defiant, prison-based offending and/or (c) who continue to protest their innocence, who get stuck at this stage. Some of them are referred to Grendon, the therapeutic community prison, or to the TC unit at Gartree (specifically for lifers) but many are in a log jam which often adds years to their imprisonment.

4. *Category C Prison:* Rather more a staging post and time filler, the years spent in Cat Cs are officially meant to be for:
    (a) the first review reference suitability for release;
    (b) the introduction of some outside activities at the discretion of HQ staff; and
    (c) testing in less secure conditions.

5 *Category D (Open) Prison:* This is the ultimate prize for lifers and, yet, many of them resent this stage the most. Transfer to Cat D is 'in preparation for eventual release on licence'. Cat D is meant to test lifers in 'more challenging' conditions before they are considered for the final stage. It is here that lifers are given most trust and freedom, often going into local communities to work or to take part in voluntary projects, as well as more opportunities for home leave. A survey of lifers (89) at HMP Kingston (Portsmouth), where the whole population is lifers aiming for release, found that the overwhelming majority considered it an unnecessary stage which mainly determined how well they could cope with Cat D prison conditions rather than practical preparation for release on life licence. In spite of the directive which says lifers should 'usually' go to Cat D, before transfer to a PRES hostel, almost all do so. Transfer to a Cat D prison can only occur on recommendation from the Parole Board.

6. *Pre-release Employment Schemes (PRES):* Release is 'generally preceded by a period of six to nine months in a PRES hostel or Latchmere House resettlement prison'. Here, the lifer will:
    (a) undergo final testing in conditions comparable to those of release;
    (b) be offered work experience in the community;
    (c) have final reports prepared on him by both the hostel staff and the Probation Service.

The above stages typically take place over a period in excess of ten years. The average tariff in recent years has been around the 13 year mark so that, with an additional period allowed for whatever 'risk' there is felt to be, most lifers are destined to serve at least 14 or 15 years with some doing 20 years and more. The net result is that many young men will spend most of their prime adult years imprisoned, with periods of several years passing in each prison along the way. Although it has never been explicitly stated, HM Prison Service depends upon these largely compliant prisoners to act as a stabilising or at least buffering influence on their more fractious determinate colleagues (see *Chapter 4*). What is proven is that the rates of institutional offending are directly related to the proportion of lifers a prison has. *Table 3* provides the figures for a sample of nine Cat B prisons' rates of institutional offending and their percentages of lifers.

Table 3: Governors' Reports
Rates of Offending and Number of Lifers, 1 April to 31 December 1989

PRISON	Population	Reports	Rate/Inmate	Lifers	(%)
Bedford	312	317	1.0	0	0
Oxford [now closed]	189	150	.8	0	0
Shepton Mallet	239	132	.6	0	0
Blundeston	402	222	.5	24	6
Frankland	386	205	.5	36	9
Nottingham	291	114	.4	39	13
Lewes	131	29	.3	36	27
Gartree	313	128	.4	130	42
Kingston	148	5	.03	148	100

Source: Prison Statistics, England and Wales, 1989, HMSO

There is a clear inverse correlation, i.e. the higher the proportion of lifers, the lower the rate of offending, regardless of the size or nature of the prison. Even when controlling for the influence of the regime of the prison, lifers are significantly less likely to offend against Prison Rules. Of the total of all governors' reports at Gartree in 1991, 75% of the 77 non-lifers (58) were placed on report at least once, compared with only 41% (65) of the lifers, a result which is statistically significant at the $P = 0.001$ level ($X^2 = 24.6$, df = 1, $P = 0.001$). However, the lifers who did offend were slightly more likely to commit more than one offence, with the 65 lifers averaging 2.4 reports compared with two each for the non-lifers. The majority of lifers are less likely to be in trouble inside than are non-lifers.

THE *VICTIM'S CHARTER*

Another positive aspect of the *Lifer Manual* is that it refers to the latest edition of the *Victim's Charter*, advocating that probation staff responsible for lifers who are nearing release should contact the victims or victims' families in order to assuage anxieties about the imminent release, consider any restrictions which might need to be imposed upon the lifer in order to reassure them and inform him or her as to the general procedures which will apply. This innovative dimension, whilst opening the prospect of some risk of retaliation (probation are admonished not to provide any personal details as to date of release, area the lifer would be going to, etc.), obviously serves both to reassure those on the victim's side who were most affected by the crime and addresses the oft-mooted complaint that the scales of justice are tipped unfairly in favour of the offender.

INDIVIDUAL CASES

Where appropriate in the chapters which follow, we have provided information about individual cases to illustrate the particular nature of life imprisonment and to assist in understanding murderers and other life sentence prisoners. These examples are not meant to necessarily typify their population but rather to highlight some of the issues which the authors most want to address. A selection of lifers direct accounts is contained in *Chapter 2*. Also, *Appendix A* to this work contains the story of Anthony ('Alex') Alexandrowicz (perhaps somewhat atypical, yet sadly far from unique) which underscores many of the underlying themes of this book including the problem which occurs when a lifer insists on maintaining innocence in the face of Prison Service policies which, notwithstanding a proliferation of miscarriage of justice cases, do not acknowledge or cater for this eventuality. Alex's case involves a discretionary life sentence where the hope of the sentencing judge (as expressed at the time) that a short period in custody would be served was patently not honoured. This in turn serves to emphasise why there was such a need for the open justice provided by the relatively new Discretionary Lifer Panels outlined in *Chapter 5*.

TWO STRIKES AND YOU'RE IN

One of the most controversial aspects of the Crime (Sentences) Act 1997 is that which obliges an automatic sentence for serious, second, violent or sex offences (a 'Section 2' life sentence). This was the brainchild of a Conservative government influenced, perhaps inevitably, by the absurd Californian policy of giving life sentences to offenders for their third indictable offence of *whatever* severity. Passed in 1994, the American legislation has resulted in over 17,000 people being sentenced under its provisions. Wilson (1998) has highlighted some of the life sentence prisoners now safely behind bars as a consequence:

> Duane Silva for house burglary, but who had two previous sentences for setting fire to two rubbish bins and a parked car. Under California law Mr Silva's mitigating circumstances cannot be taken into account. These relate to the fact that Mr Silva suffers from a mental handicap, and was found to be incompetent to stand trial.

Wilson goes on to report that this was:

> By no means an isolated example, and life sentences have also been awarded to a man in Sacramento for stealing two cigarette packets; another in San Bernardino who stole a slice of pizza; and another in Santa Ana who stole four chocolate chip cookies.

In their White Paper, the Government proposed that an automatic life sentence be imposed on offenders aged 18 or over who are convicted for the second time of a serious violent or sex offence, unless there are genuinely exceptional circumstances. The crimes which are determined to be sufficiently serious are:

(a) violent offences
- attempted murder
- threat or conspiracy to murder
- manslaughter
- wounding with intent to do grievous bodily harm
- robbery involving the use of firearms
- possession of a firearm with intent to endanger life or to commit an indictable offence or to resist arrest.

(b) sexual offences
- rape or attempted rape
- unlawful sexual intercourse with a girl under 13.

The power to impose a discretionary life sentence for the offences of kidnapping, arson or false imprisonment remains. According to the White Paper:

> The grounds for this new law are compelling. There are offenders who leave prison with a high risk of reoffending. Anyone who has worked in prisons knows this to be true and will no doubt have felt acute frustration, and no little apprehension, at having to watch such people leave the prison, some of whom have actually said they will re-offend.

The proposals actually refer to this fear:

But if a determinate sentence is imposed the offender must be released once that sentence has been served, even if there is every reason to believe that he or she will commit further serious offences.

The government argued that it is the *indeterminacy* rather than the *length* of the sentence which is critical, leaving the discretion as to the risk in the hand of a quasi-judicial panel as currently obtains with discretionary lifers. The sentence, they argued, is more accurately described as an 'automatic indeterminate sentence', which amounts to the same thing.

What then are the reservations? If, as argued by government, the process puts the safety of the public first, and there are safeguards against the extreme abuses of the Californian system which imprisons petty thieves for life, and 'ministers will play no part in this process', and courts have some discretion not to pass the sentence in exceptional cases, and it would only be passed for second serious offences, and release is via a 'judicial' panel, what are the objections?

There are at least three of substance. The first concerns the resource implications and was anticipated by the White Paper; the second concerns the ethical issues; and the third the question of justice.

The government anticipated (in 1996) that 'The proposals on sentencing are likely to result in a substantial increase in the prison population over time'. Those proposals also included that determinate sentence prisoners should serve their full terms of imprisonment, i.e. that automatic early release should be abolished, that a minimum sentence of seven years should be imposed for those who traffic in Class A drugs with two or more previous similar offences and that a three year minimum sentence be imposed for burglary where the offender has, again, two previous similar convictions. They estimated that, allowing for reductions in prison numbers brought about by other, deterrent, effects, the overall increase in prisoner numbers would be 'around 10,800 by 2011-12', and that these new places 'would be provided through the Private Finance Initiative (PFI)'. They further acknowledged additional resource implications for the courts, legal aid, the Crown Prosecution Service and the Probation Service, 'although these will take until around 2009-10 to reach a peak'.

Even by conservative estimates then, the implications are very substantial indeed. These estimates, which may be well under the actual figures (government estimates often are), would mean an additional 1,000 long-term prisoners joining the prison system each year. Although the White Paper does not say how many of these would be lifers, it is not unreasonable to assume that, as anything between 30 per cent and 60 per cent of violent and sex offenders re-offend, their numbers would increase dramatically within the first few years.

Ethically, the authors of this work are concerned that imposing indeterminate sentences on offenders for a whole new tier of crimes (presumably regarded as less serious than those to which such sentences previously pertained) raises the 'domino' question 'Who next?'. What should we do with other 'serious' criminals like burglars, robbers, persistent car thieves and those who cause the death of children by reckless driving, etc. who, having received a custodial sentence, go out and do it—or something comparable—again. These are the groups most at risk of re-offending. How many common assaults is equivalent to one grievous bodily harm (GBH)? How many houses robbed and their occupants traumatised equates to two arsons? The reality is that discretionary lifers already serve, on average, longer sentences than do mandatory lifers although the latter are presumed to be the worse offenders. We may now have cases of offenders whose conditions (e.g. mental state) will have deteriorated because of their life imprisonment such that they may become 'natural lifers' as a consequence of having wounded with intent as an 18 year old and, 20 years later, attempted rape, offences which, according to the Home Office's own statistics, would normally attract sentence of under ten years combined.

Finally, as Wilson (above) also observed:

> In England and Wales our "two strikes" law is framed to take exceptional circumstances into account. What might these consist of? Someone high on drugs? . . . Or perhaps someone who has spent his entire life in care, and whose first serious offence was committed using a toy gun? Clearly not, as James Hall committed this offence on the day he was released from prison, whilst he was high on a mixture of amphetamines and drink, has a history of institutional care and attention and whose first serious offence—a robbery—saw him pull out a toy pistol.

James Hall—aged 24 and of no fixed abode—was the first offender in England and Wales to be given an automatic life sentence under the 'two strikes' law.

CHAPTER 2

The Psychology of the Murderer

When you enter the mind of a murderer, you approach with caution. There is an understandable concern about what you'll find there. A chamber of horrors? Memories too painful or too frightening to share? How can we come to terms with these fellow citizens who have broken the cardinal commandment 'Thou shalt not kill'. Just as importantly, why should we try? Wouldn't it be better to live our lives, already full enough with problems, without having to hear such horrific tales? The only answer we have is that in better understanding the worst in them we understand the worst which could be in ourselves. If we aren't afraid to discover that the differences between murderers and the rest of us are smaller than comfort would allow, we might better come to accept their ultimate return to society. If the reader is working with offenders who have killed or occasioned extreme violence to other people, then hopefully this chapter may help in both understanding and facilitating the personal change necessary to live their future lives without doing further harm.

This chapter is in three sections. *Section I* provides a summary overview of some of the major theoretical explanations for extreme violence and murder. *Section II* illustrates the nature and circumstances of individual cases by a close scrutiny of a selection of interviews with murderers who are currently in prison. They are on special regimes which encourage them to explore their lives, personalities and crimes—the Therapeutic Communities at Grendon and Gartree. These interviews afford the reader rare insights into how the murderers themselves view what they did and how they were capable of murder. *Section III* summarises some practical views as to how we can better approach, understand and help such men.

I. THEORIES OF VIOLENCE AND MURDER

Lethal Violence
Any attempt at understanding those who have been extremely violent, particularly in taking another person's life, must start with a solid theoretical and research review. This is often difficult to establish as criminological theory on these issues is constantly changing. Some of the main areas of perspective include:

- *biological determinants* of aggression, such as the XYY chromosome, testosterone levels, neurophysiology issues like brain lesions and biochemistry/psychopharmacology (e.g. the effects of drugs on behaviour)

- *socio-cultural determinants* including the influence of anomie, alienation and sub-cultural and peer group pressure; and
- *psychological* aspects including mental instability, interpersonal conflicts and psychopathy.

More recently, Hodge, McMurran and Hollin (1997) conclude that addiction to violence '. . . may be a real phenomenon for some people'. Other partial explanations covered include *situational determinants, psychiatric determinants* and *political motivation.*

Biological determinants

The belief common in the 1960s and 1970s that men with an extra Y chromosome had greater criminal proclivity was largely dispelled by a large scale study by Witkin *et al* (1977) and extended by Volavka *et a l* (1979) in Denmark. These studies concluded that men with XYY chromosomes were no more statistically likely to have committed crimes than those without. Mednick *et al* (1982) conclude that 'The literature reviewed strongly suggests that many violent offenders suffer organic brain dysfunction' but go on to caution that environmental events and factors will usually moderate the expression and severity of violence such that

> . . . in cases where aggressive criminal behaviour is manifested by an individual reared in noncriminogenic social conditions, we must look to individual (biological) characteristics for the bases of deviance.

Males are significantly more likely to commit violent acts, and to kill, than are females. Some of this difference may be attributable to levels of testosterone, the principal androgenic steroid hormone. Research (Rada *et al* 1976, etc.) has indicated that violent criminals had higher levels than either non-violent criminals or non-criminals. Obviously other, non-biological factors account for much of the gender-based differences in violence. There is also some evidence (Zuckerman, 1980) that many violent criminals suffer from organic brain dysfunction.

Excessive alcohol consumption is often associated with violence and aggressive behaviour, including murder and manslaughter. There is little evidence however to confirm a causal relationship proving that:

> alcohol directly stimulates violent behaviour. Social circumstances may mediate the relationship between alcohol intake and manifestations of aggression. (Mednick *et al*, 1982)

The problem is essentially that:

It is not clear whether alcohol induces violent behaviour directly or whether it acts primarily as a disinhibitor of pre-existing aggressive tendencies. (op cit)

Probably the single most discussed enduring concept said to contribute to anti-social behaviour in general, and violent behaviour in particular is that of psychopathy. There is now a very considerable body of evidence (Cleckley, 1964; Hare, 1978, 1981; Hare and Hart, 1993; Blackburn, 1974, 1980) adding weight to the assertion that men identified either by clinical assessment and/or use of the Psychopathy Checklist PCL-R 90 as psychopaths are significantly more likely to have histories of violence than those (offenders and non-offenders) who do not. The clinical definition itself is however no longer in the Mental Health Act due to widespread lack of agreement as to the delineating characteristics. Hare's later work from 1981 onwards of determining five specific factors which help identify the true psychopath indicated that the main factor of a lack of empathy or concern for others may be a signal dynamic in helping to explain the personality of a substantial proportion of murderers and other violent criminals. Current research at Grendon, the therapeutic community prison for personality disordered offenders, is addressing the extent to which the Hare Psychopathy Checklist can identify people for whom therapy may be contra-indicated by virtue of high scores. Their potential for damaging the general culture and life of the communities in prison is considerable quite apart from the risk of violence they represent to others.

The concept of psychopathy probably lies as appropriately in the psychological rather than biological determinants of extreme interpersonal violence. However it has yet to be determined whether there are biological predeterminants to this cluster of dysfunctional behaviour.

Socio-cultural determinants
The literature on criminality is rich with theories of violence made attributable to social class, peer group influences, cultural 'press', alienation etc.

If we begin with broader theories of criminality generally, one of the most durable sociological perspectives is that of Merton's (1967) Anomie. This posits that 'culturally prescribed norms for appropriate goals become disassociated from the acceptable avenues for realising'. More simply, some people become 'have nots', don't like it and discover 'deviant' ways of getting what they feel entitled to. This 'anomie' is meant to be followed by normlessness, deterioration and disintegration of individual value systems. The theory stresses that, when an individual is a member of a class stratum which numbers more deviant than compliant members, they are no longer deviant. Similar to this theory is the Strain, or Motivational theory of Cohen (1955) where, again, those who are becoming delinquent adopt the antithesis of middle-class norms and values in a process called reaction formation, so that they possess sets of both conventional and deviant values to which they can situationally subscribe. The large-scale alienation of black and Hispanic young people in America and their subsequent subscribing to the violent code of gang life is a painful illustration of how powerful the influences of peer-group norms can be. The added ingredient of advocating violence both as a 'rite of passage' for gaining greater group respect and dominance, and for expressing what must be formidable reserves of hatred for the (perceived or real) suppression and rejection by the (largely white) cultural norms, is a lethal mix.

Whether it is at a deeply personal level or part of a sub-cultural value system, the part that a sense of alienation plays in creating a potentially lethally violent person is strong. When you find a group which accepts you, having previously been rejected by others, your loyalty to that group and their prevailing value system can overwhelm prior parental socialisation and a sense of personal conscience.

When this pattern is enacted against a cultural or societal backcloth which advocates the possession of weapons as an *inalienable right*, the conventional proscriptions and constraints of 'civilised' society are weakened and can, ultimately, be broken. In this scenario, the American scenario, the sense of risk, and the concomitant defensive 'bearing of arms' simply increases the potential for violent deaths. We have observed the explosion in the numbers of murders in the United States across four decades, from a time in the 1950s when the dominant atmosphere was one of peace, growth and prosperity aligned to a tradition of independence and self-sufficiency, to the 1990s with record levels of violence, murder and imprisonment in a climate of retaliation, right-wing moral backlash and record numbers dependent on welfare, and on drugs.

The availability—and cultural acceptance—of guns in America as distinct from the United Kingdom, make the decision to kill easier. Cook (1982) explains that the qualities of guns mean: (a) there is less danger of effective victim resistance during attack; (b) killing can be accomplished more quickly and impersonally and with less effort than is usually required with a knife or other object. We would note, however, that though the method may be impersonal, most US murder victims know their perpetrators. It would seem that perceived vulnerability of the victim is also a factor in choosing a gun as the means to that end. Almost all law enforcement officers in the US in recent years who were murdered were shot: in 1978, 91 of 93 murdered officers were killed by guns. Cook looked at FBI figures for homicides in 50 large American cities in the mid-1970s and examined killer-victim characteristics. He found consistent proof that there is a relative vulnerability factor, i.e. that the use of guns was significantly related to the gender and age of the parties. Wherever the killer was disadvantaged, e.g. a woman or an older man, the percentage using guns, as opposed to other weapons, increased. This aspect of the cultural press on individuals is clearly linked with situational determinants discussed shortly.

Given the popular presumption that American cultural dynamics cross to the United Kingdom within a few years, it comes as a relief to see the passing of gun control legislation in the wake of Dunblane. Sadly, this must be contrasted with the growing frequency of firearm use in offences in the United Kingdom with the concomitant pressure to arm police.

Psychological determinants
Thornton and Reid (1982) applied Kohlberg's stages of moral reasoning to criminal behaviour. They defined preconventional moral reasoning as where 'right action is identified with action that serves one's self-interest', and they made a distinction between prudent and imprudent offending based on the offender's judgement as to the probability of evading detection. They evaluated serious offenders (robbers, major fraudsters, murderers and rapists) in terms of verbal intelligence and 'moral maturity scores' and found that prudent offending was equated to serious dishonesty while imprudent offending was equated to serious offences against the person not committed for financial gain. This sheds some light on one aspect of the psychology of murderers where the probability of evading detection is not considered, but, in the majority of cases these authors deal with, most premeditated murders involve an element of assessing the risk of detection and many murders committed in extreme emotional states have an overwhelming self-preservation element soon after the crime.

Probably the most well-known, and possibly the most tendentious, theory of personality is Eysenck's (1964). This theory holds that:

> . . . heredity, mediated through personality, plays some part in predisposing some people to act in an anti-social manner. Environment is equally important and . . . it is the interaction between the two which is perhaps the most crucial factor.

Eysenck held that criminals can be differentiated along three bi-polar dimensions:

—*Extraversion-Introversion (E):* Typical extroverts are sociable, outgoing, excitement seeking, talkative and impulsive, while introverts are quiet, retiring, introspective and distant apart from with intimate friends. These, and the other descriptions should be viewed as extremes on a continuum.

— *Neuroticism (N):* High scorers are described as anxious, worrying, moody and frequently depressed, with a tendency to worry and become preoccupied with things that may go wrong. Low scorers tend to be calm, even tempered, controlled and unworried.

— *Psychoticism (P) or 'Tough mindedness':* High scorers are described as solitary uncaring towards others, i.e. lacking in empathy, hostile with a disregard for danger and '... empathy, feelings of guilt, sensitivity to other people are notions that are strange and unfamiliar to them'.

He found that there were significant differences on these scales for different types of criminals, e.g. 'domestic' murderers were 'significantly introverted' while 'professional gunmen' were 'significantly extroverted'. Eysenck was able to support many of his findings with a massive reference list of research work while acknowledging a not inconsiderable alternative list which countered or questioned his own.

Behavioural psychology focuses on the reinforcement patterns of behaviour, i.e. what happens before, during and after a crime determines whether that experience was positive (rewarding) or negative (punishing) for that individual. Williams (1987) asked three questions:

'What was the purpose of the offence?'

'What constitutes the kind of situation in which the offence was committed?'

'Was the offence primarily verbal or non-verbal?'

In discussing a classification of serious offenders, he cites murderers as a good example of a group of criminals with obvious sub-groups in terms of reinforcement contingencies. The sadistic murderers he posits as being obviously positively reinforced, i.e. 'turned on' by the sexual pleasure derived by inflicting pain, contrasted to the 'domestic' murderers who are generally negatively reinforced, i.e. the murder 'turned off' some aversive stimuli or state such as the threat of the loss of a wife or girlfriend to another man (or equally the escape from aversive stimuli from a wife who the murderer hated).

One of the most common phenomena the authors have observed in working with hundreds of murderers and other life sentenced offenders is the dissociation they have created between themselves and their crimes. When asked or obliged to refer to the specific crime, many refer to it in the second or third person, i.e. they don't say 'I stabbed him several times in the chest and stomach' but rather 'When he had been stabbed' or 'The bloke was hit with the knife over and over'. This distancing obviously performs a protective service, but can also be a barometer to the extent of acceptance or denial the offender feels. In therapy, many individuals pass through several stages of increasingly personalised statements until they are able to say clearly that they killed a specific individual in a specific way and own that act.

This pattern of detachment reflects a similar phenomenon observed in descriptions of events immediately prior to the violent outbursts. Murderers often describe how the victim became depersonalised, an object. Equally, accounts often refer to the victim personifying other people generally or an amorphous cluster of those who the attacker had previously experienced as having been abusive or rejecting of him or her, i.e. those for whom the attacker bore grudges or even hated. In this sense, there are no 'innocent victims' in the eyes of most murderers.

A sub-group of murderers which seems to be over-represented in post-crime treatment such as Special Hospitals and Therapeutic Community prisons are the 'lust murderers'. Several authors (e.g. Hazelwood and Douglas, 1980) have described this cluster of men as characteristically maiming or disfiguring the body—usually female—of their victim. They differentiated between the 'organized nonsocial' and 'disorganized asocial' types, with the former tending to be 'egocentric, amoral individuals'. They tended to commit methodical and well-organized murders with considerable effort expended in calculated plans to avoid capture. The disorganized asocial lust murderer was described as 'a loner who had great difficulty in interpersonal relationships and [who] felt rejected and alienated'. Their murders tended to be impulsive and so they had little thought of escape. Hazelwood and Douglas go on to assert that the nonsocial types were more likely to rape the victims before or after death, while the asocial types rarely did so but would sometimes insert foreign bodies into the victim's orifices. Sadly, these tragic profiles are all too common in murderers currently in Prison Services establishments.

Certain personality characteristics recur in taxonomies of murderers, among them low self-esteem, high levels of general hostility especially extra-punitiveness, poor impulse control, a fear of rejection and a tendency to feel alienated either from society generally or from the victim or the group which the victim represents for the murderer, e.g. all women.

Situational determinants of violence.
Stress and the related inability to cope plays a part in most, if not all, explosions of extreme interpersonal violence. McGrath (1970) describes

this as '. . . a state of imbalance between the demands of the social and physical environment and the capabilities of an individual to cope with these demands'.

The literature on stress and a model of anger arousal as a form of reacting to it is the province of Novaco (1979). His model of the factors to be assessed in the prediction of violent behaviour gives a clear relational image of how events and internal cognitions relate:

STRESSFUL EVENTS	COGNITIVE PROCESSES
e.g. frustrations, annoyances, insults, taunting	(a) Predisposing appraisals and expectations (e.g. violent fantasies and self-statements, perceived intentionally)
	(b) Inhibiting appraisals and expectations (e.g. non-violent self-statements, expectations of punishment).
BEHAVIOURAL COPING RESPONSES	AFFECTIVE REACTIONS
(a) Violent (e.g. murder, rape, robbery)	(a) Predisposing (e.g. anger, hatred, assault)
(b) Non-violent (e.g. withdrawal, avoidance)	(b) Inhibiting (e.g. empathy, guilt anxiety, fear)

Our earlier reference to those lifers who seem to have a permanent chip on their shoulders (pp.33-35) serves to illustrate the model. For example, lifer Smith hears a reference to being like an 'animal' at the dining table. Although a relatively innocent reference to his eating habits, for Smith this is a potential stressor. His 'predisposing appraisal' that this is a direct reference to his offence means that his 'behavioural coping response' is to react with an aggressive insult or physical confrontation directed at the 'offender', which results in the 'affective reaction' that several of those who witnessed the incident conclude that Smith is, indeed, 'a bit of a nutter', or dangerously quick-tempered. Thus the cycle is repeated and more potential provoking stressors are 'recruited' to the ranks of those who might trigger aggression or violence from Smith.

Thus, in this model, stressful situations are filtered through certain cognitive processes in the individual largely in two ways: appraisals and expectations. One individual will appraise a situation or other person as provocative more than another and might further interpret the provocation to have been intentional. As Monahan and Klassen (1982) put it: 'The chips on their shoulders may be precariously balanced'.

Expectations operate to determine whether or not someone is violent in similar ways. If he has experienced aggression as being successful in most events or as a useful means to an end, the aggressor is more likely to expect it to work in future.

Some murders occur when what individuals expect to happen (e.g. compliance or an empty house) do not materialise. The violence then can be both instrumental in terms of aiding escape and gratifying in terms of a reassuring demonstration of importance and power. The Novaco model of anger, while not comprehensive, helps us to understand more of the internal workings of the potential murderer.

Psychiatric determinants

Unquestionably, psychiatrists remain at the forefront of traditional approaches in the United Kingdom to the related problems of assessing, treating and predicting future risk for criminals determined to be mentally 'ill' or unstable. In the community, psychiatrists are often expected to inform the police or social services of patients who they feel represent a danger to themselves or other people, normally by way of a confidential register. When people kill or commit crimes of extreme violence, the psychiatrist is usually among the first to be asked for an assessment for the court, either for the defence or the prosecution. If the murderer is found guilty and sentenced to imprisonment or to be detained in a special secure hospital (e.g. Rampton or Broadmoor), their treatment is inevitably the responsibility of a psychiatrist (or medical officer) and, finally, when the question of release comes, it is to the psychiatrists that officialdom usually turns for the medical authority to release or detain. Ultimate freedom is the greatest prize for the man (or woman) imprisoned for life and the greatest risk for those responsible. Those subject to the closest scrutiny within this group are people with histories of mental instability or illness, or sometimes those who have had even the question of state of mind raised in their records. Far too many medical records and reports on lifers—by medical officers and other staff not qualified to pass clinical judgement—label lifers schizophrenic, psychopathic, delusional, paranoid, etc. The most common labels used, in the authors' experience, were 'personality disordered' and 'psychopathic tendencies'.

The temptation to so label was not confined to non-psychiatrists in the medical professions. Labels were often used as well by probation officers, psychologists and prison officers without any attempt to explain or justify the stigmatisation beyond often general accounts of unusual, bizarre or deviant prison behaviour.

Gunn (1996), in *The Management and Discharge of Violent Patients*, opined that patients suffering from psychosis, the most extreme dissociation from reality, were clearly linked with violence. Referring to an earlier study by Taylor and Gunn (1984) which had found that 'Eleven per cent of men charged with homicide suffer from schizophrenia', he goes on to remind us that this was '. . . a long way from saying that a high proportion of patients with schizophrenia commit violence', given also that only about one per cent of the general population are afflicted by schizophrenia, and that only about one in nine of these are dangerous, the risk must be kept in perspective. The psychiatric labels which feature most frequently in cases of homicidal violence are those of paranoid, persecution complex and other schizophrenic clusters where the individual becomes trapped in a mind set of fearing the abuse, victimisation or humiliation from others and, often with the additional factor of having abused drink or drugs, attacks the perceived tormentor (or a safer, displaced, alternative target). There is often a history of violence, psychiatric or prison containment and, sadly, all too prophetically, predictions of future, more extreme violence, to come.

Political motivation

There is a relatively small but significant minority of murderers and other lifers for whom taking life is an operational objective or, at least, an occupational hazard. Those who are either obvious or self-styled political prisoners (e.g. Irish republicans) and various Middle Eastern terrorists fall clearly into this category. While we may attempt to apply psychological labels to their behaviour, the counter argument is simply that they do what they do for a 'higher goal', e.g. for the sake of political freedom or to defy real or perceived subjugation. Although it would be tempting to set aside this category of murderer, to do so would risk dismissing the obvious human capacity to justify even the most extreme violence against one's fellow man in the name of some often selectively applied political concepts such as 'patriotism', 'liberation' or even 'tit for tat' reciprocal killing. The most significant implications for our text are more to do with the difficulty of engaging these individuals in any dialogue which challenges their behaviour at an *individual responsibility* rather than *political operative* level.

II. WHAT THE MURDERERS SAY

Reviewing the literature and the authors' experiences of men who have killed affords the reader large parts of the overall picture but the accounts of *the offenders themselves* inevitably provide more compelling and often far more revealing pictures. These interviews were carried out with the full consent and cooperation of the men concerned who understood they were being interviewed for a book in preparation, that they would not be identified individually and that some aspects of their accounts would be altered in an effort to ensure anonymity. This was done to protect the families of both the victims and the offenders as well from any possible further stress.

SIX CASE STUDIES

CASE A

I've been something different all my life from what I should have been. I should have been an ordinary geezer.

When he came into the room, A carried with him an atmosphere of menace. There was an immediate tension where none had been the moment before. A is a large man, with generous tattooing and some scarring. Yet there was also a strange sense of vulnerability at the same time. As he spoke, the reasons for both sensations quickly became obvious.

When A came out of prison in 1985, he was 30. He was 'a villain and a gangster', married to a 'gangster's moll and she loved it. Believed I was one of the Krays'. He was going through a divorce, 'ugly'. Although he'd only been out a few months, he was struggling and was required to work in a church centre where he met his victim—a 69 year old lady. They became acquainted and she loaned A money—'a couple of quid'—which he had not paid back. Not long before the murder, A had been to see a plastic surgeon about having a large tattoo removed from the back of his hand which was quite prominent and which he felt was holding him back from getting on with a 'straight' life. He felt gutted, blaming the tattoo which he now saw as a major disfigurement. He started drinking, going out and doing drugs and burglaries. On the day of the murder, A says he had decided to repay the loan and got dressed up. He said 'I had the evening all planned out but even that got f . . ked up for me'. He had been drinking but says he wasn't drunk and does not blame what happened on that. He went to the lady's house and knocked on the door but that is '. . . where it all goes schizo on me'. Recalling that she opened the door and immediately said: 'Oh, it's you. I hope you've got my money'. This apparently incensed A so much that 'Fifteen seconds later, I picked up an ornament and hit her over the head several times then went to the kitchen, got a knife and stabbed her 80 times. Since then, I've been one horrible f . . . ker'.

A explains the explosion of such violence with so little—indeed no— provocation in terms of a resentment towards and alienation from society and people generally which had grown so great and was so near the surface that the victim saying what she did was like a slap in the face. It said to him that he was not to be trusted, had taken advantage of her and that she doubted if he would ever repay her. Once he hit her, she was no longer a person, but the target for all his frustrated rage towards everyone who had ever slighted him or not given him a chance. After the attack, A recalls having felt am immense sense of release and relief.

There are at least two related themes in this man's case which seem relevant to our exploration of the psychology of murder. First is the obvious pattern of feeling himself a victim: a victim first of some kind of fate whereby he feels that, no matter what he tried to do, he was destined to fail or be rejected. This growing conviction—grown to a full-blown persecution 'complex'—seemed to have left A almost convinced that it was pointless to try. Given that his youth and young adult years had been spent in relatively successful and profitable crimes of acquisition, he may have concluded that this was at least one vocation in which he could be both rewarded and extract some measure of retaliation upon this society which had become *malevolent towards him*.

Second, he recounted how the victim was innocent but doomed from the moment of her—perceived—slight. It is often difficult for many people to understand how someone could attack and kill an old lady with such ferocity and cold-bloodedness, but this is to miss the point entirely. For A, the victim literally personified his hatred for all people who slighted, ridiculed or put him down and did so *unfairly*, i.e. he was not just belittled but was belittled even when he intended to do good (in this case by returning the money owed). The image of a *time bomb* is often invoked to summarise this type of murderer. These are recurring themes in a significant proportion of murder cases, which we return to in a later case and in the final section on what forms positive intervention can take.

Returning briefly to A, I asked him if he had a future:

A. No. Have I f . . . k.
Q. Are they going to let you out?
A. I'm not even sure I want to go out. I've been something different all my life from what I should have been. I should have been an ordinary geezer.

A had been given a tariff (i.e. minimum) sentence of 17 years but seemed likely to serve a good deal longer. Throughout his imprisonment, he had been in trouble, smashing up and going on hunger strikes. He had been placed on the highest security category, Category A, which meant his movements within prison had been severely constrained and he had managed to alienate the management of pretty nearly every prison he had been in over 12 years.

CASE B

I suppose I always felt I was going to kill someone

B is a 26 year old, bespectacled young man with dark, lank hair who looks younger, more like a university student than a murderer. He had served seven years of his sentence for murder and attempted murder. He was clearly bright, articulate and rather personable, quick-witted and helpful on interview.

B's childhood was fractured. Although he described the family as 'very close' this excluded his father who had tried to kill B's mother when he was very young. His mother was left disabled and his father was sent to prison. B hated his father and only re-established contact with him recently in order—he said—to have some kind of relationship before it was too late.

B volunteered that he had 'never been in a serious relationship'. At home, he had been pleasant and kind; outside of home, 'violent and nasty'. He recalled having been very badly bullied and sent to a special school because he was thought to be 'stupid'. A physical education teacher took pity on him and eventually got him to try rugby which he was not much good at but found that he really enjoyed the tackling: 'It was hard. I liked it. I threw off sheep's clothing and became a lion'. He recalled how when other boys got hurt he enjoyed it and the sense of power he felt. He said that before this he had '. . . felt like being nothing. I couldn't protect myself and that's a scary thing'. B said that he then began to get involved in minor crimes and that this had happened partly because he began to 'hang around with heavies'.

When he was 18, B began an affair with a married Asian woman, the wife of the victim. He says it was 'lust' and that the victim was very wealthy. He became part of a conspiracy, along with the wife, the victim's son and an accomplice who was persuaded to actually do the shooting. In return, B would have '. . . the "widow" and part of the considerable fortune, £8.5 million pounds'.

A first attempt failed but left the victim hospitalised. As soon as he was released from hospital, B and his accomplice 'tracked' him and a second, successful, attempt was made with a shotgun. B arranged to have an alibi by being in a nearby pub where he recalls hearing the shots of the killing occurring just down the road and continuing to play on a vending machine. When invited to explain how he was able to conspire to commit murder, B said he had 'omnipotent fantasies where he had God-like powers going back to the beginning of time'.

I suppose I always felt I was going to kill someone. I suppose I never really lived in reality. It was like a film.

I don't think his life meant anything to me.

To look back, it seems so bizarre and weird.

B explained that the victim had been a brutal man—so much so that his wife and son had wanted him dead, so B felt nothing for him. He repeated 'It was like everything in my life was from a film'. He had previously admitted that he had acquired an image of a hard man, capable of violence and of enjoying it, an image he had learned to live up to. Perhaps the most revealing observation from B was:

My whole world meant more to me than someone's life. I'd built myself up to be this person and if I'd gone against it, what would I have been?

There was an emptiness about B as he recounted his crime and the events surrounding it. Apart from his near worship of his mother ('I'd give my life for my mum. She's never judged me. Her love means so much for me') the only feelings I saw which seemed genuine were a deep regret for the crime but in the sense that B was the victim having been condemned to life in prison.

It is this sense of intense egocentricity, partly attributable to his age (he was only 18 at the time of the murder) and partly his inordinately overdeveloped sense of being special, that his life was a kind of film—at once unreal and inevitable, already recorded—which stand out. There was also an obvious—and strong—element of avarice, as well presumably as of anticipating that he would then also have his lover to himself. This was from B's accounts a cold, premeditated killing where those restraining qualities of humanity were conspicuously absent. B was even prepared to cynically exploit another young man to commit the killing. Yet B impressed as an intelligent, sensitive and sociable young man. Perhaps this is what he had become in the ensuing years and possibly in part as a result of his having been in therapy for the past three. Yet much of his account of the younger B coupled with this now personable and persuasive man is similar to that of the psychopathic personality type. Although this label might not definitely apply to B, and not on the basis of so brief a contact, his case does illustrate the human capacity to kill in a detached, calculated manner simply for money and for 'lust'.

CASE C

If I hadn't had that dad, I wouldn't be here now.

The sixth of seven children from a poor family, C experienced years of psychological and physical abuse from his violent, aggressive and unpredictable father. He says this had a 'profound' effect on him, one of fear and sadness such that he feels unfairly treated because of his family and the reputation his father had. He kept returning to the genative influences his father had had, e.g. 'Dad was the weak link in the whole thing'. C's two older sisters left home as soon as they were old enought to support themselves and at critical times in C's development. Father was violent indiscriminately towards all the children and their mother and C was tremendously relieved when he, too, finally left home.

C married young and in so doing continued the dysfunctional nature of family relationships. He had a five year affair with the wife of his older brother: 'She seduced me'. C claims she wanted a child but could not conceive normally so was on the waiting list for in-vitro fertilisation. C feels she used him and did not love him, but they had a child who C loved deeply, becoming very attached to the baby boy. Tragically, C recounts that his wife was unfaithful to him and told him she was leaving him and taking their son to move in with another man. C says he had then decided to kill himself, collecting assorted memorabilia about him for his son, but that he decided to make one last 'pathetic' appeal to his wife not to leave. He says that he pleaded with her to at least let him have their son, but that they argued. The argument worsened until C went into the kitchen to collect some of their son's things and try to leave with him. He recalled the sequence which follows in horrific detail. C says he was aware of trying to

... dehumanise her enough to kill her—she was insulting me but I was now detached. I went to the kitchen to get some of . . . 's things and the sun shone through onto the metal part of the handle of some knives. I had a vision of a demonic beast. I was already a dead man.

C picked up a knife and stabbed his wife nine times. 'For the rest of my life, I can only be that person that killed . . . '. 'I suffer from horror fatigue sometimes'.

Although there was an element of blaming his childhood abuse and 'a very painful life', C was definitely more fully accepting of his guilt and responsibilities. He credited the therapeutic regime he was in for helping him to this acceptance, summarising the process as enabling him (and others) to: 'Have the courage to stop protecting the person you are in order to become the person you want to be'.

This case is illustrative of another large cluster of our study, the so-called 'domestic murderer'. C had little prior criminality, with only one previous conviction—for shop-lifting when aged 11—and no prior custodial experience. His dependence upon his relationship with his wife and, more significantly, his son, made the threat of her taking all that from him intolerable and he came to see her as his tormentor, the source of all his unhappiness and of a gross injustice. The situational determinants of an escalating argument, and those few seconds in the kitchen prior to the attack, seem to have been the key contributors to his losing control and killing. Although a somewhat speculative view, the longer term influences of his father on C's personality cannot have helped, teaching him tragic lessons in the power of physical aggression to (a) inflict great pain and (b) as a means to an end.

CASE D

> I believe I killed lots of women on that night—mother, sister—all those that treated me like shit all my life.

Like C, this man killed his cohabitee. Like C, D had experienced years of abuse while growing up, not only from his father but from being 'bullied every day of my school life'. During our interview, D rarely stopped smiling; a nervous, distracted smile which signalled how uncomfortable he was talking about these matters.

D also featured his father when invited to talk about his parents. He never felt loved by his father, who he said ignored him and never took him out to the normal things, e.g. football. 'I had no hero, no love or respect from my father'. His parents separated and eventually divorced. At school, D was

> ... quiet and undemonstrative. Everyone picked on me and bullied me. I didn't stand up for myself. I did well in school but felt useless; worthless. I thought "Is this what I'm destined to be forever?"

He recalled having a girlfriend when aged eight who was his best friend and who he trusted. One day, she left town—the family moved—without telling him and he felt betrayed. Aged 12, D again became close with a girl who began to 'pester' D for sex which he refused to have. He recalls that she finished the relationship and told everyone that D would not have sex with her and how useless and worthless he was. He felt humiliated and inadequate.

When he grew up, D eventually settled with a woman who he recalls as 'timid and gullible'. They lived together for nine years and had two children, but D says he regularly 'used and abused' her and that he never loved her. He met another woman who was beautiful and he was very surprised that she could have been attracted to him. He soon abandoned his family to live with this new woman, but the relationship quickly deteriorated with her being unfaithful to D on a regular basis, culminating in her announcement that she was having affairs with three other men—two being friends of D—and was leaving him. Rather than face this further rejection and humiliation from a woman with whom D was besotted, he plotted to kill her, planning the assault for three days before the event. He lured her to woods which they'd been to before, strangled her and buried the body, telling everyone she'd gone away for a few days.

D is very clear about why he killed her:

> Because I couldn't control her any longer. She wouldn't be what I wanted her to be—there for me and me only—a housewife. I didn't want to let her go off. . . She made me feel 20 feet tall—the ultimate woman I'd ever desired. I'd given up so much for her. I was jealous. If I couldn't have her, no-one would. I believe I killed lots of women that night—mother, sister—all those that treated me like shit all my life. I've always had this problem with women. Not trusting women, despising certain types of women. I picked on my sister and resented her for taking mother's love from me. I despise women who can frighten me. More intelligent and self-confident. Women who can speak their minds and put me down.

The lifelong sense of resentment, even hatred, which D felt towards many women had generalised and deepened to such an extent that to be rejected and labelled as inadequate by one who he had come to love and for whom he had given up so much was too much for his fragile self-esteem to take. There are many men who have had to face similar circumstances but most of them have not accumulated such a deep reserve of vulnerability and hatred, not become so selfish, egocentric and insecure. It is bad enough to be self-centred, but to have a low self-esteem as well and then be rejected by someone towards whom you have become obsessional must be terrible to endure.

To his credit, D now sees these things about himself and is working towards changing them. Ironically, he continues to be bullied by some of the other inmates which he takes with an understandable long-suffering shrug. He says he hopes to get out in about another ten years and 'would like a relationship with a woman', but that he 'won't go in the deep end'.

CASE E

> For a couple of seconds, I felt like I got my life back.

Like most of the others, E was abused in childhood. He recalls this to have been by his 'natural mother': 'I used to have quick flashbacks of . .

. . . me flying across the kitchen'. He lived with his natural parents until the age of about 4, then moved with his natural father to live with his step-mother. He recalled becoming confused, then angry and resentful and misbehaving. He was put into 'voluntary' care when aged 14. He recalls:

> I never lived at home again. Only visited for weekends, holidays. Step-mother gave ultimatum to natural father . . . I was showing signs of violence from an early age. At eleven, I was taken to a school psychologist. I think it was just before I found out my stepmother wasn't my natural mother and when I saw the psychologist, I found out I had a younger brother who had died. All other appointments were not kept. After finding out this, I shut myself away from my family . . .

When he was 16, E was raped coming out of a nightclub and 'After that, I just disappeared from the world'.

He committed the index offence just before his eighteenth birthday. He was living in a bed and breadfast which was 'recognised by the Probation Service' in the area. The majority of residents were on probation. E reflected that another resident 'seemed like he'd been on Rule 43 (a prison status used to protect vulnerable offenders—often sex offenders—from other prisoners) and that 'It all came back to me about having been raped. I saw him as like my victim—we were drunk anyway'. E's account is rather confused, but he recalled arguing with the victim about having got his (E's) girlfriend barred from the B and B (even though officially no-one was supposed to have girls in, E had asked the landlord for permission). The victim had—E asserts—had boyfriends in. The victim came towards E and said 'Is it like that?', which E says he took to mean that he would carry it—the argument—on later, so E felt threatened and struck out, hitting the victim three or four times. Two of his 'co-accuseds' than started to punch and kick the victim and another gave E a knife without getting involved himself.

> We took him to the canal. At various times, he was like my raper; then my father. We took him to this canal bridge. I stabbed him and we threw him in and for a couple of seconds I thought like I got my life back.

E said that he felt ashamed about what he'd done and sorry for his victim but that he'd 'met so many similar (to him) since that I'm better about it'. At times, he has felt as though he never deserved to be released from prison. When he was originally sentenced, the judge recommended he serve a minimum of 20 years, which was quickly reduced he explained 'due to being under age for a recommendation. Apparently there was a debate between prosecution—Judge—defence in a chambers, then I was taken back into the court and re-sentenced to life. My tariff was set at 14 years by the Home Secretary at the time'.

E said that having been in therapy has helped him to come to terms with his crimes and his sexuality, that he had got rid of barriers in relationships and has better relationships with his parents. He acknowledges part of this in saying that he was drunk and that he is an alcoholic. He also seemed to appreciate the link between his having been raped and then attacking, beating and stabbing to death an apparently aggressive homosexual less than two years later.

CASE F

I think I'd have gone any distance to keep my image.

G is 37 and coming to the end of a period of therapy which has lasted over three years and '. . . given me back my life and self-respect'. He spoke quietly but eloquently about himself, his crime and the powerful therapeutic process he'd experienced.

In spite of an unexceptional childhood, F says he was most influenced by his grandfather who died when he was four years old and that he ran away from home when he was 14 to begin a 'criminal lifestyle' including, he estimated, well over 50 crimes of burglary, taking and driving away a motor vehicle (as it then was), and assaults. He had gone to borstal and been in prison before the index crime of murder. The crime itself was not exceptional by the standards of murder: a vengeful stabbing to death of his estranged wife's new lover. F said he had wanted to kill them both, indeed had had enough of life himself but '. . . didn't know how to get out of it'. Having confronted the couple, and their having denied the affair, he admits that he set up the subsequent confrontation on the pretence of wanting to resolve their differences. He says part of the motivation was wanting his wife to suffer for the rest of her life. The victim, formally a close friend of F, was stabbed by him 40 times. Asked why, F explained that he'd felt justified at the time: 'I felt like I'd lost everything in life—son, girlfriend, image and ego'.

Asked to reflect on the events which had led up to the killing, F confessed that he'd 'Always known I was a very dangerous man, that I had to come to prison until it was safe to go out'. In the past, he'd known that as soon as he left prison he became dangerous. Now, after seven years inside and almost half of that in a therapeutic community regime, F felt safe. He has voluntarily, at his own request, gone through the official 'scene of crime' photographs which number in their dozens and which are extremely graphic and detailed. This process, of confronting the clearest possible evidence of his crime, and of his violence, was intended to serve both to refute any subsequent distortions in his recall (minimisation) as to the horrific nature of the crime, and to assist the therapeutic process—guided by the staff team—on internal emotional reconciliation.

F has a 14 year tariff and no illusions but that he will serve many more years before being freed. He was impressive in his resolve and clearly respected by the other members of the prison community for his courage, sound advice to others and his commitment.

The lessons from these six cases, and from the authors' experience of having worked closely with many hundreds of other murderers over careers each spanning three decades, are briefly highlighted in *Section III* of this chapter.

III. HOW TO KNOW AND HOW TO HELP

STRATEGIES FOR HELPING MURDERERS AND OTHER LIFERS TO CHANGE

The only thing murderers have in common is their victim's death. The diversity of men and women who kill is axiomatic. That given, there are things which those of us who are asked to understand these fellow humans—and hopefully help them to both come to terms with what they've done and to exert some positive influence upon their various efforts to change for the better—can proffer.

We have already seen that it is possible to identify a small number of relatively discreet parts to the overall picture:

- the *biological* factors which influence our limitations, drives and capacities
- the *historical* aspects of childhood and the influences of parents, etc.
- the *social and cultural* influences and pressures which often cause our parents to refer to 'bad influences', peer pressures, etc. as well as the lottery of which nationality we are and how that nation views individual freedom and crime
- the *psychological* cards we are all dealt and the personalities we present
- the *situational* pressures which can determine whether we kill, argue, discuss or acquiesce.

As with these factors, there are also many specific circumstances which help to identify taxonomies of murder, those types or clusters which make us feel as though we understand better but which mainly serve only to oversimplify. Nevertheless, we see sufficient patterns to risk identifying (as others have before us):

- *domestic murderers* who kill a wife, girlfriend, parents. Recurring factors include fear of loss/rejection, infidelity, rage and an intense explosion of anger which is often said to have (a) built up over long periods, often years and which often is (b) dissipated immediately the act is done.

- *escape murderers* who are surprised in the course of a burglary or who are engaged in a robbery where the victim behaves in an unexpected, challenging and aggressive manner. Such individuals are often relatively normal, profit-motivated criminals who kill almost accidentally in order to escape capture/detention.

- *profit murderers* who kill as a means to an end, i.e. in order to inherit money or benefit indirectly or who are profit-motivated criminals prepared to see life taking as an 'occupational hazard'.

- *irrational murderers* who kill without any apparent motive. Such people are often mentally unstable or mentally ill, with a number of highly publicised cases of individuals released from mental hospitals to 'care in the community' only to have obviously not been cared for.

- *explosion murderers* who are often over-controlled, even timid people with little or no prior criminality.

There are many strategies of intervention which have the potential to help these people. The starting point must be one of understanding; of seeing another human rather than a murderer. It is difficult if not impossible, but the *first strategy* we would suggest is to *imagine how you would feel if it were you who had killed.* Do not pass this suggestion; stop and concentrate on that prospect. You have only to reflect on the worst thing that you ever did to another person. Was it someone you cared for? Were you ever able to make amends? Were you reconciled? If you kill, you can never be reconciled with your victim and it is extremely rare for murderers to ever be reconciled with their victims' families and friends. From the day you are confirmed as a murderer, you are forever a murderer first, a person second. Does this process of 'role reversal' provoke any introspection?

The literature on interpersonal relationships, e.g. social skills, is full of information about first impressions and how to make good ones. With murderers, and lifers generally in my experience, there tends to be an additional layer of defensiveness and an anticipation that they will be poorly judged. Experience again suggests that another helpful strategy is *to treat each man as if he's normal*—because he probably is. And, if he is not, he probably wants to be, so it cannot hurt and will probably help. This suggestion flies in the face of traditional psychiatric and psychotherapeutic advice which would be concerned that 'patients' who have been classified as 'suffering' from disorders of personality are, by definition, not normal and that we must be careful not to exacerbate their 'conditions' by attempting to intervene without extensive, specialised training in psychiatry or psychotherapy. This prescription means, in practice, that they have a dual agenda whereby they address the 'patient' as if he or she were normal, but are interpreting his or her behaviour for signs—'symptoms'—of the underlying disorder which then must be factored into the therapist's 'diagnosis' and recommended form of treatment: if, indeed, the individual is fortunate to be 'suffering' from one of the conditions which this professional avenue dictates is amenable to treatment. The delight of the therapeutic community approach is that it demedicalises the entire process, saves considerable complexity in this convoluted—and unproven—process and allows people who are simply stable, motivated and humane to contribute to helping others to become the same.

Understand the person first and you will understand the crime
This is is our third strategy although the more appropriate word is probably principle, as strategy seems too much like tactics used as a means to an end, a form of manipulation for self-purposes and that is not what we are advocating. The best way to understand someone, in our experience, is to let them talk about themselves and, when you have established a level of trust, to try to encourage a closer exploration of those aspects of their account of their life which seem confused or discordant. It is not about facts, it is about honesty and that is about both what we say and what we do not say. A lifer once said

... the best lies are the ones wrapped in truths.

and he was right. We are most often misled by partial truths which are 'as true as they aren't' and by partial disclosures which seem full enough to allow the worst to remain hidden. One of the great and, in our experience unique, strengths of the Therapeutic Community (TC) approach to treating serious offenders is that it is a form of therapy which reaches the feelings, and parts of minds, other therapies cannot reach. It does this by a sustained scrutiny of each man's life by a party of his peers who are resolved to stay with him until the truth is out. While one-to-one therapy, and other group-based therapies can achieve these insights, a TC obliges them to *demonstrate* that they really have changed as a consequence of those insights and, further still, that the new, pro-social behaviours resulting aren't simply temporarily 'learned' to satisfy the authorities. Being a 24-hour form of living therapy means that it is impossible to sustain pretences, particularly when your peers (and sometime former accomplices) are now your scrutineers!

Another maxim which has come to us through the therapeutic community process is that you are not obliged to find solutions.

Collective responsibility means collective exploration

If you are fortunate enough to be working within groups or communities, it is so important not to take on board too much of the onus or responsibility for an individual's treatment. Share it. If, on the other hand, you are working primarily in a one-to-one situation, consider involving a colleague as a sounding board and alternative view. This would obviously only be done with the consent of the inmate or patient and on a agreed basis of confidentiality.

Another traditional approach which often occurs in treating serious offenders is heard through the assertion 'I don't hate you, I hate your crime'. This theme, and variations on it, presume that, if we detach the crime from the criminal, it will (a) make it easier for him or her to be accepted and (b) send a message of encouragement.

Our view is that it is far more difficult, but also far more important, to be able to honestly assert that we aim to accept the person even though it means accepting his or her crime. This is not the same as diminishing the seriousness of the crime—murder is murder. It is a recognition that the offender can *never* not be responsible for taking the life of another human being but can come to be accepted again even though he or she did. To do otherwise—in our view—is to collude in a form of denial. The understanding is that this alternative strategy is saying, effectively, 'I hate what you did and I'm prepared to help you never do it again'. We would summarise this strategy as a variant on the classic therapeutic aspiration of *unconditional positive regard.*

There are of course many other strategies for positive intervention with lifers generally and murderers in particular. For our purpose, hopefully this brief list will help the reader to consider the image of this whole process as being comparable to putting *one* arm around the man or woman and, when they trust you, slowly moving a mirror into place so that they see themselves as others see them.

CHAPTER THREE

Delusions of Innocence[1]

This chapter addresses the question of the number of prisoners, especially life sentenced prisoners, who are innocent of the crime for which they have been convicted, but who nonetheless have been imprisoned. It describes the experiences of prisoners who were wrongly convicted and imprisoned, and who have now been released, and others who remain in custody. The chapter argues that HM Prison Service should develop suitable procedures for prisoners who maintain their innocence, and who as a consequence are pursuing their case with the CCRC. In particular, it is argued that the current procedures involved in the SOTP, and more generally parole, which require prisoners to "acknowledge" their guilt amount to a "throffer" — the combination of a threat with an offer. This chapter suggests that this fundamentally undermines the concept of justice in prisons.

I. LIFERS, INNOCENCE AND HM PRISON SERVICE: THE SCALE OF THE PROBLEM

On 27 November 1997 more than 60 prisoners at HMPs Frankland, Long Lartin, Durham, Gartree, and Maidstone went on hunger strike to highlight the number of alleged miscarriage of justice cases within the criminal justice system (CJS).[2] It is estimated that at present there are over 1,000 such cases, and that the Criminal Cases Review Commission (CCRC), an independent body set up under the Criminal Appeal Act 1995 to investigate suspected miscarriage cases, receives new cases at the rate of five per day. A significant number of those who took part in the hunger strike are life sentenced prisoners. They included Winston Silcott, who, having been cleared of the murder of PC Keith Blakelock, is serving life for another murder, which he claims was self-defence; Susan May, serving life for the murder of an elderly aunt; Gary Mills and Tony Poole, whose case has been taken up by the campaigning TV

---

[1] I am grateful to Campbell Malone, Stefan Kiszko's solicitor, who advised me about this entry in Mr Kiszko's medical notes. This miscarriage case is discussed in detail within the text. I would also like to thank the Prison Reform Trust for allowing me to use their excellent library and research facilities, and for permission to quote from letters sent to them by serving prisoners.

[2] *The Guardian*, 27 November 1997, p.4. The hunger strike was jointly organized by Action Against Injustice, who state that they are fighting 'against corruption in the police and legal system', and Birmingham Prisoners Solidarity. On the day in question they also organized a march to the CCRC. They stated in their flyer advertising the march that their aim was to 'have a big effect in highlighting individual campaigns and the level of corruption in the police and justice system in Britain today, and also build solidarity among campaigns'. A copy of the leaflet advertising the march was sent to the Prison Reform Trust, dated 31 October 1997.

series, *Trial and Error*; and Eddie Gilfoyle, serving life for the murder of his wife.

It is of course difficult to establish a definitive number of prisoners who are alleging to be wrongly convicted at any one time. Nor is it possible to establish how many of those who allege that they are innocent are in fact eventually proven to be innocent of the crime for which they have been convicted. Indeed, HM Prison Service is even reluctant to acknowledge that this might be an issue, and allow or commission research which could establish the extent of the problem.[3] However, the figures produced by the CCRC are confirmed by the number of cases currently being worked on by *Trial and Error*, and evidence from other secondary sources.[4] For example, in 1989 the organization JUSTICE estimated that the number of defendants per year, sentenced to four years or more by the Crown Court, who had been wrongly convicted, suggested that there will be well over 1,000 people in prison wrongly convicted at any one time. Similarly, the Prison Officers Association estimated that in 1992 there might be up to 700 innocent people in prison after conviction.[5] This variety of evidence would seem to indicate that about 2 per cent of the prison population, or 1,300 people, mostly concentrated in long-term prisons, are innocent of the crime for which they have been convicted, and that a substantial proportion of this number are life sentenced prisoners.

This estimate is likely to be on the low side, given that there are many disincentives for prisoners, especially long-term prisoners to maintain their innocence. Such issues as parole, transfer, incentives, categorization (see below) might all depend on the willingness of the prisoner to 'acknowledge' his or her guilt. As the former Home Affairs specialist at *The Observer* writes,

> . . . for life sentenced prisoners, protesting innocence is a sure-fire way to remain in gaol forever. The inmate will be accused of having failed to "address his offending behaviour", so making it impossible for the authorities to assess his future risk to the public.[6]

A number of high profile 'miscarriage cases' are visible proof of some aspects of this problem. A miscarriage case can be seen as having three

---

[3] The Prison Reform Trust has attempted to raise this matter with the Director General of HM Prison Service, but with no success. The author was Senior Policy Advisor at the Prison Reform Trust, prior to taking up an academic post.

[4] The ITV programme *Trial and Error* is currently working on 190 cases, of which approximately 100 relate to life sentenced prisoners. Personal correspondence between John Ashton, researcher on *Trial and Error* and the author, dated 9 December 1997.

[5] Both estimates are reported in C Walker, K Starmer (1993), *Justice in Error*, London: Blackstone, pp. 11-12.

[6] D Rose (1996) *In The Name of the Law: The Collapse of Criminal Justice*, London: Vintage, p.34

inter-related elements: firstly, one in which an individual or individuals are treated by the state in a way which breaches their rights; secondly, where someone is treated adversely by the state in that the punishment is disproportionate to the aim of protecting the rights of others; and finally where the rights of others are not properly vindicated or protected by state action. Thus in relation to the first of these three elements, the breaching of the rights of an individual would occur when that individual is subjected to arrest or imprisonment without due cause. Clearly this is of relevance to the present chapter, as imprisoning people who are innocent of crime falls within this definition. However, it can also be argued that imprisoning someone who is guilty of crime, but on the basis of inadequate proof, is similarly tainted. Some will argue that those who are 'truly innocent' should be seen as a separate category from those who are 'innocent by way of a legal technicality'. However, as Clive Walker has argued, a person who has in fact committed a crime could be said 'to have suffered a miscarriage if convicted on evidence which is legally inadmissible or which is not proven beyond reasonable doubt'.[7]

II. MISCARRIAGE OF JUSTICE CASES

The most prominent recent miscarriage cases begin with the Guildford Four, who were wrongly convicted of IRA pub bombings in Guildford and Woolwich; the Maguire Seven; Judith Ward; and the Birmingham Six.[8] Thereafter, most of the high profile cases relate to the work of the West Midlands Serious Crime Squad, which was disbanded in 1989. Perhaps the most notorious case arising from its work was that of Derek Treadaway who confessed to four armed robberies. He received a sentence of 15 years, having 'confessed' only after police had placed a series of plastic bags over his head. In 1994 he was awarded £50,000 in damages.[9] Other cases from different police areas relate to those convicted after the Broadwater Farm riot in 1985; those who were alleged to have murdered the paper boy Carl Bridgewater; Michelle and Lisa Taylor, who were wrongly convicted of murdering the wife of Michelle's lover; and Stefan Kiszko.

Stefan Kiszko spent 16 years in prison wrongly convicted of the sexual murder of the schoolgirl Lesley Molseed, in October 1975. When Stefan was arrested in December of that year there was no forensic evidence to link him to Lesley's death. He was an overweight tax clerk

---

[7] Walker, Starmer (1993), p. 4. The definition of what constitutes a miscarriage case follows Walker's analysis closely.

[8] Of interest are G Conlon (1990), *Proved Innocent*, London: Hamilton; and, C Mullin (1990), *Error of Judgment*, London: Chatto and Windus

[9] An account of the Treadaway case can be found in Rose (1996), pp.260-274

from Rochdale, who until that winter had never been in trouble with the police. When he went with the police on Christmas Eve in 1975 he had absolute confidence that the police investigation would exonerate him. After two days in police custody Stefan signed a 'confession' to the murder, which he subsequently withdrew. It took 16 years for Stefan to be released, when his solicitors discovered that he had a zero sperm count, and that tests on his semen, and semen found on Lesley were incompatible. Stefan's biographers describe the toll of his years of incarceration:

> Was it the very fact of Kiszko's incarceration that had rendered him "quite mad", or was it the fact that he was never regarded as a likely candidate for parole, notwithstanding that he had served longer than other convicted murderers who were released after a much shorter period of time inside. Was it his immovable belief in his own innocence . . . or was it merely the failure of any other person to consider that he might be telling the truth when he declared his innocence? Was it the persistence of those who sought to persaude him to admit his crime or was it simply an inevitable consequence of an underdeveloped and fragile personality dealt the most enormous wrong by a system of justice in which he placed so much faith?[10]

All these cases are proof of a number of prisoners who are wrongly convicted and incarcerated, sometimes for very long periods of time, for crimes which they did not commit. Indeed it is interesting to note that during Prisoners' Week, an annual event since 1975 organized by Prison Chaplains and other Christians, and largely celebrated in the local community, which in 1997 took place between 16-22 November, one of the daily prayers was to 'Pray for Prisoners who are Not Guilty'.

> Some prisoners are not guilty of the crimes with which they are charged. Do we listen to them and support them in their quest for justice?[11]

A variety of evidence would suggest that the manner in which HM Prison Service treats prisoners who allege that they are innocent falls far short of the spirit of the question within the prayer. Vincent Hickey, for example, who together with his cousin Michael, Jimmy Robinson and the late Pat Malloy were wrongly convicted of the murder of Carl Bridgewater, gives a flavour of how those alleging to be innocent are treated. Having been released in February 1997 after spending 18 years in jail, he wrote that '. . . they pulled every stroke in the book to keep us in prison. They lied and lied'. He also claims:

---

[10] J Rose, S Panter, T Wilkinson (1997), *Innocents: How Justice Failed Stefan Kiszko and Lesley Molseed*, Fourth Estate: London, p.244

[11] Prisoners' Week is a registered charity. Its Patrons are the Archbishop of Canterbury, the Archbishop of Westminster and the Moderator of the Free Church Federal Council. The text of the prayer is taken from their leaflet for 1997.

I am still haunted by the flashbacks. In the middle of the night my cell door used to fly open and drunken screws would burst in and beat me. Then they pissed on me. I'd be fast asleep, the next thing I know my face has hit the floor. Now every night when I go to bed I lie down and I see it all over again. I can't sleep. The thing that gets to me most is the fact that they pissed on me. The lack of dignity. In the day I can sometimes forget. It's the nights that it gets bad, and it doesn't leave me.[12]

Of course not all those who claim to be innocent of the crime for which they have been convicted are able to generate the publicity, support, and campaigns which characterised, for example, the Birmingham Six. One journalist wrote of being 'almost inured to the pleas of innocence from men in gaol which regularly cross my desk'. He acknowledges that very few cases have an infra-structure of support, which in turn will generate media interest.

One first fights to convince one's newspaper executive that the subject is worthy of space; a battle which, in the late 1990s, is increasingly hard to win, as miscarriages of justice no longer command the mainstream of political debate. At last the story is published: in the life of a prisoner, an event of incalculable significance. And then nothing, for years on end.[13]

This was certainly true for Andy Evans, e.g. who served 25 years of a life sentence having been convicted of killing a teenage girl in Tamworth. At the time of the killing, Evans, on the verge of a nervous breakdown, had dreamt that he had seen the victim, and gone to the local police station to ask to see a photograph of the girl to put his mind at rest. After being held in custody for three days, without being allowed to see a solicitor, he confessed to murder, and was convicted on the basis of that confession, despite the absence of corroborating evidence. Only in November 1997 was he at last released from prison, having won his appeal.[14]

Alf Fox has not been so lucky. Fox was convicted and sentenced to life imprisonment in 1980, despite the fact that the evidence against him was largely circumstantial. Police became convinced that Fox had started the fire which killed his estranged wife and her mother, as their child had been spared from the same fate. The police's only evidence against Fox was the testimony of Myrtle Westhead, who lived opposite the house where the murders took place, and who alleged that she had seen a car similar to Fox's speeding away from the scene of the crime. However, in 1992 Fox's solicitor was given access

---

[12] *The Observer*, 17 August 1997. For an outline of the case, which is essentially accurate despite being published eleven years before their release, see P Foot (1986), *Murder at the Farm: Who Killed Carl Bridgewater?*, Harmondsworth: Penguin

[13] Rose (1996), p.34

[14] ibid, p.36. Rose's book was published before Evans won his appeal and release

to police documents which had not been disclosed at the time of the trial. These showed that Mrs Westhead had claimed to have seen a car entirely different from the type owned by Fox, and was only persuaded to change her mind about the make of the car after several weeks of detectives paying visits to her.[15] As yet, Fox remains in prison.

III. PRISON AND INNOCENCE: PROTESTS AND THE OFFICIAL SIDE

Why should HM Prison Service care if the prisoners it houses are innocent or guilty? Indeed, at one level some prison staff might argue that as this is an issue which is determined elsewhere within the criminal justice system, as are appeals against conviction, that HM Prison Service really cannot get involved with issues relating to miscarriages of justice; or, even more broadly, with innocence, which in any event can be investigated by the CCRC. Similarly some prisoners will declare themselves innocent, despite the fact that they are guilty, in the hope of, e.g. protecting their family, or more simply because they are 'in denial'. This does make all of this problematic for prison staff. Nonetheless the remainder of this chapter will present a series of arguments to show that views such as these are at best short sighted, and in the long run contribute to the general undermining of confidence that many people currently sense in relation to the criminal justice system in England and Wales. Prisons are an integral part of this system, and have themselves adopted measures which require offenders to 'acknowledge' their guilt in order to gain parole, or improvements in regime conditions. This adversely affects prisoners who are innocent of the crime for which they have been convicted. An outline of the origins and development of the CCRC will also be presented, and the chapter will conclude with some tentative suggestions as to a possible strategy that HM Prison Service could adopt to deal with this issue.

Managing prisoners who claim to be innocent is not always easy. If they are organized they will be able to generate media interest, and this in itself creates work for the prison. However, of greater concern is that the prisoners themselves often refuse to accept the realities of prison life. This is no small matter, and Michael and Vincent Hickey, e.g. took their protestations of innocence onto the roof of HMP Long Lartin, one of the country's dispersal prisons, and thus theoretically one of the most secure, between 26 February and 20 March 1983.[16] The 22

---

[15] The outline of the case is contained in Rose (1996), pp.34-36
[16] There are many standard text books which explain the origins of the 'dispersal system': see, e.g. D Wilson, S Bryans (1998), *The Prison Governor: Theory and Practice, Prison Service*

days that they spent on the prison roof compares poorly with the 89 days that Michael spent on the roof at HMP Gartree between 24 November 1983 and 21 February 1984. This was a truly astonishing feat, which in turn generated substantial media interest, but which could not have been sustained without the support of other prisoners within HMP Gartree. Clearly, no matter how well prepared a prisoner who wants to adopt this approach is, food sooner or later runs out, it gets bitterly cold, and lonely. However, describing the course of the events, Paul Foot explains how Michael was able to sustain the protest for so long:

> He could not have survived for more than a few days without the sudden, spontaneous and almost unanimous support of the inmates of Gartree prison. Before long, all sorts of useful things started arriving on the roof. By the end of the second week Michael had amassed 100 new bin liners, and a huge assortment of coat hangers, broom handles, pillows, and blankets. There was also an endless supply of radios – perhaps the most precious of all prisoners' possessions – which kept breaking down in the frost and damp, but were instantly replaced.[17]

Michael was also able to build a shelter against the weather, and given that prison staff had decided upon a strategy of 'starving him down', proved adept at maintaining stocks of food. Foot advises us that Michael '. . . got a hot meal almost every night', by adopting a covert plan with collaborators in the prison's residential units.

> The plan contained an intricate code with letters and numbers which would be held out of the windows to let him know where his food parcel was coming from. After a few weeks, Michael had string with hooks hanging down to almost every window in the prison. He would then watch out for the code, and, after a dummy run or two to confuse the warders, he would rush to the correct window and haul up his food.[18]

Leaving on one side how embarrassing this must have been to the prison, especially given the strategy adopted to have him end the protest, it clearly also must have been a drain on resources in the prison. Managing roof-top protests, as with other demonstrations, demands the implementation of contingency plans which involve staff at a variety of grades working outside of their normal roles; co-ordination of those plans with HM Prison Service Headquarters at Cleland House in

Journal: HMP Leyhill. However, in brief, the policy of dispersing Cat A prisoners—the highest security category for prisoners, which is itself divided into three sub-categories—was introduced following the Mountbatten Report into prison security in 1966, even though this was not recommended in the report. In effect prisoners in Cat A are 'dispersed' amongst a few prisons deemed to have appropriate levels of security.

[17] Foot (1986), p.242
[18] ibid, p.244

London; and continued anxiety that the protest might spread, or be used as cover for other incidents such as escapes. In the often tense culture of long-term prisons,[19] where the balance of power between staff and inmates is almost constantly being tested, having a prisoner on the roof, and being able to sustain that prisoner for over 12 weeks, would give encouragement to many other prisoners for different protests of their own.

Not all prisoners who are innocent engage in protests of this kind. However, if refusing to acknowledge innocence, or the possibility of a miscarriage of justice can lead in extreme circumstances to situations of the type described above, perhaps it is in HM Prison Service's interests to deal with this issue in more positive ways. Indeed, if the estimate of those who are incarcerated who are innocent is accepted, sheer numbers alone suggests that a strategy to accommodate these prisoners should be developed. There are clearly better reasons for HM Prison Service to deal with all of this positively than a desire for good prison management.

The concept of justice in prisons is one which several commentators have argued should be at the heart of what HM Prison Service does. Lord Justice Woolf, e.g. commented in the report of his inquiry after the disturbances prompted by the riot at HMP Strangeways in 1990:

> . . . a recurring theme in the evidence from prisoners who may have instigated, and who were involved in, the riots was that their actions were a response to the manner in which they were treated by the prison system. If what they say is true, the failure of the Prison Service to fulfil its responsibilities to act with justice created in April 1990 serious difficulties in maintaining security and control in prisons.[20]

This led Woolf to conclude that there should be improved standards of justice inside prison—partly as a means to improve security and control—which would involve 'giving reasons to a prisoner for any decision which materially and adversely affects him; a grievance procedure and disciplinary proceedings which ensure that the Governor deals with most matters under his present powers; relieving Boards of Visitors of their adjudicatory role; and providing for final access to an independent complaints adjudicator'.[21] This last point led directly to the creation of the Prisons Ombudsman.

---

[19] Issues related to the culture and sub-cultures of prisons are beyond the scope of this chapter. However, of note, especially as he is now in charge of the Dispersals Directorate, Phil Wheatley wrote about this issue in 'Riots and Mass Disorder in Male Prisons', in J Reynolds, U Smartt (1996), *Prison Policy and Practice: Selected Papers from 35 Years of the Prison Service Journal*, Leyhill: Prison Service Journal, pp. 223-231

[20] *Prison Disturbances, April 1990: Report of an Inquiry* (1991), London: HMSO, p. 226

[21] ibid, p.434

The Woolf Inquiry raises the issue of justice in a way which both relates to the actual experience of imprisonment and at the same time places what happens in prison within a broader context of the criminal justice system as a whole. Indeed this was evident in the recommendation that there should be much clearer cooperation between all the component parts of that system through the establishment of the Criminal Justice Consultative Council, and 24 Area Criminal Justice Liaison Committees. Thus it could be argued that in the same way that the police had to respond to the miscarriage cases, with the subsequent introduction of the Police and Criminal Evidence Act 1984, and then the establishment of the Crown Prosecution Service, both of which altered the way in which the CJS operated, so should HM Prison Service be prepared to develop accordingly.

Whether this view is accepted or not, the position which HM Prison Service currently adopts is to deny that there is an issue. Not only that, it has gone further, and also requires prisoners in a variety of circumstances to actively acknowledge their guilt. If they refuse to do so, they potentially worsen their position in relation to release. Andy Evans, e.g. had by 1991 managed to progress within the prison system by falsely acknowledging his guilt, and as a consequence had gained a transfer to the open prison HMP Leyhill. Despite being trusted to work in the local Gloucester community, Evans decided that he could no longer maintain his deceit in relation to the offence for which he had been sentenced, and advised the Governor accordingly. That same afternoon he was transferred back into maximum security conditions.[22]

This comes very close to what political philosophers describe as 'throffers'—the combination of an offer or promise of a reward if a course of action is pursued, with a threat or penalty if this course of action is refused.[23] This is obviously an exercise in power. The choice structure offers incentives to the prisoner to follow the course of action desired by the prison, making that 'choice' appear rational. It is of course rare for prison policy or regulations to be presented or openly described in this way—although many prisoners will describe their experiences as such[24]—and David Rose, for example, who has written about these matters did not provide any specific examples of 'throffers' operating in practice, but rather in terms of outcomes affecting prisoners, which could be explained in other ways. However, glimpses

---

[22] Rose (1996), p.36

[23] The term 'throffer' was coined by Hillel Steiner, but for a general introduction to throffers see M A Taylor (1982), *Community, Anarchy and Liberty*, Cambridge: Cambridge University Press. The term has also been in general use by police and in British courts for many years to describe any situation where an offer implies some less desirable alternative.

[24] I have previously written about this issue in 'Prisoners' Postbag', *Criminal Justice Matters*, No. 29, Autumn 1997, pp.19-20

of 'throffers' occasionally come to the surface, and the sex offender treatment programme is a case in point.

IV. THE SEX OFFENDER TREATMENT PROGRAMME AND THE PROBLEMS OF INNOCENCE

The Sex Offender Treatment Programme (SOTP) was introduced into HM Prison Service in the early 1990s. Building upon the cognitive behavioural programmes developed in Canada, the SOTP seemed to promise much in the face of growing media and moral panics about sex offenders in the community. According to an editorial in the *Journal of Forensic Psychiatry*, a '. . . combination of public concern, political expediency and policy initiative' saw the number of sex offenders in prison more than double between 1981 and 1988, when 2,692 prisoners were incarcerated with a sexual offence as their main index offence. The desire to do something about this growing number of sex offenders meant that, in the words of the Senior Medical Officer at HMP Grendon, 'Sex offenders have become sexy'.[25]

The basis of the SOTP was explained in almost breathless terms by Eddie Guy, the civil servant in charge of DIP2, which at the time was the division of HM Prison Service which had responsibility for 'programmes for problem behaviour'. He described the four main features of HM Prison Service's strategy towards sex offenders:

- sex offenders would be held in fewer prisons
- priority for treatment would be given to those who were likely to represent the greatest risk to the community on release
- prisoners would be assessed following conviction and sentence to determine which of them was in most need of treatment; and
- treatment programmes would be based on admission of offences, challenging attitudes, and tackling offending behaviour.[26]

There are two main programmes within the SOTP, both of which are offence specific: the 'extended programme', for those who represent the greatest risk to the public; and a 'core programme', which requires less specialist resources. Of note, Guy advises that the core programme

> . . . will tackle offenders' distorted beliefs about relationships, enhance their awareness of the effect of sexual offences on the victim, and seek to get

---

[25] *The Journal of Forensic Psychiatry*, Vol. 2, No. 1, May 1991, pp.8-9
[26] E Guy, 'The Prison Service's Strategy', in *The Penal Response to Sex Offending* (1992), London: Prison Reform Trust, pp.1-7

prisoners to take responsibility for, and face up to the consequences of, their own offending behaviour.[27]

This is all well and good, unless of course you actually did not commit the sexual offence for which you have been convicted. Indeed it becomes doubly difficult for the convicted sex offender who just happens to be innocent, for as Guy advises us, sex offenders are particularly prone to 'cognitive distortions', which allow them to 'rationalise' their offending.[28] Protestations of innocence can thus be seen as merely 'delusions', or the product of cognitive distortions.

In relation to the 'throffer', the explicit 'offer' is the treatment with its promise of release; the 'threat' the failure to secure release, and possibly beyond the time at which this could have been expected. This threat is quite explicit, despite the fact that the SOTP wants 'volunteers' to engage in the programme. In determining 'priorities for treatment', e.g. Guy explains that the programme will prioritise those with the longest sentence, as this reflects the seriousness of the offence, and the fact that

> such offenders will be subject to a selective system of parole. The extent to which their offending behaviour has been addressed in prison is likely to be an important factor in reaching that parole decision.[29]

It is thus quite clear that to get parole any sex offender would have to admit guilt, and participate in programmes to work on his offence and any cognitive distortions. At the time that all of this was being written, Stefan Kiszko (although later found to be innocent: see above) was one of this growing number of sex offenders who were to be targeted for treatment. One prisoner who still is wrote to the Prison Reform Trust from HMP Risley about the predicament which he faced:

> I am currently serving a seven year sentence for alleged rape which I always maintained that I did not commit . . . I have settled into my sentence in a peaceful manor, worked everyday available and only had one adjudication upheld against me . . . 12 months ago I made enquiries with me personal officer about obtaining Category 'D' status. I was advised by him to use the request complaints procedure which I did, and have in my possession the reply stating the prison system will not consider me for Category 'D' status without addressing my alleged 'offending behaviour' . . . obviously I am of the opinion that this constitutes a rather vulgar form of blackmail, in that my refusal to lie, by taking part in the 'core programme' and pretending that I *did* commit the offence, even though I didn't — which they would like me to do, gives them the right to say that I have no chance of being given

---

[27] ibid, p.1
[28] ibid, p.5
[29] ibid, p.4

parole, though this was not a condition imposed upon me at the time of my sentencing by the Judge who handled my case.[30]

Policy and internal procedures related to HM Prison Service are not always as open in their rationale as that applied to the SOTP.. Another exception is the *Lifer Manual* (LM) mentioned earlier, which is the formal source document about how life sentenced prisoners should be managed.[31] As such it maintains that lifers who maintain their innocence are 'undeniably difficult', but goes on to suggest that as a strategy for dealing with this difficulty '. . . it may not help to get involved in discussions about guilt or innocence'.[32] This is underscored by the fact that it makes it clear that 'the Prison Service must take as its starting point the assumption that the prisoner was rightly convicted'.[33] Given this position it provides advice to staff concerning the information required on life sentenced prisoners when they are to be considered for parole, or re-categorization to a lower security category. It states that such reports 'must concentrate on the degree to which the lifer has addressed his or her offending behaviour', and as such outlines some criteria to be included in the ideal report. This would include attitude to the offence:

- Does the prisoner deny guilt?
- Has the prisoner come to terms with his or her part in the offence, and accepted responsibility for it?
- Is he or she ready to talk about it?
- Assess the prisoner's attitude towards others who may have been involved, and the victim.
- State the degree of remorse, if any, expressed.[34]

The Training Guidance within the manual for staff considering transferring a lifer to open conditions applies these questions in a very direct way, and also explains why Andy Evans was removed so quickly

---

[30] Letter to Prison Reform Trust in March 1997, from HMP Risley. I have retained the spelling, style and emphasis of the original letter. It should be noted that five sex offenders at HMP Wymott went to the High Court in March 1997 arguing much the same as the letter writer to the Prison Reform Trust. In this test case, Edward Tabachnik QC claimed that in effect HM Prison Service were 'punishing the deniers for denying', who were in a 'Catch 22' situation, unable to show that they had addressed their 'offending behaviour', given that they maintained their innocence. This argument was rejected by the judge.

[31] All quotes are taken from the *Lifer Manual: A Guide for Members of the Prison and Probation Services Working with Life Sentenced Prisoners*, HM Prison Service, 1996. This document is not particularly 'user friendly', and anyone wishing to understand a little more of the complexities of the lifer system should see instead, N Stone (1997) *A Companion Guide to Life Sentences*, Ilkley: Owen Wells Publisher.

[32] *Lifer Manual*, paras 7.4 - 7.5

[33] *Lifer Manual*, para 7.4

[34] *Lifer Manual*, para 7.3.2

from HMP Leyhill. For example, it recommends that the following factors should generally be taken into account when recommending transfer to open conditions: the nature and circumstances of the original offence and the reasons for it; 'areas of concern in the lifer's offending behaviour'; and 'insight into attitudes and behavioural problems, attitude to the offence and degree of remorse and steps taken to achieve the treatment and training objectives set out in the Life Sentence Plan'.[35] As can be imagined, a prisoner maintaining his or her innocence is going to find it very difficult indeed to benefit from transfer to a prison in a lower security category. One life sentenced prisoner at HMP Gartree, writing about his own and others' experiences in relation to this issue, commented that 'it is regrettable that despite various trials and appeal hearings they could not get their convictions overturned for a crime they did not commit and are at a loss as to how to make progress through the prison system'.[36]

V. 'FALSE NEGATIVES'

Central to any potential response that HM Prison Service might develop to the question of innocent people being incarcerated will be the Criminal Cases Review Commission (CCRC), and it is therefore important to understand something of the recent history and development of this independent agency.

The Criminal Cases Review Commisssion

Set up by the Criminal Appeal Act 1995, the CCRC's origins stem from a Royal Commission on Criminal Justice announced by Kenneth Baker in March 1991, who at the time was Home Secretary. Baker explained his thinking in his memoirs in the following way:

> Having dealt with several cases of alleged miscarriages of justice I came to the conclusion that the system needs to be changed. Such allegations should not come to the Home Secretary for him to consider whether they should be referred to the Court of Appeal. They should instead be submitted to a separate Authority which would investigate them and examine any new evidence. That Authority should have extensive powers of investigation and examination. If it found that allegations of a miscarriage of justice were not frivolous but cast serious doubts over the soundness of a verdict, then it would refer the case either to the Court of Appeal or to a separate Court which would reopen the matter in a less formal way than the usual adversarial style of the British Courts.[37]

---

[35] *Lifer Manual*, Appendix 6, para 2
[36] Letter to Prison Reform Trust, in May 1997 from HMP Gartree
[37] K Baker (1993), *The Turbulent Years: My Life in Politics*, London: Faber and Faber, pp.431-432

Given this type of reasoning, the Royal Commission's terms of reference were therefore quite far-reaching, and its report was presented to Parliament in July 1993. It recommended the establishment of an independent body to consider suspected miscarriages of justice; where appropriate to arrange for their investigation; and, where that investigation revealed matters which ought to be considered further by the courts, to refer the case concerned to the Court of Appeal. The CCRC is therefore a 'last resort', and as such cases cannot be considered until the prisoner has exhausted the normal appeal system.

The CCRC examines each case impartially, and has to decide whether there is a real possibility of it succeeding if it is given a further hearing in an appeal court. This is done by one of the 14 members of the Commission, who are assisted by support and administration staff. However, despite what Baker seems to have intended, the CCRC has no power of investigation, and cannot, e.g. carry out searches of premises, check criminal records, use police computers, or make an arrest. If a commissioner feels that any one of these things is necessary to make a decision about a case, then the police would have to become involved to investigate on behalf of the CCRC. This might prove problematic, and potentially compromise the independence of the CCRC when reaching a decision. It should also be noted that the basis for overturning a conviction is that there are exceptional circumstances—such as a change in the law—or evidence comes to light which was not available at the time of the trial, or subsequent appeals. However, given that only five cases have so far been handed back to the Court of Appeal, the real criticism of the CCRC has been the time taken to reach a decision on a case.[38] With new cases being referred to the CCRC at the rate of five per day, many must fear that it will be many years before their case is heard.

Despite these criticisms, the CCRC has been established only recently as an independent body. As such it has to be given time to develop its own working methods, and its place within the criminal justice system. It should also be given support to do this. HM Prison Service should actively seek to establish formal contact with the CCRC so that, e.g. resources might be shared, or ideas developed in partnership to decrease the backlog of cases currently being pursued. For example, each of the 14 commissioners might be attached to a prison service area, and included in relevant meetings with the Area Manager and support team when this is appropriate. At a more immediate level the Prison Service should provide information to prisoners about the

---

[38] The first five cases referred back to the Court of Appeal are those of Danny McNamee, John Taylor, Derek Bentley, Patrick Nichols and Mahmood Mattan. Of note both Bentley and Mattan were hanged for murder in the 1950s. It is understood that a sixth case— that of James Hanratty—could be completed soon. Hanratty was also hanged for murder.

CCRC and its work, and it is disappointing to note that its 1996 *Prisoners' Information Book* did not include information about the CCRC, or even its address or telephone number in its list of 'useful organizations'[39] (This matter has been rectified in the 1998 Handbook). There are a variety of places within prisons where this sort of information should be held, such as the library, but it must go further than this. For example, the reception procedure of every prison should include information about the CCRC; with prisoners asked if they know about its work; with this being logged on the prisoner's record.

Better record keeping, administration, and inter-agency liaison will clearly help in making procedures work more effectively, and this is no small matter. As one serving life sentenced prisoner wrote to the Prison Reform Trust from HMP Whitemoor in 1997, 'Please let me make it clear, the Prison Service has effectively frustrated and undermined my trial, frustrated my Appeal, and is doing its best to prevent me getting to Europe and the CCRC'.[40] However, at the heart of this chapter has been an argument in relation to how HM Prison Service organizes itself with regard to prisoners who are innocent, or claim to be innocent. It is clearly not acceptable to require prisoners to 'acknowledge' their guilt if they are actively pursuing their case with the CCRC. Nor is it reasonable to place prisoners in this category at a disadvantage in terms of regime conditions, and the possibility of parole if they are similarly engaged. No matter how difficult it is to do this in practice, HM Prison Service has to develop arrangements accordingly, or the concept of justice being re-fashioned in other parts of the criminal justice system will remain absent in prisons, with all the consequent problems that this will bring for order and control.

The most obvious model that HM Prison Service could apply in relation to all of this is its current arrangements with regard to prisoners on remand. For example, such prisoners are not required to work, and have special arrangements in relation to wearing their own clothes, visits, and so forth. They are also, except in extraordinary circumstances, housed in local prisons. Given the number of prisoners currently estimated to be alleging their innocence it would not be possible, or practicable to do this in their circumstances, especially as each case might continue for several years, and which in effect would merely increase overcrowding in local prisons. Nonetheless to treat prisoners who are in liaison with the CCRC in a different way from those who are not contesting their conviction, acknowledges the fact that miscarriage cases affect HM Prison Service, as they have other parts of the criminal justice system. It also acknowledges the

---

[39] The *Prisoners' Information Book: Questions and Answers about Your Time in Prison* (1996), London: HM Prison Service, is a joint publication with the Prison Reform Trust
[40] Letter to Prison Reform Trust in July 1997 from HMP Whitemoor

importance and the potential of the CCRC as an integral part of the criminal justice system, and gives status to its role and powers. More importantly, it would underscore the fact that HM Prison Service cares about justice, and is prepared to demonstrate a commitment to that principle, no matter how difficult it is in practice to do so.

We should also acknowledge the alternative problem that to posit the innocence of significant numbers of convicted prisoners—even one is to risk undermining confidence in the criminal justice system and possibly the judiciary's integrity. It is also beyond the duties and responsibilities given to the Prison Service. If we are to advocate that those lifers who are in liaison with the CCRC are given status equivalent to those on remand, we have shifted the assumption from one of guilt to implied or not proven innocence. Of course the assumption is not the same. Remand prisoners are innocent unless and until proved guilty. CCRC cases are guilty until proven otherwise or until convictions are overturned. Nevertheless, there should be no impediments placed between those prisoners protesting their innocence and legal representation. At the least, when a case has been accepted by the CCRC, this should be taken into consideration when referring those individuals for specific treatment programmes which require a presumption of guilt.

Guilty but denying

The other side of the coin reveals a group of offenders of at least equivalent size and vociferousness. For every inmate who claims innocence who is in fact innocent, there is at least one such who is in fact guilty. Whilst it is hardly surprising to find significant numbers of these souls amongst the unconvicted populations, it is more interesting to explore those who continue to maintain their innocence in the face of often irrefutable evidence, after being found guilty and sometimes long after their imprisonment might be legally challenged. What motivates these people?

Obviously, for many of them, there is the simple expedient of being on formal appeal, either against their conviction or against the length of their sentence. The former group obviously need to sustain the plea of innocence in order to stand any chance of a successful appeal. But the latter must, in most cases, sustain at least a variation on the innocence position. The majority of these are more likely to submit to a lesser charge in order to challenge sentence length.

For many lifers, particularly those who have continuing strong relationships within their families, the need to maintain their innocence is critical to keeping their families support—at least in their eyes. Equally, they would argue that the pain of telling their families, usually 'Mom', of their real culpability, is too much for them to face and that the plea of innocence allows the family to continue their solidarity in opposition to what can then be sustained as an unfair conviction of their 'innocent' son or daughter. This not only supports the family who will continue to visit the unjustly imprisoned child, but also the offender who can perpetuate the belief—at least within this small circle willing to believe—that they are in fact the victim.

Finally, sustaining a 'delusion' of innocence in therapeutic terms allows the offender to sustain an often fragile ego—strength due to the mind's extraordinary capacity to self-delude, to gradually blur recall and modify memory even to the extent that, on one level of consciousness, they come to believe (almost) the lie. For most of us, it is probably difficult to imagine how someone who has killed another, usually in close and vivid circumstances, could possibly succeed in deluding themselves into believing it had not happened or, at least, in evolving or fabricating a version of events which allows them to reduce culpability, e.g. to exaggerate the provocation, blame the influence of drink or drugs, or simply so as to be unable to recall the crucial few seconds of the actual killing which would establish their guilt incontrovertibly.

The authors are fortunate in having observed first hand the uniquely powerful process of therapy at Grendon Therapeutic Community prison, where countless murderers and other lifers have been obliged to face the facts of their crimes and, in this dynamic, have confessed to their guilt and accepted their responsibilities. This terribly painful but ultimately cathartic and healing process is one of the most rewarding experiences in our lives and the consequences for the offenders are often, sometimes unexpectedly, positive. Take, e.g. the case of the young man who had been convicted of being an accomplice to murder, of having played a secondary role to a murder committed by two accomplices. In therapy, this man eventually, after several months, confessed that he had in fact done the killing while the other two had played secondary, passive roles. Tragically, the two accomplices were also serving life sentences but their solicitors were informed of the confession and have been able to appeal on their clients behalf to have their sentences reduced. The related, albeit lesser, tragedy for this young man was in having to tell his family what he had done after having managed to convince them—for several years—that his role had been relatively minor.

The psychological dynamic of denial and the related process of minimisation, are strong forces in the individual framework of survival. They help people survive the personal horror of facing the fact that they have killed another person and the knowledge that there are many people—the victim's family, often wife, husband, children and usually parents—whose lives are forever damaged and diminished by their deeds. Helping these offenders to stop living their biggest lie takes a clear understanding that to do so is justified in terms of living honestly, of helping others to know the truth and, ultimately, of beginning the journey towards personal reconciliation and allowing others also hurt to recover through knowing the worst and surviving it.

*This chapter was contributed by **Dr David Wilson** who is the Course Director for the MA in Criminal Justice, Policy and Practice at the University of Central England in Birmingham. He is the former Head of Prison Officer and Operational Training for HM Prison Service, a post from which he resigned in 1997. The closing paragraphs were added by the authors.*

© David Wilson 1998

CHAPTER 4

Containment and Treatment

This chapter looks at what life is like inside lifer prisons and the effects of this imprisonment. How do Administrators and Governors view lifers and what do national policies tell us about Prison Service priorities in terms of control, positive containment and the treatment needs of lifers generally and murderers in particular? The central section of the chapter provides an innovative, detailed guide for staff in terms of the essential skills and competencies necessary to help lifers change. The next following section summarises some of the treatment interventions most likely to have positive impact and the final section reviews the risks and consequences of releasing lifers on licence.

I. CONTAINMENT

The concept of control is at the heart of prison management mentality. Efforts to run prisons or, indeed, any form of secure imposed containment, start from the need to keep prisoners in custody against their will and to do so without riot or concerted acts of indiscipline. The first act of imprisonment, normally remand in custody, is to ensure a measure of physical control over someone presumed too dangerous or unreliable to be left free. For life sentence prisoners, this imprisonment is automatic and long-term (and it is quite rare that someone charged with murder obtains bail pending their trial). Control mechanisms in prison fall within two broad categories, *physical* controls and *psychological* controls.

Physical controls
The first and most obvious form of control is the perimeter security. This varies in the UK from marked boundaries for open prisons to double perimeter walls/fences with ultrasonic sensors and electronic scanning TV. Related to perimeter security are the gate complexes, potentially the most vulnerable area of ingress/egress, which have to be controlled so as to never have both sets of doors open at the same time. Recent escalations of first line security in many prisons include electronic surveillance, X-ray machines similar to those used in international airports and closer scrutiny of personal identification. Perimeter walls and fences in all Category A and B prisons have additional rings of 'barbed' or dannet wiring completely around the perimeters and often around internal boundaries and any walls or roofs which might be accessible. All of the higher security prisons have extensive TV

surveillance facilities. Most lifers and murderers spend the greater part of their sentences in these prisons.

The architecture of prisons plays another central role in creating the perception of control. Most internal residential buildings are massive, thickset and strategically distanced from the perimeter with the areas between usually being deliberately barren, clear of impediments to vision and potential aids to escape, secretion etc. In the highest security prisons, many buildings are linked by passageways broken by a series of secure gates designed to compartmentalise and control. Most Victorian prisons have a particularly useful design, the panopticon, which denies the congregating of large numbers of prisoners and, with its classic radial design and central control rooms, gives maximum visual access. More recently, some of these older prisons have taken to closing off the radial wings with secure gates and, in some cases, boarding in order to further control inmates' movements and unofficial or unauthorised communication. The claustrophobic effect is powerful.

Staff control the physical movement of inmates around the majority of prisons in highly structured ways, none more so than with Category A prisoners. Most of these maximum security prisoners are lifers and they number in the hundreds. Cat A men can only be unlocked when a minimum of two staff are present and only during certain times of the day. They are not allowed to work in normal locations where the roll is large and their movements are recorded in individual daily logs. This process is reviewed annually and can continue for years. The security departments of each prison with Cat A prisoners maintain especial vigilance over these cases, with extensive records and procedures to maintain and follow. All Cat A mens' records are supervised centrally. Such is the concern following the much publicised escapes from Whitemoor and Parkhurst, the Prison Service's number one Key Performance Indicator or KPI target for 1996-97 was to ensure that no Cat A prisoners escaped (and that the number of escapes overall was significantly lower than the year before).

Other obvious forms of physical control include the locking/unlocking procedures—which are either by security keys or eletronic unlock or both—and control of contact with the outside world, e.g. via letters, telephone and home leave. The use of punishment is both a psychological and physical control including the use of the Segregation Unit, or punishment block. Prison Rules allow a member of staff to place an inmate 'on report' for any one of 23 rule violations including the comprehensive 'offends against good order and discipline'. Probably the gravest form of punishment (ironically termed an 'award' in prison vocabulary) which a prison Governor can give is loss of time, or delay in a prisoner's earliest date of release, both of which mean longer imprisonment. If an inmate is found guilty, he can have up to 42 days added by the Governor. While this might presumably have a diminished impact on a lifer who might feel that he has no time to lose in a sense, few lifers like risking a black mark on their permanent record which subsequent deliberating Parole Boards might see as weighing against release.

Virtually every prison (except for the therapeutic regime at Grendon) has a separate punishment unit, usually called a Segregation Unit but popularly known as 'The Block', to which inmates are removed when placed on a Governor's report for serious offences or when they have reacted violently to being placed on report otherwise. A prisoner can also be removed to the block without having committed an offence.

Governors have discretion, under Rule 43—usually called 'Good Order and Discipline' (GOAD)—to do this if they have good reason to believe the individual is behaving in a seriously subversive manner, e.g. plotting to riot or provoke some major act of collective indiscipline or if they are believed to be a major drug dealer, etc. On a surprisingly frequent incidence, prisoners can also choose to be removed for their own protection, under Rule 43—'Own Protection' (OP)—as when they are in debt to the 'heavy mob' or at risk of being assaulted or sexually abused. This does not necessarily mean their removal to a segregation unit; this depends on whether the prison has alternative facilities such as one of the Rule 43 or Vulnerable Prisoner Units.[1] Blocks tend to be the least commodious environments in prisons, with the worst coming close to sensory deprivation, even closer if a man is placed in 'strip conditions'. This final and most extreme act of explicit control involves stripping the man of all his clothing and often forcibly placing him in a special nylon or reinforced cloth jacket in a room stripped of all furnishings save a specially constructed cardboard table and chair. Bedding may be a thin special mattress placed on a slightly raised concrete corner section of a small cell. Perhaps the most extraordinary fact of all is that these are almost exactly the same conditions in which suicidal patients may be placed in some prison hospitals. This apparently perverse process means that the most violent or disruptive prisoners are treated in conditions almost identical to those for the most disturbed and vulnerable. Whether the motivation is restraint or safety, the effects are the same.

The report which has had the greatest effect on lifers in the past 15 years is arguably the report of the Control Review Committee in 1984. The brief was to review the 'dispersal system' for long-term prisoners with particular reference to issues of control. Primary among

---

[1] It is of some considerable concern that, in 1990, there were over 3,200 prisoners in the system on either Rule 43 ('own protection') or a national Vulnerable Persons Unit (VPU)

the recommendations were three points summarised by Bottoms in *The Aims of Imprisonment* (1990):

- *First,* there is the explicit statement in the preamble that "imprisonment itself . . . is the punishment inflicted by law and no further avoidable hardship should be imposed on a prisoner except by way of formal disciplinary action".
- *Second,* the explicit statement ". . . that prisoners' lawful rights should be respected" introduces a new concept . . .
- **Third** . . . this formulation incorporates a basic distinction between "core" tasks and "opportunity" tasks.

Psychological controls

The controls which staff can exert upon prisoners to achieve cooperation and compliance are considerable. The obvious 'stick' is that prisoners are a society of captives and therefore dependent upon staff. Lifers, or at least those who expect or hope for eventual release, have additional pressures to comply. The use of the punishment block is however, a blunt and double-edged tool. If an inmate has been injured, forcibly removed or is seen to have been unjustly punished, his peers sense of injustice may provide a serious demonstration. This can develop very quickly and the potential loss of control is commensurate. Explosive backlashes even riots have frequently been triggered in just this way, whether precipitated by genuine concern or used as an excuse to threaten the prison with violence to secure better conditions etc. In any potential riot scenario, lifers become particularly vulnerable to the double bind conflicts generated by these 'us and them' forced choices, i.e. loyalty to the inmate code at the possible cost of several years being added to their sentence or loyalty to the system at the cost of possible physical assaults in retaliation, ostracising or both.

Positive control is the more common dynamic by which the staff and inmates co-exist peacefully in their closed worlds. The natural instinct and will in most of the people inside prison is to develop positive relationships and to minimise the harsher effects of working and living inside. The incidence of positive relationships, and friendships, between the two groups is probably higher than the public would imagine, with the human instinct to get to know our fellow men primary. It is probably this dynamic, identified so clearly in Dunbar's *A Sense of Direction* (1985), which is at the heart of positive control for long-term prisoners. The main thrust of this internal policy paper is with the need for clarity of aims, tasks and performance measures, but it goes beyond these to advise that the principles of relationships and activities are essential to the future and not just attention to the Prison Services's responsibilities to the public or the need for 'positive custody' and 'humane containment', catchphrases of the 1980s. In this respect, policy makers were finally catching up with the arguments put forward by criminologists like Rutherford, King and McDermott and Bottoms, and by groups like the Prison Reform Trust (see Stern, 1989) for years. This, in a real sense, elevates the idea beyond one of control to one of stability within prisons for long-term prisoners through cooperation.

As powerful as the staff pressures, influences and cooperation on and with prisoners might be, they are less so than the power of the peer group. The most powerful form of punishment in prison is not written in the *Staff Handbook*, it is written on the walls of the recess areas and in the traditions of the prison code. The range and severity of 'awards' meted out in summary 'justice' by other prisoners—up to and including death—are far more fearsome than staffs sanctions. The fear of assault, including rape, is not confined to the 'grassing' code, or informing on another inmate. It is pervasive, the currency of control in all areas of life—including particular debts unhonoured, drugs transactions and insults (presumed or real)—and a manifestation of the customs of accountability which operate inside.

Loss of control
When control breaks down, or when relationships deteriorate to a crisis level, the potential for riots and serious mass disorders increases. The traditional attitude of many prison managers prior to the Strangeways riot of 1990 was summarised by Wheatley (1981), who recommended prison managers, especially Governors, to cultivate a sub-culture with enlightened self-interest in maintaining a 'quiet prison' whilst seeking to 'prevent its worst aspects'; maintaining a healthy flow of informers amongst the prisoner population and for discipline staff to 'be employed in an aggressive rule enforcement role'. He also implicitly advocated the selective rewarding of informers and enforcers within the inmate population as staff normally control access to 'the best jobs, the best cells, education classes, home leave, pre-release employment schemes and parole; concluding that 'If in taking decisions on these sort of topics, the need to maintain a stable sub-culture is borne in mind it is possible to see that the deserving are rewarded and the undeserving are not successful'. There was no reference, in this article, or by anyone working within the Prison Department, to the need to respond to complaints about prison conditions or other grievances which might be legitimate or that staff may bear any portion of the responsibility for creating the conditions preceding and leading to the riot or disorder.

In their analysis of the most significant riot in a British prison this century before Strangeways, at Hull prison in 1976, *The Exploding Prison* (1980), Thomas and Pooley concluded that the main causes of the disruption were:

- a process of transition from a more to a less liberal regime
- the consequent denial to prisoners of 'perks' that had become customary
- increased use of cellular confinement; and
- strain in staff-prisoner relations.

Following the Strangeways riot in 1990, and a series of other disturbances in five other establishments, Lord Justice Woolf reported not only on the events specific to the disturbances but also on wider issues of prison policy, prisoner control and the responsibility of the state to provide justice in prisons. If, e.g. it is proven that a prison has contained prisoners in conditions which 'are inhumane or degrading, or which are otherwise wholly inappropriate, then a punishment of imprisonment which was justly imposed will result in injustice' (Sparks, 1992). On the wider issues of justice in prisons in terms of discipline, grievances and the management of trouble, Woolf concluded:

> If there is an absence of justice, prisoners will be aggrieved. Control and security will be threatened. This is part of what happened in April. The scale of each of the riots indicates that in each establishment there was a substantial number of prisoners who were prepared to turn what otherwise would have been a limited disturbance into a full scale riot . . . If a proper level of justice is provided in prisons, then it is less likely that prisoners will behave in this way. (Woolf, 1991).

Lifers as a stabilising influence.
One of the most enduring assumptions made generally by management and staff in the Prison Service is that lifers are a more stable, less disruptive group than are non-lifers and that they provide a stabilising influence on the other inmates making wings and landings less susceptible to the 'concerted acts of indiscipline', protests and riots which prison Governors fear most. The Governor responsible for policy for lifers in 1991 avowed:

> Lifers are not different in any way to determinate prisoners except that they understand it was in their interest to behave . . .

and that '. . . it is in their best interest to be more stable'.

As for such positive influence as lifers might have, it was 'almost entirely the weight of numbers, proportion and aversion, i.e. a form of enlightened self-interest'.[2]

---

[2] This same Governor, asked what the average life sentence was, explained: 'I've never really bothered. I see it as largely irrelevant. Comparisons are not helpful'. Also, when asked how he reacted to European Court rulings on judicial panels considering discretionary life sentence prisoners for release, he concluded 'It won't apply'.

The results of interviews, surveys and questionnaires of 42 Governors and 25 other discipline staff as well as over 230 inmates, lifers and non-lifers formed the basis of one author's doctorate research (Cullen, 1992) which addressed just this question. The overwhelming majority of all involved affirmed that life sentence prisoners exercise a stabilising influence on the behaviour or other prisoners and the regimes of their prisons: whether in terms of rates of institutional offending, staff perceptions of cooperation, Governors' reflections over careers ranging from 5 to 35 years or the views of inmates from three Main Lifer centres and three young offender institutions with both lifers and fixed sentence populations, the results were the same.

If, however, we can confidently conclude that lifers are a positive, even stabilising influence on the regimes which contain them and the other prisoners around them, it rather begs the question *'Should* lifers be used (mixed) deliberately or should they be separated in the name of more equitable and just containment?' If the only argument for separation is that it is the choice of the majority of lifers—partly because mixing with non-lifers is more vexatious and more distressing when the lifers see the others being released, presumably the weight of argument is not particularly strong. The alternative, one which is already practised to an extent, is a combination of separation at the beginning and end of lifers' sentences and of mixing in between. The logic of this is that, at the beginning of their sentences, the particular problems of life imprisonment and the extensive obligatory documentation and assessment requires a concentration of lifers such as is seen at Wormwood Scrubs D Wing and Gartree. Toward the end of their sentences, lifers, it might be argued, need to focus much more on freedom and community-orientated issues, preparing for release after many years imprisoned and that to do so with the distractions and risks imposed by mixing with non-lifers is counterproductive. The logic follows that, for the intervening years between these two extremes, lifers should of necessity cope with living in prison in much the same ways as non-lifers, i.e. when there are more similarities than differences.

II. STAFF COMPETENCIES: SKILLS REQUIRED TO WORK EFFECTIVELY WITH LIFERS

Core competencies developed in the Prison Service

The Prison Service has developed a framework of core competencies to identify the skills required of its staff to carry out the service's functions at its many levels. These competencies can be seen as relevant in the management of lifers at different levels and will prove particularly effective in determining the training needs of staff and in ensuring their long term personal development. Recruitment, selection and the development of staff will be informed in future by the Core Competence Framework. There are 12 competencies, grouped into four clusters as follows:

Custodial Skills

1. Security Awareness
2. Concern for Prisoner Care
3. Rehabilitation—Orientation

Systematic and Procedural Skills

4. Systematic Approach
5. Planning and Reviewing
6. Organizing and Empowering

Interpersonal Skills

7. Team Playing /Networking
8. Team Building / Liaising
9. Motivation and Commitment

Innovative and Informing Skills

10. Communicating Clearly
11. Problem Solving /Continuous Improvement
12. Leadership and Decision-making.

Given the intensity and variety of managerial and supervisory abilities necessary for working effectively with lifers the comprehensive framework provides a sound structure to explore the nature of staff skills required.

Custodial skills

1. Security Awareness

- Contributes fully to the security requirements of keeping prisoners in custody.
- Encourages disciplined and cooperative behaviour in prisoners.
- Supports the provision of an orderly controlled and safe environment.

An awareness of the security risks represented by lifers is a vital part of their management. Full information about their motivation to escape, to accept their sentence and to work effectively towards release is critical in carrying out the service's responsibility to the public and in creating confidence that the highest risk population is being managed properly. Confidence of staff and other prisoners is also developed by having effective risk assessments made regularly about lifers in the security context. The more effective this can be seen to be the more confident the Prison Service will become in taking the sort of risks with lifers which are vital if they are to proceed towards tariff with a realistic chance of being assessed for release when legally possible. The progress through security levels of prisons and the need for lifers to be released through open conditions make security and control awareness of lifers a key skill for staff at all levels.

The expectation that lifers will not be a control problem because of the indeterminacy of their sentence is an underlying assumption with many staff and there is thus a need to be aware of their manipulation as a result of this factor which may often be exaggerated. Lifers are a very diverse group, some representing great potential for disturbance within the prison setting whilst others are completely overcome and subdued by the prison experience and the nature of their sentence. Those who see themselves as political prisoners—the terrorists—may well challenge authority in many ways, overtly or subversively. The domestic murderer may well be so overcome by personal tragedy that he or she cannot make sense of the alien culture of prison and so retreats into complete conformity in order to survive. Without a culture of engagement and the personal development of individual plans and systems of reviewing progress they can as a group become anxious and potentially disruptive to good order in a prison. Lifers are often respected by other prisoners because of their indeterminate status, because of their experience of prisons and their potential dangerousness at a personal level. They should never be taken for granted, as sometimes is evident in tactical management of population movement. Sensitivity towards their position should be developed in all staff. Particularly sensitive are the needs of the small group of lifers who are becoming aware that they will never be considered for release—the 'natural life' lifers. Although there are legal challenges upon which many place their trust there will be a group for whom future prospects of release do not play a part in their motivation. Loss of hope is often experienced by lifers and those who realise there is nothing they can do to affect future decisions present the Prison Service with unique issues of management which will focus attention on the continuing quality of life within prison.

Expected behaviour in demonstrating this competence include:

- checking the environment for threats to security
- being alert and attentive to events and behaviour
- identifying risks and taking appropriate steps to minimise them
- reporting unusual events and objects
- maintaining appropriate levels of confidentiality at all times
- carrying out established procedures
- being observant of threats to safety and security associated with a prisoner's mood change
- exercising authority when required
- using persuasion and encouragement to obtain cooperation
- issuing appropriate and consistent instructions
- using the minimum of force as a last resort and employing only approved techniques.

2. Concern for Prisoner Care

- Contributes to ensuring that decent physical conditions prevail.
- Is vigilant that recognised standards are achieved.
- Shows concern that prisoner needs, including health care, are met with fairness, justice and respect.

It is in this area that staff skills should be fully developed because of the extreme sensitivities and the great needs of lifers. They represent the highest risk in terms of dangerousness within the prison population, in terms of their potential for self-harm and suicide and their potential dangerous behaviour on release. There is the dynamic at certain stages of their sentence of having 'nothing to lose'. They are often the most difficult people to assess, carrying the burden of their guilt which has to be explored through their time in custody. The nature of their indeterminate sentence places the most pressure on them which calls for a level of personal care and support not always overtly called for by other prisoners. Lifers are the group calling for the most developed skills in staff.

This factor of care extends to all levels of those involved with lifers, not solely with those in daily contact. Thus decisions about requests made by lifers, decisions about their location, the activities they can take part in, how they can be escorted outside prison and the minutiae of regular communication can have a significant impact on the perception by them of their status and their feelings of self worth. Similarly, pronouncements through speeches reported through the media about how lifers are to be treated in the system have a disproportionate impact on the morale of individuals.

Expected behaviour in demonstrating this competence include:

- persuading colleagues to meet care standards
- informing prisoners correctly of procedures
- giving helpful advice, guidance and information to prisoners and visitors
- behaving with consideration of both prisoners and visitors
- encouraging prisoners' self-management
- acting to protect prisoners from abuse and violence from any quarter
- upholding the suicide awareness policy and acting to prevent self-harm
- promoting individual's rights
- honouring undertakings to assist individuals
- understanding prisoners' needs for privacy and offering appropriate respect for confidentiality.

3. *Rehabilitation—Orientation*

- Contributes to provide a positive regime.
- Encourages prisoners to address causes of offending behaviour and adopt a responsible approach to their circumstances.
- Acts to encourage the aim of a successful return to the community.

The encouragement staff provide to lifers to make constructive use of their time and particularly to address the causes of their offending behaviour through focusing on the areas of concern identified in their Lifer Sentence Plan is central to their sound management. The provision of sufficient opportunities to formally address criminogenic needs is an increasing problem for the Prison Service. Evidence from research has given increasing proof that there are effective courses of work which can reduce recidivism and as a consequence there is an expectation that lifers will participate in such work to demonstrate that they have addressed elements of their risk. The limited provision of such courses such as the Sex Offender Treatment Programme, the Violent Offender Treatment Programme and Reasoning and Rehabilitation courses means that not all lifers can participate in such work in time for that experience to be considered before tariff to enable location in open conditions to be decided upon. With the likelihood of shorter tariff dates following the 1997 legislation, there is a pressing need to provide the sort of opportunity that the Parole Board is looking for to assess the risk having been addressed. There is thus an impetus required in developing such relatively expensive courses at a time of reducing resources for prisons. The experience of staff in being trained and participating in such work is some of the most rewarding of their service—and the skills they gain through that discipline is of the highest relevance in achieving the long-term development of a culture of care in prisons.

Preparing lifers to return to the community calls for considerable co-ordination of effort from those involved both in the prisons and those concerned with responsibility for their care in the community. The throughcare of lifers calls for long-term commitment from Probation Services working with prisoners. The reduction of resources in probation areas has contributed towards this work often being given a limited priority which can lead to frustration for staff in prisons and feelings of being abandoned by lifers. There are examples of excellent practice which could provide a model for the future of regular visiting and attendance at case conferences bringing external agencies to bear in assisting the progress towards release.

Expected behaviour arising from this competence include:

- supporting prisoner rights and choices within the system
- encouraging prisoner involvement in regime activities
- demonstrating fairness by personal examples
- challenging behaviour which may be seen as anti-social
- offering guidance and counselling to promote prisoners' self-esteem and behaviour
- encouraging actively and facilitating prisoners' preparation for release
- encouraging prisoners to address their offending behaviour
- encouraging prisoners to make constructive use of their time, setting realistic targets and evaluating their progress
- upholding prisoners' access to family, friends and their community
- guaranteeing prisoners' access to legal advisers and outside agencies.

Systematic and procedural skills

4. Adopting a Systematic Approach

- Is systematic and methodical.
- Identifies measures, costs benefits and standards in order to maximise efficiency.
- Demonstrates attention to best practice.

There is a need when working with lifers to ensure that some certainty is introduced into dealings with them because of the high level of uncertainty in other areas. Thus it is important for staff to establish milestones with lifers and these should be met as much as possible to avoid further feelings of being forgotten. The introduction of efficient systems into the management of lifers would greatly facilitate the aim of preparing them to have addressed their areas of concern in good time to enable them to be considered for transfer to open conditions in time for their tariff completion.

The collection and collation of information available about lifers— although the best in the system in terms of building up a chronological sequence and establishing detail—still presents those assessing risk with partial and sometimes inaccurate material. Collating further detail and referring to sources in a methodical manner will improve systems and enable due weighting to be given to aspects of the data to help reduce the subjectivity often inevitable as each reader approaches the file *de novo*.

The lack of awareness of the systems of lifer management by lifers is surprising and calls for a full technical awareness among staff who manage them so that there can be a confidence and certainty in setting their sentence into context with structure. The recent changes in lifer management have not always kept pace with a general awareness and certainty amongst staff who regularly effect daily decisions and share information. Changes in the expectations of Ministers that all lifers have to go through Category B and C prisons before they can proceed to open conditions is an example that has taken some time for all lifers to appreciate.

Expected behaviour arising from this competence include:

- allocating and evaluating work schedules
- reviewing regularly methods of working
- setting realistic timetables
- being precise and paying attention to detail
- working systematically through routine
- making effective use of resources
- checking the accuracy or validity of information or questionable instructions
- proposing improvements in systems and procedures
- identifying and implementing opportunities to improve operational effectiveness
- extracting important detail from random information
- producing systems that people can understand and work to
- identifying measures of performance to assess effectiveness of strategy.

5. Planning and Reviewing

- Accumulates and analyses data, in order to prioritise and project a view.
- Assesses risks and foresees consequences.
- Plans activities and reviews progress against plans.

Managing the careers of lifers calls for a capacity from staff to hold a long-term view of their personal development and interaction with prison conditions and facilities. The management of groups of lifers within an establishment also calls for sensitivity towards the dynamics of prisoner populations so that control elements do not dominate the need for opportunities for personal development, risk taking and a recognition of the special needs of indeterminate sentenced prisoners. The management of lifers on a service-wide basis calls for vision and political sensitivity in developing programmes and systems of creativity and hope whilst retaining political and public confidence. This involves ensuring that staff working with lifers are well trained and can be confidently responsive within the policy arrangements which should ensure that areas of concern are addressed pro-actively by the prison in which the lifer is located as well as ensuring if necessary that the lifer is moved to a place where he or she can tackle the issues himself or herself. The sensitivity of networking about decisions lifers receive must be appreciated by all concerned as well as the effect of speeches and signals about the testing of risk and the unacceptability of serious offending. With the expected rise in the lifer population this aspect of staff skills will be more critical in the next few years.

The planning of careers with lifers is a critical aspect of their management, leading to the long-term reduction of risk to the community to which they will eventually return as well as to the prison community in which they are held during their sentence. The capacity of the individual to have a life in the community having made reparation for his or her offence can only be achieved through sound planning which involves the lifer. The development and establishing of objectives for lifers to work upon as identified areas of risk is critical in ensuring that their time is used to maximum effect and that legal requirements with regard to tariff are met.

Expected behaviour arising from this competence include;

- collecting and appraising information
- assimilating new and previous information
- making plans appropriate to the situation
- standing back and taking a longer view
- identifying political ramifications of options for change
- identifying risks in options
- revising objectives in the light of new information
- setting realistic objectives and priorities
- providing timetables with costing, staffing and resource requirements
- monitoring progress towards objectives
- predicting outcomes from careful projection

- promoting understanding of strategy for change.

6. *Organizing and Empowering*

- Is able to clarify objectives, and set realistic goals and deadlines for self and for others.
- Delegates, and allocates adequate resources.
- Defines the boundaries within which people can be free to exercise authority.

The importance of setting objectives for lifers and for the staff who work closely with them is clearly established as one of the key aspects of successful lifer management. The role of the Lifer Liaison Officer in each prison which holds lifers has been established now for many years but there remains very little clarity about the expectations from this person who is the focus of lifers and of the Lifer Management Unit at headquarters. When this role is carried with enthusiasm and personal commitment there can be a considerable effect on the morale of staff and lifers. The skills in this section are central to the effective carrying out of the role. The organizing of the complex procedures contained in the *Lifer Manual* and keeping to the schedules of reports and activities places a considerable burden upon busy managers. With the reduction of resources in prisons and the need to slim down management structures there is evidence that this role is not always given the due weight of focus it requires, with the consequent complaints from those who do not receive reports on time. There is a need for a reappraisal of the resource implication of managing lifers in order to provide the drive to achieve the important work to a standard of quality.

Expected behaviour arising from this competence include:

- seeing the potential in others
- offering reassurance and showing patience with slow learners
- coaching staff
- supporting training actively
- acting as a mentor and encouraging a mentoring system
- giving opportunity for self development and learning
- encouraging self development plans
- making sure that performance information goes direct to the job holder
- demonstrating clear ideas of desirable goals and the strategies to achieve them
- setting realistic personal objectives and priorities
- supporting staff in times of stress

- creating and maintaining a supportive environment in which teams and individuals can fulfil their potential.

Interpersonal skills

7. Team Playing/Networking

- Is a good team player who encourages others to contribute.
- Is capable of interacting easily with a wide range of people both colleagues and public.
- Upholds equality of opportunity and actively rejects discrimination.

Given the complexity of the work with lifers there are major responsibilities for close team working in devising strategies and systems to manage the many dimensions entailed. Staff can often become as uncertain about the context within which lifers are carrying out their sentence as the prisoners unless there is good sharing of information and a clear sense of purpose in the individual and within collective policy. Feelings of dependency upon a distant bureaucracy have been experienced in the past which must be changed to enable those staff working closely with lifers to feel empowered to carry out the work of engagement, challenge and stimulation which is called for in managing them. Headquarters should see the staff in prisons as part of their team in managing lifers.

The confidence with which staff operate with lifers can lead to considerable advantages or to many problems due to the levels of uncertainty that prevail in any lifer's experience. The willingness to risk oneself in a relationship is an important part of enriching the quality of dialogue which can ultimately lead to change and to an accurate assessment of what has been achieved, what remains to be done and how to proceed to the next step. The awareness of the benefits of operating with an informal, non-directive style in daily contacts within the context of formal procedures which often direct the lifer to work at certain issues should be an important competency for those working with lifers.

Expected behaviour arising from this competence include:

- demonstrating support for all colleagues
- showing confidence in others and establishing mutual trust
- being aware of the impact of their own behaviour on others
- following instructions and yet using initiative
- completing tasks on time whenever possible
- addressing issues in a positive manner
- developing networks to learn from others

- focusing on team goals and priorities
- rejecting any form of discriminatory practice.

8. Team Building/Liaising

- Is able to get people to work well together.
- Gains understanding of the need for trust and cooperation to achieve effective working.
- Can reconcile conflict and build group identity.

The role of the Lifer Liaison Officer calls for considerable skills in working across many groups of staff who have functional responsibilities in other areas and yet have the demanding work of assessing and reporting on the progress which lifers are making at any time. To lead staff to establish sound working relationships with lifers is demanding but essential in order to carry out the work of managing them with expertise.

The development of sound positive relationships within the boundaries of the sentence and the setting is the most demanding and yet most necessary part of working with lifers. There can sometimes be a reluctance from staff to enter too closely into relationships with lifers because of the extreme sensitivities of their situation and yet they are the group with the most need for personal contact and interaction in order to make a deeper experience of their time in custody. The risk that staff take is of becoming bound up in the hopelessness of the lifer's experience. There is also often the fear and repugnance about the offence to manage within any contact. Skills of remaining professionally detached and yet humanly in touch are developed by experienced staff working regularly with lifers within a context of close staff support and personal supervision. The matter cannot be left to chance and must be managed so that there is sufficient awareness of the inner life of the lifers upon which to make judgements being regularly expected of staff, such as about the risk they represent to themselves and others. Such roles can be modelled by sound managers so that members of the team of staff working with lifers can all develop the expertise to assess and relate to a high level. Working together as a team encourages others to share information and enhance the quality of awareness of all members.

Expected behaviour arising from this competence include:

- combining individuals' styles and skills to build an effective team
- identifying strengths and development needs of teams and individuals
- guiding the work of teams and individuals to achieve objectives
- showing interest in each team member's achievement

- acknowledging good work and celebrating success
- challenging poor work
- disciplining and reprimanding if required
- fostering an atmosphere of honesty, trust and mutual support
- consulting members before making changes which affect the team
- briefing teams and individuals on current issues and priorities
- dealing with grievances promptly
- accepting responsibility for the action of the team.

9. Motivation and Commitment

- Gives personal example of commitment to the Prison Service purpose, vision, goals and values.
- Is capable of energising people and encouraging them to want to contribute.
- Takes personal responsibility for achieving results and performs well under pressure.

The selection of staff to work in prisons concentrates on their motivation to work with people and their capacity to relate with sensitivity and confidence with prisoners in difficult and potentially stressful circumstances. This is very demanding work and depends not only on successful selection but on good training and opportunities for continuous development. The organization of human resource management is developing to provide prison staff with clear objectives for their personal development in order to achieve the objectives of the establishment in which they work and relevant training to achieve that work. The number of prisons which have achieved or are in the process of achieving the national standard of Investors in People is a mark of this commitment to ensuring sound personnel development.

Working with lifers calls for particularly strong motivation and commitment because of the manifold problems of sensitivity and complexity involved in such activity. The training provided for staff working with lifers is of a high standard but like many aspects of training in prisons provides a good initial grounding without always the opportunity to take the subject further. Particularly there is a need to provide for a clearer focus on the leadership role of the lifer liaison officer and to train them to enable the prison systems to support the important processes of working with lifers.

Expected behaviour arising from this competence include:

- being highly motivated to achieve
- organizing own work to a high standard
- seeking feedback on own performance
- being able to subordinate self-interest to achieve objectives

- being prepared to admit mistakes and learn from them
- generating enthusiasm
- taking personal responsibility for making things happen
- remaining calm under pressure
- following through on commitments
- maintaining commitment and effort in spite of setbacks
- helping others to develop.

Innovative and informing skills

10. Communicating Clearly

- Is articulate and able to communicate well both to individuals and groups.
- Practises accuracy, brevity and clarity in the written word.
- Promotes good communication by others, actively supporting techniques to encourage open behaviour.

All staff working with prisoners should have well developed oral communication skills as it is through the regular sharing of information and views that the quality of life for prisoners is sustained. For lifers this is particularly important in that they are more dependent for making sense of their experience upon staff than other prisoners who have clearer boundaries. Sensitivity and awareness of the effect of words are key competencies for those in relationships of control and for the encouragement of motivation. The culture of prisons tends to be predominantly verbal and thus the quality of dialogue and life is much influenced by these skills.

Lifers build up files of material about themselves and the consideration of their case. Since the decision that all material upon which decisions being made about lifers is disclosed to them, the competency of report writing has increased in sensitivity. Lifers are acutely conscious that what is written about them has a major impact upon decisions made about them. The skill of writing accurately about relationships, about progress in attitudinal changes and the interpretation of incidents and overt behaviour is thus vital in providing material for risk assessment in the future. The tension between the culture of verbal communication at establishment level and that of a predominantly written culture at headquarters and the Parole Board is clearly evident at times when there appears to be a lack of awareness of the progress lifers are making. Skills in writing need developing in order to ensure the decision makers' culture receives accurate and full information.

Expected behaviour arising from this competence include:

- listening accurately
- contributing positively to discussions
- being articulate and making effective presentations
- conducting interviews well
- writing with accuracy, brevity and clarity
- using correct grammar and spelling
- presenting information in a manner appropriate to receivers
- mastering a brief quickly
- appreciating the importance of good communication to teamwork
- ensuring effective communication systems are used
- acting to prevent barriers to effective communications.

11. *Problem Solving/Continuous Improvement*

- Applies concepts and builds frameworks to produce solutions.
- Endeavours to offer continuous improvement.
- Is innovative and encourages creativity in others.

Skills in this area are concerned with how lifers can demonstrate learning about future behaviour within a tightly constrained setting and with limited resources. Developing problem solving and life skills amongst lifers is an important aspect of their development. Their awareness of opportunities for learning and integrating such learning within their demonstrated behaviour must be encouraged and managed within relationships of casework management. The need to balance the requirements and expectations of the court, the politicians, the victims, the staff and other prisoners is a considerable challenge to the skills of those who manage lifers.

Staff attitudes of flexibility and imagination are vital in providing imaginative opportunities for lifers to develop and demonstrate new skills and attitudes as well as to show they can be trusted with increasing responsibility as they progress through their sentence. The willingness to take initiatives has led to the development of activities for lifers and their families which have increased opportunities for them commensurate with their needs.

Expected behaviour arising from this competence include:

- differentiating between relevant and irrelevant information
- recognising that information may be interpreted in different ways
- interpreting a problem into logical steps
- questioning existing practice
- reconciling conflicting views
- putting theory into practice
- looking for continuous improvement
- seeing connections and producing original solutions

- analysing situations in terms of deliverables and outputs
- testing out ideas in consultation.

12. Leadership and Decision-making

- Is self assured and decisive, creating a good impression.
- Is impartial and inspires confidence.
- Has vision and knows when to react quickly or take a longer-term view.

Working with lifers represents some of the most difficult decisions of assessing risk for the public and calls for leadership from staff in confronting sensitive issues openly. The need for clear judgement and courage in stating what may be unpopular views are significant skills for staff to develop. Examples of this can be seen in the need to confront sensitive issues of addressing lifers areas of concern even after many years of them being in prison in order to be sure that the judgements made and the reports written have been carefully considered by the writer. The need to also state when the member of staff is convinced of the reduced risk of a lifer despite concerns of public opinion can place the individual in an isolated position, but one which should be represented to the decision-makers. The need to share bad news with the lifer can place considerable personal demands upon those staff near to him or her who have to help the lifer make sense of the situation and to look forward to the possibilities within the setback.

Critical decisions about lifers are regularly made by staff managing them. These range across day-to-day recognition of the particular sensitivities of mood changes in coming to terms with indeterminacy, with guilt, with bereavement, with hopelessness, with the rebuilding of expectations within an uncertain world in which much emphasis is placed upon preparing for leaving prison. The particular sensitivity of anniversaries of the offence should be borne in mind as should the effect of mixing with those who are about to be released.

Expected behaviour arising from this competence include:

- having vision and communicating it
- inspiring confidence and loyalty
- giving praise and recognition where appropriate
- confronting difficult issues openly
- being realistic about strengths and weaknesses
- accepting challenges but moderating risks
- making judgements which carry conviction
- taking decisions within time constraints and delegated authority
- taking decisions with restricted information when necessary

- amending decisions where appropriate in the light of new information.

Conclusion

Working with lifers is recognised as being some of the most demanding and rewarding work for prison staff. With the increase in the number of lifers the Prison Service is facing this is likely to become even more stressful and pressured in the future. Similarly the development of clearer expectations defined through legal precedent makes this aspect of prison work more examined than many others and ensures a closer accountability of delivery than experienced elsewhere. All the more need to develop the competencies and skills of those staff trusted with the responsibility of managing lifers to meet the need of this demanding and important work.

Action Learning Points

- The skills required by staff in each setting need to be identified by managers.
- A training needs assessment should be carried out for staff working with lifers.
- Training for staff should be focused on developing and supporting the practice of the skills identified as necessary for the task.
- The role of Lifer Liaison Officer should be developed formally with specific training to ensure sound management systems in all prisons.
- Reviews of staff concerns about working with lifers should be carried out in order to ensure continuous improvement.
- The national forum of key workers with lifers should be developed to ensure good practice is spread.

III. TREATMENT

We have seen the problems of containing the record growth of lifers in the 1990s in the prisons of England and Wales and provided a detailed framework of skills for the staff obliged to work with them. There remains however the question of how lifers are treated in both the daily routine and the 'curative' senses. It is one thing for the Prison Service to talk of managing the life sentence population. It is a very different matter for lifers to explain the reality of managing their life imprisonment.

The context and framework within which staff and prisoners relate are important in determining the quality of the management of the life sentence. Without purposeful and focused activity directed towards the reduction of risk all the good relationships and skilful involvement of staff may well prove pointless to the lifer who remains concerned with issues relating to release and the processes which lead to it.

How the Prison Service 'manages' lifers
A small but very significant number of innovations since 1990 have significantly improved the services which the Prison Service provides for life sentence prisoners. Among these are:

- the creation of the *Lifer Manual* which is an extremely thorough reference document covering all procedures to do with the management, documentation, and review of all lifers.
- the decision to combine the Prison Service and Probation Service under the joint responsibility of the Minister for Prisons, thus facilitating the integration of throughcare and community support/supervision.
- the development of centrally created and controlled *treatment programmes* for targeted groups of serious offenders including sex offenders, violent offenders and a more generic course called 'Reasoning and Rehabilitation'.

Credit for these initiatives goes to the Programme Development Unit psychologists in Prison Service headquarters.

The *Lifer Manual*
The management of lifers is said to be based on three principles:

- they are treated as a group whose special needs are recognised within the prison, though not necessarily by separation or special privileges;
- they have a planned and structured career through the prison system and, where appropriate, progress to conditions of lower security; and
- their allocation to establishments is managed centrally by Custody Group.

The qualification about separate treatment is as much an acknowledgement that lifers would cause serious logistical and financial problems were they to be separated throughout their sentences, as the concerns about destabilising regimes expressed earlier. Equality of privileges ensures that non-lifer prisoners do not have grounds for grievances about unfair preferential treatment, particularly sensitive in the public's eyes as lifers would be amongst the least sympathetically viewed offenders.

The convention of obliging all lifers, with few exceptions, to go through the full sequence of establishments from a Main Centre to a Pre-release Employment Scheme is, in the view of at least one of us, unnecessarily rigid. The manual does not explain or attempt to justify this prescription. The logic of it has, to our knowledge, never been tested nor has its efficacy. As it concedes: 'No two life sentences will be identical'. Why then oblige all lifers to jump through all six hoops? Given the wide range of sentence lengths—from well under ten years to in excess of 30—presumably a not insignificant minority of lifers could justify missing out one or more stages due to their progress, the length of sentence or by virtue of having extremely good release provision. Presumably, if the Prison Service is obliging all lifers to go through the same sequence, those individuals who subsequently re-offend cannot be blamed on the policy-makers using individual discretion to give such individuals a by-pass over one or more stages.

THE ROLE OF PROBATION

A probation officer *must* be appointed in the home area of every defendant who would face a possible life sentence on conviction.

Thus the manual opens the process of liasion between the lifer and probation which, once found guilty, extends, literally, to the end of the lifer's life. This continuity of contact is an excellent safeguard against the fragmentation, or compartmentalising, of a life sentence. There are, however, at least three different probation officers involved:

- the 'home probation officer' refers to those responsible for the case in the prisoner's home area.
- the 'seconded probation officer' refers to those attached to the prison where the lifer is held and allocated to that lifer only for the period he or she is in that prison.
- the 'supervising probation officer' refers to those who supervise the life licensee after release from prison.

There are consequently many probation officers involved in each lifer case over the full term of his or her life. Some of the main duties of POs dealing with lifers (backed by agreement between HM Prison Service and the Probation Service and set out in the *Lifer Manual*) include:

Home probation officer:

(a) creating a file of press clippings showing local reaction to the offence and all contact with the remanded prisoner and his/her family or friends;

(b) providing assistance and information to the court including pre-trial and post-trial reports as required;

(c) visiting the prisoner to establish contact and build rapport;

(d) honouring the requirements of the *Victim's Charter* (1996) by contacting the victim's family. This task is very labour-intensive and sensitive, involving detailed instructions for each stage of the procedures (and it applies retrospectively to all current lifers as well as those newly convicted).

Seconded probation officer:

(a) establishing contact as soon as possible and opening a prison file;

(b) maintaining close contact with the home probation officer;

(c) contributing to most aspects of the Life Sentence Plan including report writing, working on individual and group-based treatment and courses addressing offending behaviour;

(d) dealing with lifers' ongoing personal needs, especially informal contacts with family and friends;

(e) liaising with the supervising probation officer when the lifer reaches the preparation for release stage and providing a pre-release report which emphasises any risk factors for the future; and

(f) ensuring that appropriate resettlement arrangements are made.

Supervising probation officer:

(a) ensuring regular contact with the lifer after release (e.g. 'at least weekly for the first four weeks . . . fortnightly for the next two months, and thereafter not less than monthly');

(b) providing reports to Parole and Lifer Review Group (PLRG) if there is concern about the licensee, e.g. a risk of re-offending or the probation officer loses touch; and

(c) taking responsibility for recommending a recall to the relevant senior probation officer or assistant chief probation officer.

It is obvious from this abridged list of PO tasks why the recent extension of the Minister for Prison's brief to include probation is so logical and right and why the new *Lifer Manual* is a guide for members of both the Prison Service *and* the *Probation Service*. What the manual does not explain though is the vital role which the hundreds of probation officers based in prison establishments play for offenders generally and lifers in particular. The services of probation officers are purchased by prisons contractually from local Probation Services and these agreements must be re-negotiated annually in the context of tightening financial budgets. This has led in the mid-1990s to a growing pressure on prison Governors to cut this service as it is one of the few personnel groups where the people concerned are not civil servants, so cutting their numbers from prisons does not result in redundancies for the staff concerned, who are redeployed.

The unfortunate consequence for prisoners however can be a diminution of the quality and regularity of contact with the outside world including their families, as well as losing one of the few 'civilian' contacts they have in prison. As POs are often also amongst the relatively few women that lifers get to meet on a regular basis, the positive normalising effects of this contact are also diminished.

Combining the two services under the same accountability line to a Minister of State has the positive potential of bringing much greater continuity to the supervision of prisoners during and after imprisonment. It should also reduce the complexity and duplication of effort in the administration of the process and give a national reference point to probation which had heretofore been a county-based entity.

PRISON SERVICE COURSES

The Programme Development Section of HM Prison Service developed what has become the largest centrally-coordinated treatment programmes ever in England and Wales under the astute leadership of Dr David Thornton. There are currently three accredited offending behaviour programmes running in prisons:

- the Sex Offender Treatment Programme (SOTP)
- two Cognitive Skills Programmes
  —Reasoning and Rehabilitation
  —Enhanced Thinking Skills.

SOTP
The SOTP is available for any male prisoner who has been convicted of a sexual offence and who has enough time left to complete the course. In practice, this means that prisoners serving less than two years are not usually able to attend. All prisoners are assessed before joining a group. Assessment involves interviews with a psychologist trained to conduct SOTP, completion of a large number of questionnaires and, in some prisons, a penile plethysmograph (PPG) which indicates physical responses to sexual preference images. The official information leaflet identifies four 'Practice Issues':

- In each treatment centre, the programme is managed by a team consisting of a Programme Manager (usually a Governor grade), a Treatment Manager (a Psychologist) and a Senior Probation Officer.

- The Prison Service is committed to developing throughcare procedures so that sex offenders receive consistent support throughout their sentence and on release.
- All tutors delivering the programme have undertaken a comprehensive training course equipping them with the necessary knowledge and skills.
- The programme is set out in a manual, thereby ensuring consistency of delivery.
- The Prison Service is committed to anti-discriminatory practice in the delivery of offending behaviour programmes, as in all other areas of its work. '

The description of the SOTP explains that it is 'based on established cognitive-behavioural principles of the type known to be most effective in reducing risk of reoffending'. There is (or was, at time of writing) a *Core Programme* of about 180 hours of groupwork, and an *Extended Programme* with an additional 16 session *Thinking Skills Course* and a 24 session *Relapse Prevention Module* intended to 'develop and rehearse' the relapse prevention plan created in the Core Programme.

The Extended programme is also meant to help course members '. . . tackle any related treatment needs such as anger management, deviant sexual arousal, interpersonal relationships or alcohol/drug abuse. We understand that the service plans to run only the Extended Programme in the future.

Cognitive Behavioural Programmes

The Programme Development Section offers establishments a choice of programmes designed to '. . . tackle the thinking and attitudes which underpin anti-social and criminal behaviour'. They are called the *Reasoning and Rehabilitation Programme* (R&R) and the *Thinking Skills Course*. The essential philosophy behind these programmes is that offenders' thinking, values and reasoning play important parts in their criminal conduct, with developmental factors such as '. . . poverty, lack of opportunity, limited intellectual stimulation, and insufficient or inadequate education' preventing offenders from acquiring the cognitive skills necessary for 'effective and non-criminal social adaptation'. The descriptions and contents of the two programmes are very similar, prompting the assumption that the in-house package developed by Programme Development Section—the Thinking Skills Course—is intended eventually to replace the R&R programme which has had to be purchased from a Canadian business group. Programme goals include teaching offenders:

- Thinking skills, problem solving and decision-making.
- General strategies for recognising problems, analysing them, conceiving and considering alternative non-criminal solutions to them.

- How to formulate plans.
- To think logically, objectively and rationally, without over-generalising or distorting facts.
- To calculate consequence of their behaviour—to stop and think before they act.
- To go beyond an egocentric view of the world and comprehend and consider the thoughts and feelings of other people.
- To improve interpersonal problem solving skills and develop coping behaviours which can serve as effective alternatives to anti-social or criminal behaviour.
- To view frustrations as problem-solving tasks rather than personal threats.
- To develop a self-regulatory system so that their pro-social behaviour is not dependent on external controls.

These programmes will also teach offenders that they can control their lives; that what happens to them depends in large measure on their thinking and the behaviour it leads them to.

As with the SOTP, referrals are thoroughly assessed using standardised methods conducted by well-trained staff. All Cognitive Skills Training courses also have clear, manual-based programmes, local resourcing and managerial support, and establishments approved to run the courses are obliged to maintain regular contact with Programme Development Section for quality control and monitoring. The official information provided indicates a range of relatively well proven pro-social changes as well as research from Canada that there is a '20 per cent overall reduction in recidivism rates for programme completers. These reductions on the recidivism rates were even higher for sex offenders, violent offenders and substance abusers'.

The Programme Development Section provided figures for the numbers of offenders who had completed the programmes through 1996/97 as well as projected figures for 1997/98. Unfortunately, they do not have separate figures for lifers who had received this treatment.

	SOTP	REASONING REHABILITATION	THINKING SKILLS
1992/3	284	Not Started	Not Started
1993/4	439	63	46
1994/5	554	44	241
1995/6	406	115	631
1996/7	564	190	580
Total	2247	412	1498

(Projected 1997/8   SOTP 588   Cognitive Skills combined 1489)

There have also been 149 offenders who have completed the 'Relapse Prevention/Booster' courses and another 154 projected to complete it in 1997/98.

These offender programmes, being centrally co-ordinated, based on proven efficacy and with detailed manuals of instruction and quality control procedures, represent the most outstanding initiative in treatment from the Prison Service and it is very much to be wished that life sentence prisoners are given every opportunity to attend and complete whichever programmes are relevant to them.

The Offending Behaviour Programme Unit (OBPU) of the Adult Males, Parole and Lifer Group of HM Prison Service is currently expanding both the range of courses offered and the numbers of prisoners targeted. This growth is based partly on encouraging preliminary assessments of the first courses and on a growing expectation within the service—from both the managerial hierarchy and lifers themselves— that lifers' attendance at offending behaviour courses affect their progress towards release. The aim of the Prison Board for 2001-02 is that at least 6,000 'successful completions' will be achieved, of which 1,200 should be through Sex Offender Treatment Programmes.

Morrisey (1994) surveyed all prisons with psychologists in England and Wales with lifers for information on what groupwork was available specifically for lifers. Of these, 37 (90%) provided information including all six Main Centres, 90% of the dispersal prisons and Cat B prisons and about half each of the Cat C and Cat D establishments. She grouped the results into three primary function types of groups: providing *information* or *support* or *addressing offending behaviour*.

The importance of group-based courses about life sentences and how to cope and manage them is highest at the early stages and it is not reassuring to find that not all Main Centres provided this—and that those that did were variable in length and content. The author concluded that it would be 'desirable at the main centre stage' to have a comprehensive information course for all lifers, and we would add that these courses should also be uniform in their content, i.e. centrally co-ordinated.

Only four of 18 prisons in 'mid-sentence stage', i.e. the dispersals and Cat B and C prisons, provided information groups or courses for lifers. Those groups which were run were generally well-received and well attended.

Given evidence that lifers require a great deal of support particularly during the early stages of their sentences, it was disappointing to find that only two of the six Main Centres provided groups which focused on the range of emotional problems including 'shock, disbelief and anger . . . grief and remorse . . . anxiety fear and confusion' which all lifers experience in varying degrees. Pooley (1990) found that murderers accounted for almost one-sixth (15.6%) of all suicides in prison between 1972 and 1987, while only constituting 3.6% of the population and Sapsford (1983) found high levels of emotional disturbance in the first year of life sentences. Here too there seems a strong argument for support groups targeted at lifers in *all* Main Centres, perhaps especially so for young offenders.

Of the three themes, groups addressing offending behaviour should be perhaps the highest priority, as Morrisey concluded:

> Comprehensive provision of groupwork with those (address their offending behaviour and related behaviour) objectives therefore is crucially important for lifers.

She refers to a 1991 review (Morrissey and Towl) of the treatment provisions for lifers finding that only a very small number of establishments had provision for group-based treatment interventions with lifers at that time. This later study found that all Main Centres had some kind of offending-related groupwork which lifers could attend, but that only half had courses directed specifically for lifers. Only a third of the Cat C and half of the Cat B prisons with lifers ran treatment oriented courses specifically for lifers. The research concludes that

> ... while there are some establishments providing well for lifers on the three key areas ... these are relatively few in number and tend to be confined to the prisons that specialise in lifer management.

while also endorsing the nationally co-ordinated programmes such as the Sex Offender Treatment Programme, Cognitive Skills and Anger Management courses mentioned above and the therapeutic community regimes at Gartree and Grendon which offer intensive therapy for selected lifers.

MENTALLY DISORDERED OFFENDERS

The report of the Committee on the Penalty for Homicide (1993) revealed that

> Hospital orders (section 37 and 38 of the Mental Health Act) cannot, *ex hypothesi* be made where the sentence of life imprisonment is fixed by law.

With the benefit of the views of the full membership of the Executive of the Royal College of Psychiatrists (Forensic Section), the report concludes that the expulsion of those accused of murder from this opportunity is regarded as 'inexplicable' by psychiatrists. Although lifers who are subsequently so classified may be transferred under section 48, most psychiatrist regard this as inappropriate as it requires that the patient is in 'urgent need of treatment', obliging the sectioning doctor to stretch the definition in many cases to justify the act of transfer.

Although it may be generally viewed as preferable to send life sentence prisoners who are deemed to be 'suffering' from disorders of personality including psychopathy to a Special Hospital rather than to prison, this is not the view of a significant proportion of the prisoners. The Lane Report referred to Dell and Robertson, in *Sentenced to Hospital* (1988), and opined that

> . . . there are many good reasons for pausing to consider whether a prisoner's best interests are served by a transfer to hospital, particularly in the light of the potential for misuse of the Mental Health Act to prolong the detention of dangerous individuals (so called psychopaths) under the guise of treatment they neither want nor can benefit from.

Many lifers will also explain that they are extremely opposed to having any psychiatric diagnosis or label attached to them, as the label alone is sufficient to prolong their imprisonment. The general perception is that the Parole Board are more likely to exercise caution, and to ascribe presumptions of unpredictability, to lifers who have been so labelled. Indeed, a former chairman of the Parole Board told the authors that men who are transferred to Grendon 'psychiatric' prison for treatment are generally viewed as higher risks of reoffending than otherwise comparable prisoners who do not go for treatment by virtue of the presumption of a psychiatric instability, regardless of their treatment outcome.

But what is the size of the problem? How many life sentence prisoners 'suffer' from a mental disorder? Swinton, Maden and Gunn (1994) looked at a representative cross-section of 170 lifers from the total lifer population (2,587) in 1991 and compared them with 1,630 fixed-term prisoners. Their assessments included reference to subjects' files, interviews using the Clinical Interview Schedule (CIS)—a standardised assessment of mental state and psychiatric diagnoses using the ICD—9 nomenclature. Of an original group of 193 lifers selected, 23 (12%) refused. Psychiatric diagnoses 'were made in 71 (42%) of those interviewed', although the correct figure is 40%, including six cases with psychotic disorders!

Diagnoses included personality disorder—31 (18%); alcohol or drug abuse/dependence 17 (10%); and sexual deviation 7 (4%). Although some readers might query defining alcohol abuse (or indeed 'pathological gambling' and 'mental handicap') as a psychiatric disorder, if we extrapolate these figures to the whole lifer population, there are roughly 1,400 imprisoned lifers suffering from some form of psychiatric condition. The authors conclude that:

> ... there was evidence of increased psychological vulnerability in the lifers, who were significantly more likely to report episodes of self-harm before their index offence and after sentence ... [and that] nearly a quarter of the lifers had a history of self-harm and one in six had probably attempted suicide (substantially more than reported by other sentenced prisoners.

> The figures suggest that among the 2,587 male lifers in prison, 91 would have psychotic disorder ... and that 198 would need hospital admission ... This figure would approximately double the number of life-sentenced prisoner currently in hospital.

> The lifers were found to have a significantly higher rate of personality disorder than other male sentenced prisoners.

If we accept these estimates of the number of lifers with some form of psychiatric disorder, then the unmet need in terms of prison-based treatment is massive. The only facility which might be defined as 'psychiatric' in the prison service is Grendon, which has a capacity of 345 places. None of the other 80 or so places in Therapeutic Community prisons require a psychiatric classification for referral.

Woolf and Tumim (1991), in their far-reaching report, *Prison Disturbances April 1990*, which also addressed the wider issues facing the Prison Service, concluded:

> The range of initiatives being undertaken to minimise the number of mentally disordered people within the penal system should be continued and further developed.

> There should be research into the services at present available for the mentally disordered and how well they work.

> The Prison Service should recognise the special responsibility it has for those in its care who are mentally disordered.

> The Prison Service should ensure that clearer and more specific attention is paid to mentally handicapped offenders in its care.

The authors of *Murderers and Life Imprisonment* are not aware of any substantive formal initiatives which have followed from the Prison Service from these conclusions.

A significant number of mentally disordered offenders reside in the Special Secure Hospitals, Broadmoor, Rampton and Ashworth. A report entitled *Strategy for Patients with Personality Disorder*

(Special Hospitals Authority Statistics, 1995), observed that the Special Hospitals have

> . . . a substantial role to play in the future development of services for mentally disordered offenders with personality disorder and currently provide for the largest concentrations of such patients in therapeutic settings in conditions of security.

There were 265 referrals to the Special Hospitals in 1994 with a 'mental illness' classification and another 131 described as suffering from a 'psychopathic disorder'. Of these 396 people, only 168 (42%) were accepted. Less than a third (43) of the 'psychopaths' were accepted. Many informed prison staff, especially psychologists and psychiatrists, feel there are significant numbers of prisoners who might accurately be described as suffering from a psychopathic disorder, which is a legal, rather than medical, classification under the Mental Health Act 1983. These men are also often felt to be amongst those least responsive to treatment intervention, often being labelled 'untreatable', or detainable in order to prevent a deterioration of their condition (an option under the 1983 Act). Although the report does not record how many of the 40% of all Special Hospital referrals in 1994 from prisons were lifers, those who were accepted automatically became indeterminate patients, or prisoners under treatment. Over the years since 1986, the percentage of referrals which are successful has dropped from 82% to 47% for mental illness and from 74% to 33% for psychopathic disorder. If these disordered offenders are not being accepted into hospitals, then presumably more and more of them are being contained in prisons, precisely the opposite to the Woolf recommendations.

It would seem that, with the closure of large numbers of community hospitals, the pressure on the Special Hospitals to take an increasing number of referrals for mentally disordered offenders has grown tremendously in recent years. As there are no commensurate increases in the places available, fewer referrals are accepted. As the greatest number of these referrals come from prisons, and as lifers have a higher incidence of mental disorder (according to available 'research' by psychiatrists), then it follows that the psychiatric treatment opportunities for mentally disordered lifers are decreasing rather than improving. This seems more probable as well given that there have been no increases in the numbers of psychiatrists or psychologists employed by the Prison Service either (indeed there is considerable pressure to cut their numbers in the light of recent financial imperatives from the Treasury).

While it may be regarded as right that lifers who have been mentally disordered are viewed as higher risks if released, those who have been treated and undergone the intensive therapeutic scrutiny of the Therapeutic Community regimes are actually lower risks of reoffending than other prisoners generally and other lifers in particular.

It might rather be regarded as perverse to oblige them to have their 'conditions' treated only to punish them further if they do so.

HOW LIFERS (AND THE STAFF WHO WORK WITH THEM) MANAGE PRISON

One of the more insightful articles on the psychology of lifers comes from Woodward and Hodkin (1997), describing the experience of lifers in the Therapeutic Community exclusively for lifers at HMP Gartree. In their article *Surviving Violent Death,* they posit that:

> There exists amongst murderers a continuum of attitudes toward the deed that they have carried out. On one extreme a prisoner feels that he has no right to life himself, having destroyed that of his victim . . . On the other, an attitude of indifference prevails, which often stems from their unwillingness to acknowledge the enormity of the crime they have committed.

For the staff who must work at a vulnerably close level with these men, there is a tremendous tension between the feelings of 'empathy for the victims' and possible anger for their suffering and that of their survivors, against the need to understand and accept the prisoners' efforts to become better people and their struggle to come to terms with the enormity of their deeds. Within this dynamic, staff must hear the most horrific details of the most horrific crimes and hear them from men who are sometimes unsympathetic in many ways. They may be self-pitying, presenting more as victim than as offender. They may seek to deny or minimise their murders, excusing much of what they've done as out of character, induced by drugs or drink, provoked by the 'bad influence' of others or the betrayal of their victims. Most of these men, as well as the majority of the rest of those in Therapeutic Community treatment regimes like Gartree and Grendon, will come to accept their responsibility and, through that, their guilt.

When this stage is reached, it becomes possible for them to address what Woodward and Hodkin refer to as

> . . . the primary issue of our very existence and its impermanence.

In a quote from Heidegger, they assert that:

Personal existence is self projecting; it is not formed and finished but an open future; therefore structurally it is in advance of itself; there is something to come.

The fact that for the imprisoned lifers, there is no open future for their victims focuses the treatment imperative and brings staff inevitably closer to the realities of death which this form of treatment obliges. When, as has recently occurred, a lifer addressed his crimes by facing the scene of crime photographs, staff were even more vulnerable and their capacity to care ever more strained. But this is what must happen in order for those lifers ever to live 'good and useful' lives again. For the staff, people who have themselves

lost loved ones, faced their own and their loved ones' illnesses and have become aware of the vulnerabilities of new life as they became parents or grandparents

this proximity to those who have destroyed life can be, at times, difficult to bear.

The heightened sense of outrage, of anger and injustice, towards the criminals can test their professionalism and objectivity to the limit. Yet, in facing these feelings and life issues, the authors conclude that the staff have 'become increasingly successful at dealing with the most fundamental issue to face us all, death', ending their article with a quote from Emmy van Deurzen-Smith:

What may seem like negative conditions initially, may turn out to contain the promise of much positive learning and experience. There are no lives without positive possibilities.

'Natural lifers'
The special management challenges represented by prisoners who have been informed by the Home Secretary that they will never be released (i.e. that they have a 'whole life' tariff) is mentioned in *Chapter 1* (see p.22) and *Chapter 7* (p.163).

CHAPTER 5

Discretionary Lifer Panels

The introduction of Discretionary Lifer Panels (DLPs) through the Criminal Justice Act 1991 was a very significant development in the way that lifers are managed in that the power of the executive was defined in a clear and precise manner and decisions about the release of discretionary lifers were made the responsibility of a judicial process carried out by the Parole Board. The implications of this change are considerable for the lifer and for the managers of his or her sentence in custody. It involves the beginnings of a cultural change which will have an effect on all lifers in due course.

I. INTRODUCTION

In the House of Commons on 25 June 1991, Mrs Angela Rumbold MP, Minister of State at the Home Office, said:

> . . . The prisoner would be entitled to have his continued detention after the term set by the trial judge reviewed by an independent body having the status of a court for the purposes of the European Convention On Human Rights. We propose that the body should be the Parole Board, operational under a special set of procedures which should be laid down in rules made by the Secretary of State. We intend that the panel of the Parole Board which will consider discretionary life sentence cases will be chaired by a judge who is a member of the Board, and one of its members will be a psychiatrist. The prisoner will be entitled to appear before the panel and be legally represented. If the panel concludes that the prisoner's continued detention is no longer necessary to protect the public, the Parole Board will direct the Secretary of State to release him. (*Hansard,* cols 903-4)

Changes in release assessment procedures for discretionary lifers which were brought about by the judiciary for determining decisions about release were accompanied by changes in procedures for due process, openness and accountability. The significance of the move of responsibility from the executive to the judiciary is considerable given the sensitivity of the risk involved in releasing those who have committed the most serious of offences. The move can be seen in the context of increasing the rights of the individual to have access to due process in considering their release. The previous bureaucratic procedure which inevitably was cautious and appeared to be governed by political sensitivities of accountability was often felt to be subject to public and media pressure. The critical considerations that underpin the new system are that there is the possibility of change for the good in even the most dangerous and damaged of individuals, and that this change can be measured and described in such a way that the risk to the public of releasing that person can be assessed through the prison experience. The meaning of this move for lifers and the staff working most closely with them is that there is increased hope for their future in terms of quality of life after prison. For staff working with lifers there is a recognition that *the experience of relationships and activity within a prison environment* can clearly contribute towards the process of rehabilitation and change. This also presents the Prison Service with the problems of structuring the lifer's career in prison in such a way as to maximise the opportunities available to him or her and also of introducing systems of close monitoring and measuring the changes which are identified as necessary to demonstrate reduced risk in the offender. The difference of decision-making processes for discretionary and mandatory lifers creates an added anxiety for the latter and much larger group which still depends on the original system of uncertain bureaucracy.

THE DISCRETIONARY LIFE SENTENCE

The discretionary life sentence developed as a measure of preventative detention for mentally unstable and dangerous offenders as a result of judicial innovation from the 1950s onwards. Judges justified the choice of an indeterminate life sentence rather than a long fixed-term sentence on the twofold basis that the sentence would then allow for review and release by the Home Secretary at an earlier stage than under a fixed-term sentence if the offender made progress, and for detention beyond the period merited as punishment for the offence if the offender was still considered dangerous at the end of such a period. The fact that release, when it came, would be on licence and subject to liability to recall was also regarded as an additional safeguard to the public. The Advisory Council on the Penal System in its 'Review of Maximum Penalties' listed no fewer than 50 statutory offences for which a discretionary life sentence could be imposed.

CHANGES IN CULTURE

The management of life sentence prisoners (already described in detail in *Chapter 4*) provides demanding challenges for the Prison Service because lifers represent the clearest image in the mind of the public of the risk to their safety. The life sentence is a uniquely serious one in that the person sentenced is never free from the effects of their crime, for although they may be released on licence, until their dying day they are subject to the possibility of recall to prison. The sentence symbolises the state's determination to protect its members from harm and thus the decisions that surround this sentence are of critical significance for all concerned with criminal justice and particularly for the Home Secretary who is ultimately accountable—for the protection of the public—in the House of Commons.

The power of the state which is represented by the life sentence calls for sensitive judgements, balancing the protection of the public against fairness to the offender. It is in examining this process that we can discern the quality of the values that reflect the nature of our society. The change brought about by the Criminal Justice Act 1991 in the arrangements for release procedures for discretionary lifers has moved the responsibility for decision-making from the executive to the judiciary. This inevitably will affect the management of lifers in the prisons in which they are held. Critical decision-making processes affect the way in which prisoners are considered within prisons and it is the study of these consideration that forms the focus of this chapter.

It would be easy to be punitive towards lifers and subject them to longer and longer periods in prison. It is far more difficult for a society that accepts the possibility that even those who have committed the most serious offences may develop in prison to such an extent that they can live safely in society. It is this concept that has led to a series of decision-making processes in order to give effect to this judgement of risk. The trial judge can decide whether to specify a minimum number of years when imposing the sentence. He can write to the Secretary of State about the case and in due course the law requires that the judge is consulted when release on licence is being considered.

The final decision about release by the Home Secretary had always been the culmination of a consideration of a wide range of reports which comprise the dossier on the lifer—the relevant file which collates information in detail. Although lifers are now becoming more numerous in prisons—there are over 4,000 at the end of 1998—they are regarded as sufficiently special to be the objects of much attention, and their dossiers are the most carefully compiled in the whole system.

Following compilation of the full dossier when a lifer was seriously being considered for release the case was referred to the Local Review Committee (LRC). The lifer submitted a report himself or herself for this review and there was a report from a member of the LRC who interviewed the lifer. There was also a report from the future supervising probation officer and the beginnings of a release plan. The dossier and the recommendations of the LRC then went to the Parole Board, which was given further information about the offence and the trial. Finally the Home Office obtained the views of the Lord Chief Justice (and the trial judge if available) and its officials prepared their own comments for the Home Secretary. These processes are listed here to show how much went into the process of decision-making. It is perhaps inevitable that the combination of so many opinions tended to result in rather cautious policies.

Culture before the introduction of Discretionary Lifer Panels
The arrangements for considering release prior to the DLPs could be described as producing a *dependency culture* in which lifers were managed. This remains largely the process for mandatory lifers at present. The main features of such a culture were:

1. *A complex bureaucracy of procedures contributing to any decision-making*—so that no staff were identified. Local staff who had regular contact and responsibility for the lifer put reports forward for the Local Review Committee to consider before recommending their views to the Parole Board about suitability for release. One member of the LRC, who sat on the review panel, would interview the lifer to help clarify their comments. The recommendations would be considered by the Parole Board at a time unknown to the prison and whose panel members were also anonymous. After their decision, the recommendation would be passed to the Parole Unit and the Lifer Management Unit of the Prison Service before being considered by Ministers who made the final decision concerning release. This decision would eventually be passed through to the prison for the lifer to be informed.

2. *Secrecy in the contributions towards decision-making*—so that no reports were made available to the lifer. Although many reports were discussed with the lifer by those at local level who were writing them, he or she was not entitled to see them nor to have copies for future reference. The lifer was not aware of the large dossier of information that had been compiled from his or her earliest days of the sentence, nor who had contributed towards this collection. This secrecy meant that no-one could challenge the truth or accuracy of statements made by reporting officers or of official documents from headquarters including depositions.

3. *Uncertainty about the timing of procedures and how long decisions would take.* Although the lifer knew when the LRC was sitting by the fact that he or she was interviewed by the individual member there was then a long period of uncertainty about where the process was being considered. The delay in getting the eventual decision could take from six to 12 months, and sometimes even longer.

4. *Uncertainty about the criteria upon which decisions were being made.* Staff writing reports had little guidance about the criteria upon which to make their assessments and sometimes included an

examination of the attitude towards the offence, behaviour in prison and support available outside in their contributions but not always so. The lifer then had little indication about the areas of work upon which he or she should concentrate to demonstrate their eligibility for release.

5. *No reasons were given for decisions when they were made.* There was only a standardised reply given to the prison which indicated the next review date, which was often several years away. Staff communicating this to the lifer had to interpret the message in the best way they could in order to help it make sense to the individual.

6. *Lack of clarity about the tariff element (punishment length of time) of the sentence for many lifers.* Many could deduce by their review date that the tariff element was likely to be associated with that event but this was rarely made explicit either by the judge in court nor by the Prison Service after some determination had been made.

7. *Staff shared this dependency*—in their local setting and often felt powerless to influence the process. The frustration of having to make sense of uncertainty and secrecy was a considerable strain for those managing lifers. This often led to men being moved form prison to prison after a decision not to release had been communicated in order to start the process again.

8. *Lack of clarity of criteria for future behaviour*—in order that progress could be demonstrated and progress made towards release—if indeed there was anything that was necessary or likely to influence such a decision.

Underlying all these features can be discerned a basic assumption about the value of the individual lifer, the rights he or she had and the ability the lifer and those immediately managing him or her had towards influencing the future. This assumption could be epitomised and was experienced as one of complete dependency upon an all-powerful executive. The height of this experience was when Leon Brittan, when Home Secretary, announced changes in the criteria for selecting lifers for release at the Conservative Party Conference—changes which extended the minimum period that lifers could expect to spend in custody before being considered for release. During this time the tariffs for many lifers were increased over and above those recommended by the judiciary and produced anxiety amongst lifers and staff managing them that there was no access to procedures of due process. There was nothing that could be done to prepare the lifer for a realistic release and nothing which could affect the eventual release date. The powerlessness and hopelessness of lifers were never more experienced than at this time. For an individual experience which had dramatic effects in that the lifer was detained for 22 years see *Alex's Story* in *Appendix A* to this work.

Prison culture changes

Changes in the culture of prisons have been taking place for many years. Sometimes these are in response to events such as disturbances—the Hull riot (1976) and the Strangeways disturbance (1990) produced significant shifts in regime planning and policy following reports about them. Sometimes change takes place as a result of personal initiative and pressure—the report in 1988 from Ian Dunbar, a member of the Prisons Board, *A Sense of Direction*, provided a platform for much developmental thinking and action on the quality of regimes and the interaction between staff and prisoners as contributing to the overall security and health of a prison. On other occasions change has been brought about as a consequence of legal rulings following individual inmate initiatives— the introduction of DLPs is an example of this change. The cases which were essential to this change follow later in this chapter. These changes have often merged and been influenced by other pressures such as overcrowding, industrial relations difficulties and controls on the use of resources. Nevertheless the dramatic and fundamental changes introduced by the DLP provisions have brought about structural, procedural and actual changes which have affected relationships and processes in a such a marked way as to be capable of examination and measurement.

Prison culture after the introduction of Discretionary Lifer Panels

The indications are that these changes could be described as bringing about a *responsive culture* with the following characteristics:

1. *Clear decision-making procedures* which have been made explicit to all lifers, with the range of reports, a timetable of delivery and a description of the process openly communicated to staff and prisoners. The presence of the members of the Parole Board who constitute the DLP in the prison meeting with the lifer and staff in the hearing makes the process far more personal.
2. *An openness of reporting* for all concerned and particularly for the lifer and his or her legal representative, including a summary of past reports to the Parole Board. The lifer gets access to the dossier in terms of having his or her own copy in good time to make their own representations, to prepare to call certain witnesses for the hearing and to be able to challenge the veracity of details included in those reports.
3. *A strict timetable* of reporting and procedures made explicit with the lifer getting the decision of the panel hearing within one

week. The process of preparation of reports is designed to enable the lifer to have sufficient time to make his or her representations after consulting their legal representative and to consider the witnesses he or she would seek to be present at the panel's hearing.

4. *The explicit nature of the criteria* upon which decisions are made was central to the legislation. The emphasis is placed upon the assessment of dangerousness that the lifer represents to the public. The elements of risk are identified through the Lifer Sentence Plan which each lifer has to have constructed. All reports from staff are now structured to address the areas of risk in a direct manner.

5. *Reasons for decisions* are given particularly when the lifer is not to be released. Indications for future action are provided as well to help with progress towards the next review. The staff and lifer are able to make sense of the decision and to consider the possible areas for future action in order to meet the needs identified.

6. *The explicit tariff* or punitive element of the sentence is now made clear to all lifers and in future will be communicated in a routine manner, as part of the sentence. This clearly adds a considerable degree of certainty to the sentence for staff and lifer to come to terms with and aid the process of planning moves and activities over the years.

7. *Staff involvement* has improved through a considerable training programme so that the relevance of their role can clearly be seen to be crucial in the progress of the individual.

8. *Clearer identification of the areas of risk* that a lifer should consider during his or her sentence. Each lifer has a 'career plan' that outlines the aspects of his or her behaviour that should be closely addressed in order for him or her to demonstrate reduction of the risk that he or she represents. There are clear courses of activity that help towards addressing criminal behaviour in prisons, such as sexual offending courses, anger management, cognitive skills courses and therapeutic community experiences that are all designed to help lifers learn about themselves and to show that they have developed more socially acceptable behaviour patterns and attitudes.

These features combine towards creating a culture in which the individual lifer's needs are respected and there is action from the authorities to meet these needs within a responsive environment. The value of the person is more enhanced by the features of the new system and although it is recognised that rules and systems do not necessarily adjust attitudes there are sufficient structural safeguards to ensure that the rights of individuals receive greater consideration than before.

The lifer himself or herself faced severe tests of his or her own judgement. They had to develop a way of life sufficiently different from their previous one to avoid the risk of repeating their crime. Such total changes in lifestyle may be desirable in theory, but given the limitations of adaptability as adult life progresses it is not surprising that some lifers slip back into ways of life (such as drinking and gambling) and methods of handling problems which have been congenial in the past but which may lead them into risky situations and relationships. The period of custody for lifers places extreme stress upon them because of the indeterminacy of their sentence. The effects of imprisonment have been well described by Gresham Sykes in *The Society of Captives* as a series of deprivations which cause men to learn methods of adaptation in order to survive the pains experienced. The lifer has to manage the pains of deprivation and to demonstrate such a change in behaviour and outlook that he or she can again be trusted with their freedom. This is a considerable demand upon any person. There are doubts that the experiences undertaken and the behaviours observed in prison can be relevant practice for life after prison. Much more could be done to assist in preparing lifers for the realities which face them.

A MODEL TO CONSIDER THE CHANGES BROUGHT ABOUT BY DLPs

Before	*After*
DEPENDENCY	RESPONSIVE
1. Complex hidden bureaucracy.	Clear decision-making procedures.
2. Secrecy of reporting.	Openness of reporting.
3. Uncertainty of timing.	Strict timetabling of process.
4. Uncertainty of criteria.	Explicit criteria for release.
5. No explanation of decisions.	Reasons for decisions given.
6. Uncertainty of tariff.	Tariff made explicit.
7. Staff as dependent as lifers.	Staff trained in proactive role.
8. Uncertainty of evidence.	Risk areas identified.

II. LEGAL BACKGROUND TO THE CHANGES

Why the change to Discretionary Lifer Panels?

The difference between the reasons for mandatory and discretionary life sentences led to questions being asked about the nature of the release process being made the same. Given the development of parole and planned release arrangements for determinate sentenced men and the clearer indication for lifers about the tariff that their offence should attract the continuing uncertainty of release timing for mandatory lifers had been severely criticised.

The length of time that the decision-making process took and the lack of openness in the procedure also led to disquiet about an essentially executive and administrative emphasis in the judicial sentencing of serious offenders. There had been evidence in many cases of the recommendations of the Parole Board to release not being accepted by the Home Secretary and indeed a clear statement from Leon Brittan when he was Home Secretary that certain lifers should not expect to be released for at least 20 years. This *blurring of responsibilities* between the executive and the judiciary caused *grave concern* amongst many people in the criminal justice system.

The growth in the movement to ensure prisoners their rights under the law led many cases to be referred to the European Court of Human Rights. In this way movement had taken place with regard to prisoners' access to confidential communications with their legal representatives and a range of other rulings which had significantly altered the expectations and status of men in indeterminate custody.

Legal considerations concerning the conviction and release of lifers

The Hodgson Pre-conditions
In *Hodgson* (1968) 52 CAR 13 the Court of Appeal laid down that the following three pre-conditions should be met before a discretionary life sentence was imposed:

1. When the offence or offences in themselves are grave enough to require a very long sentence;
2. When it appears from the nature of the offences or from the defendant's history that he is a person of unstable character likely to commit such offences in the future; and
3. When, if the offences are committed, the consequences to others may be specially injurious, as in the cases of sexual offenders or cases of violence.

These criteria have been stated and re-stated by the Court of Appeal but are not always abided by in sentencing practice. Thus, in some cases, the criterion of great gravity laid down in *Hodgson* has not been satisfied. In

Hodgson, the Court of Appeal clearly had in mind the type of case which justified a sentence of some 15 years or more; but the life sentence has been imposed for relatively trivial offences of arson that would not have justified sentences of more than three or five years in themselves. In other cases, though the offence was grave, the judge has not, in fact, gone so far as to make a finding of mental instability and of the likelihood of further offences.

The rationale of discretionary life sentences

The rationale of the discretionary life sentence was explained by the Court of Appeal in *R v Wilkinson* (1983) CAR 105:

> It seems to us that the sentence of life imprisonment, other than for an offence where it is obligatory, is really appropriate and must only be passed in the most exceptional circumstances. With few exceptions, of which this case is not one, it is reserved broadly speaking for offenders who for one reason or another cannot be dealt with under the provisions of the Mental Health Act yet who are in a mental state which makes them dangerous to the life or limb of the public. It is sometimes impossible to say when the danger will subside, therefore an indeterminate sentence is required so that the prisoner's progress may be monitored and so that he will be kept in custody only so long as public safety may be jeopardised by his being let loose at large.

In this and later cases, Lord Lane CJ stressed that it was the presence of an 'imponderable' mental element that justified the imposition of a life sentence rather than a long punitive fixed-term sentence. Where punishment was the judge's sole purpose a very long fixed-term sentence was to be imposed rather than a life sentence. It follows from the rationale of the life sentence as expounded by Lord Lane in *Wilkinson* that the prisoner was entitled to his or her release once no longer dangerous, since lifelong detention was clearly not the punishment merited by the offence.

The decision in Bradley

The clearest exposition of the rationale of the discretionary life sentence was given by Stuart-Smith LJ in the course of his judgement in *R v Parole Board, ex parte Bradley* (1991) 1 WLR 134 at 145:

> The rationale or justification for a discretionary life sentence must surely be this: that in exceptional circumstances the interests of public safety cannot be served by imposing a determinate sentence even to the maximum extent possible, i.e. the tariff sentence merited in the way of punishment, uplifted to the limited extent allowed by established case law for the protection of the public. Rather it is necessary to cater for the presently perceived risk that upon the completion of any lawful determinate sentence, the prisoner

would, if freed, remain a grave danger to security. This is achieved by passing a life sentence so as to ensure that the public will be protected and the risk re-assessed after the tariff period expires.

In the same judgement, Stuart-Smith LJ went on to recognise the potential injustice of a discretionary life sentence and the need for a 'compelling justification' for imposing it. This, he stated, could only be provided by a 'grave future risk amounting to an actual likelihood of dangerousness'.

Rights derived from the rationale of discretionary life sentences
In a succession of judgements relating to the previous parole system, the Divisional Court had already recognised that discretionary lifers could derive certain rights from the special nature of their sentence as explained by the Court of Appeal over the years. The rights that were recognised can be summarised thus:

1. In *Handscombe* (1988) 86 CAR 59 the Divisional Court held that it would be wrong to detain a discretionary lifer for punishment any longer than he or she would have been detained under a fixed-term sentence, with full remission, had he not been sentenced to life to protect the public. Thus, at the point where a fixed-term sentence determined on tariff principles would have expired (with full remission) he or she was entitled to a review, and to release unless dangerous.

2. In *Benson* (9 November 1988) the Divisional Court held that the test that should be applied in determining whether further detention was justified after the expiry of the tariff was one of whether the lifer continued to present a 'danger to life or limb', extending, of course, to a danger of rape.

3. In *Bradley* (1991) 1 WLR 134 the *Benson* test was adopted and approved. But the Court rejected the submission that, after the expiration of the tariff, a lifer was entitled to be released unless it was shown, on a balance of probabilities, that he or she was likely to re-offend in a manner of danger to life or limb. It was sufficient, the Court held, that there be a substantial risk of such further offences. The Court suggested that the longer a prisoner had served beyond their tariff, the greater the risk would have to be to justify continued detention. The Court of Appeal in *Wilson* (1992) subsequently qualified this statement of principle. Nonetheless it is clear that the necessity of further detention depends both on the degree of risk and the type of offence of which there is a danger.

What seems clear from the foregoing review is that:

1. *A discretionary lifer is entitled as a matter of law to his or her release unless there is a substantial risk of a further offence dangerous to life or limb.*
2. *The possibility or likelihood of other non-violent offences (involving danger to property, theft, burglary, etc.) is not relevant to the issue of release.*

There must be close parallels to be drawn between the risks represented by discretionary lifers and serious determinate offenders who although considered for a short period of parole towards the end of their sentence are often released without the risk they represent being reduced significantly.

The European Court decision in Weeks and Thynne, Wilson and Gunnell
The main issue before the European Court in the case of *Thynne, Wilson and Gunnell v The United Kingdom* (1990) 13 EHRR 666 was whether the parole procedures for the review of the cases of discretionary lifers who had completed their 'tariff' periods and were seeking release, or who had been released and then recalled, satisfied the requirements of Article 5(4) of the European Convention. Article 5(4) provides:

> Everyone who is deprived of his liberty by arrest or detention shall be entitled to take proceedings by which the lawfulness of his detention shall be decided speedily by a court and his release ordered if the detention is not lawful.

The argument of the applicants was that they were entitled to have a hearing before 'a court' at least at the moment when they had completed the tariff and the sole justification for their detention became their supposed 'dangerousness', and at periodic intervals thereafter; and at the time of any recall to prison from conditions of liberty of licence. By 'a court' they meant a body independent of the executive, with a power to review the substantive merits of their case for release and to release them if they were no longer dangerous; and a body that gave them a hearing in the course of which they were entitled to be heard and to see the reports written on them. Their argument therefore was that the existing system for review by the Parole Board and Home Secretary violated Article 5(4) by giving the 'final say' on release or further detention to the Home Secretary rather than an independent judicial body; and secondly, that review by a court meant review by a body which gave the prisoner notice of the case against him or her, and access to all the reports before it, which did not happen under the old Parole Board procedures.

This ruling represented a major change in the treatment of lifers and in the consideration of their release. The repercussions are still being worked through years after the event and the subsequent rulings have undoubtedly added to the hope for lifers that improvement was possible in their condition, that they were not totally dependent upon an all powerful executive and that their lives were not fully forfeited to the state.

In *Weeks v United Kingdom* (1988) 10 EHRR 293 the Court of Human Rights decided, on the special fact of Week's case, that the discretionary life sentence passed on him for a trivial offence of bungled robbery at the age of 17 was not intended to punish him but was intended, from the start, as a measure of preventative detention to rehabilitate him and protect the public from his dangerousness. The Court held that he was entitled to periodic reviews of the legality of his detention under Article 5(4) because the justification for his continuing detention depended on his continuing dangerousness.

In *Thynne, Wilson and Gunnell* the UK Government later argued that Weeks was decided on its special facts and that its reasoning did not apply to other discretionary lifer cases and particularly to those cases where the offences were very grave (all involving very serious offences of rape and buggery) and punishment played a part in the original sentence. The Court rejected this argument and recognised that all discretionary life sentences had an essentially preventative rationale, and that it was the need to protect the public from the supposed dangerousness of the offence that always justified the imposition of a life sentence rather than a fixed sentence. Therefore, the Court reasoned, the discretionary lifer was entitled to a periodic review of the legality of his or her continuing detention by 'a court' at least from the point when the tariff had expired and the sole justification for continuing detention was the presence or absence of the changeable mental quality of dangerousness.

Differences between mandatory and discretionary lifers

There are thus differences between the review and release procedures for the two types of lifer brought about by the Criminal Justice Act 1991 following a ruling in the European Court of Human Rights in the same year.

Mandatory lifers

The decision for release of a mandatory lifer is at the Home Secretary's discretion. Before release can take place, a positive recommendation must be received from the Parole Board, which reviews the case and considers the risks associated with release. Once a positive recommendation has been received, the Lord Chief Justice and the trial judge (if available) is consulted. The Home Secretary may reject the recommendation to release if he considers the risk to be unacceptable, or decides that release would undermine public confidence in the criminal justice process.

This interpretation of the law is being challenged through further cases and the uncertainty of determining the nature of public confidence by a politician has been criticised as being very unfair and lacking in accountability.

Discretionary lifers

Under the Criminal Justice Act 1991, the power to release discretionary lifers is now vested in the Parole Board which sits as a three member Discretionary Lifer Panel to consider cases under court-like procedures. The minimum period that must be served in custody to reflect the seriousness of the offence is known as the 'tariff'. This is set for discretionary lifers by the sentencing court, without Ministerial involvement, unlike the procedure for mandatory lifers. When the period has expired the Home Secretary *must* refer a prisoner's case for consideration by a DLP which *must* direct that the prisoner be released if it is satisfied that it is no longer necessary for the protection of the public for the prisoner to be confined. The prisoner is entitled to attend and participate in the hearing, to be represented, to see all relevant documentation presented to the DLP and to be given reasons for the panel's decisions.

These changes are at the forefront of the move towards greater prisoners' rights and the challenge to administrative procedures carried out in private. The implications for the management of lifers are considerable as the Prison Service seeks to implement its objectives with lifers.

The overall procedures before DLPs were introduced

Prior to the introduction of DLPs all lifers were considered under the same system in which the lifer could be released on licence when the Home Secretary of the day considered it to be justified. Life imprisonment is by law the *only* sentence that can be imposed for murder and this marks it out as a unique crime demanding an exceptional penalty. But murders vary from, e.g. the 'mercy killing' of a severely handicapped baby or a spouse suffering from an incurable disease to murder in the course of robbery or theft or by causing an explosion through to multiple, serial and motiveless child killing. Between these extremes there is a wide variety of murders of differing degrees of gravity or mitigating circumstances, for few of which detention for the remainder of the offender's life would be justified. The circumstances of each murder vary so widely that it is not possible to define categories of murder in such a way that it would make sense to set the tariff term of imprisonment for different categories.

Life imprisonment is also the maximum penalty for some other serious offences—e.g. manslaughter, armed robbery, arson, rape, kidnapping, assault and causing an explosion—but it is not normally in the mind of the sentencing judge that a person given such a sentence is likely to need keeping in prison for the rest of their days, either as a punishment or for the protection of the public. The judge's reason for passing a life sentence is often that, at the time, it is not clear when in the future the offender will be fit to return to society, and the judge considers it to be more appropriate to impose an indeterminate sentence, so that release can be considered when this is thought to be safe.

Under Section 1(2) Murder (Abolition of Death Penalty) Act 1965, a court, in sentencing to life imprisonment any person convicted of murder, may recommend a minimum period for which he or she should be detained. Such a recommendation is not binding on the Home Secretary but it must clearly carry considerable weight. The expectation is that a prisoner in respect of whom a minimum recommendation has been made will be detained for at least that period unless there are good reasons for doing otherwise. Judges initially made little use of this power. In the first 14 years after it became available about 1,400 people were convicted of murder in England and Wales but only about 110 recommendations were made. These were for periods ranging from 10 to 35 years. More recently, there have been more such recommendations including those that express the view that the prisoner should be detained for the whole of the rest of his or her life.

Life sentence prisoners are not eligible for parole as such but are released on a life licence by order of the Home Secretary. This has been the position for more than 130 years, and for most of that time the Home Secretary alone decided when a particular prisoner should be released. In recent years, however, Parliament has imposed some restrictions on the exercise of his discretion.

Under section 61 Criminal Justice Act 1967 (which still applies to mandatory lifers, but subject to a greater degree of openness) the Home Secretary may order release only if he is recommended to do so by the independent Parole Board and after consulting the Lord Chief Justice, and, if he is available, the trial judge. If the Parole Board does not recommend a prisoner's release the Home Secretary has no power to release him or her. He is not, however, bound to accept a recommendation for release and occasionally does not do so. He is also not bound by the views of the judiciary, but naturally attaches much weight to their advice.

The procedure leading to release was long and complicated, involving detailed consideration and consultation at many stages. There were no fixed times at which the release of a life sentence prisoner had to be formally considered (as there were with prisoners serving determinate sentences of 18 months or more, who had a right to be considered for parole when they had been detained for one-third of their sentence and annually thereafter). It is for the Home Secretary to decide when this should be done, but the time of the first review was usually fixed after consultation with the Parole Board, through a joint committee of representatives of the Board (the Chairman, the Vice Chairman—who is a High Court judge—and a psychiatrist) and of the Home Office. They considered all the facts of the case and the reports on the prisoner's progress in prison so far, and either recommended when the first formal review should start or, if it was clear that the prisoner could not be released for several years, or not immediately clear how soon he or she might be released, asked for the case to be brought before the committee again after a specified interval.

At each review the case was first considered by a Local Review Committee at the prison in which the prisoner was detained. This comprised representatives of the Board of Visitors of the prison and the Probation Service, independent people and the prison Governor. The committee had before them all the information available about the offence for which the life sentence was imposed and the circumstances in which it was committed; the prisoner's history, including any previous offences; the assessments and opinions of doctors who may have examined him or her before the trial; and any remarks made by the trial judge. They also had copies of all the reports made previously by the staff at the prisons in which the prisoner had been detained and others prepared specially for the review, and any representations which he or she may have made to the committee (as he or she was entitled to do). The prisoner did not—as indicated earlier in this chapter—have the right to appear before the Local Review Committee but was interviewed by one member who submitted a supplementary report to add to the written representations. In the light of all this information, the committee made a recommendation to the Home Secretary on the prisoner's apparent suitability for release.

All the papers were then sent to the Home Office, with the recommendation. There the case was carefully considered, in consultation with that Department's professional advisers. Sometimes reports from independent doctors—including psychiatrists—were obtained. An assessment was made of all the considerations, including the possible risk to the public if the prisoner were to be released (which was the Home Secretary's particular concern). The case was then referred to the Parole Board and considered by a panel of members, one of whom had to be a High Court judge and another a psychiatrist. If there seemed to be any likelihood that the Board might recommend the prisoner's release the Lord Chief Justice and the trial judge were consulted beforehand and their views were made known to the Board.

The Parole Board (which did not necessarily endorse the recommendation made by the LRC) may have recommended either that the prisoner should be given a provisional date for his or her release or that their case should be reviewed after a specified period. If it did the latter, the further review (and any successive reviews) followed the same procedure, starting again with the LRC. The date of these reviews was decided by the Home Secretary, though he normally accepted the Parole Board's recommendation.

If the Board recommended that the prisoner should be released, and the Home Secretary accepted the recommendation, a provisional date for this was fixed some time ahead—usually a year, though it may sometimes have been longer or shorter. Release was normally subject to the prisoner's continued good behaviour, the satisfactory completion of a period on the Pre-Release Employment Scheme (PRES: which involved living in a hostel attached to a prison but going out to work unsupervised) and to suitable resettlement arrangements being made. Before joining the PRES, most life sentence prisoners would also have spent a period at an open prison. This, and participation in the employment scheme, was thought to be necessary because the prisoner would have spent several years in closed prisons and needed to be gradually accustomed to conditions of greater freedom. A life sentence prisoner was not, however, moved to an open prison until thought unlikely to be a danger to anyone, and then only with the express approval of the Home Secretary or another Minister on his or her behalf.

In considering the possible release of a life sentence prisoner the very greatest care was taken by those concerned in the Home Office, the Parole Board and the prisons. Each case was considered on its individual merits, taking into account the nature of the prisoner's offence, his or her response in prison and all other relevant factors, including the views of the judiciary. The overriding consideration was the degree of risk, since the protection of the public is one of the Home Secretary's main responsibilities. It is impossible ever to be absolutely sure that there would be no future risk, but a recommendation that a life sentence prisoner should be released was not made lightly by the Parole Board and would not have been accepted unless the Home Secretary or another Home Office Minister was personally as satisfied as it is reasonably possible to be that the degree of risk was acceptable. But, despite all the care that is taken, it sometimes happened that a life sentence prisoner who had been released did commit another serious offence. The 'success' rate for lifers, however, is very high with only a seven per cent 'failure' in terms of reconviction for *any* offence following release. When a lifer does reoffend there are the inevitable questions raised about his or her suitability for release and it is this factor that makes the matter so sensitive.

Every life sentence prisoner is released on a licence, which remains in force for the whole of the remainder of their life. Initially, this is subject to conditions which require the licensee to be under the supervision of a probation officer, restrict him or her from, e.g. changing address or employment without that officer's approval, and, if necessary, imposes other special requirements. The supervising officer submits regular reports to the Home Office. After about three or four years, if the licensee has shown that he or she has settled down in the community and their behaviour has not given any cause for concern, and the supervising officer so recommends, the conditions are usually cancelled; otherwise, they are retained for as long as is thought to be necessary. But the licence itself remains in force and can be revoked at any time by the Home Secretary on the recommendation of the Parole Board or, if it has to be done immediately, subject to later confirmation by the Board. A licence would not normally be revoked if the licensee has committed a minor offence unrelated to that which led to their life sentence, but it would always be if his or her conduct gave reason for thinking that they might again be a danger to the public generally or any member of it.

If a licence is revoked, the licensee is immediately recalled to prison to continue the life sentence. He or she is given an opportunity to make representations to the Parole Board and if, after considering these, the Board recommend immediate release this must be done. If not, the question of release is considered in the same way as the initial release of a life sentence prisoner.

III. THE CHANGES

How the change has taken place
The change introduced by the establishment of Discretionary Lifer Panels due to the European ruling in *Thynne, Wilson and Gunnell* (above) has brought about significant effects in the management of lifers. The main change is in the accountability of the Prison Service to work closely within rules of due process in reviewing discretionary lifers for release.

Ministers decided that the hearings of the Parole Board would be held in the prisons in which the lifers were located. This has caused a considerable upheaval for many prisons as the space required for the hearings includes waiting and interview rooms as well as private rooms for the panel to prepare for the hearings. However the advantage of being within the prison has meant that the difficulties of moving prisoners has been overcome. There is a psychological effect on staff and prisoners in having the panel hearing with them which has still to be measured (but which will be assessed as part of research).

Hearing procedures are modelled on those used by the Mental Health Review Tribunals:

- the prisoner is entitled to see all documentation put before the panel. This has involved a significant change in the openness of the process and will cause alterations in the relationships between staff and inmates. There has had to be training for staff in the report writing procedures with open reports in mind.
- the inmate is entitled to be present during the hearing. This has altered the position of inmates to the extent of being able to participate in the hitherto secret procedures of the Parole Board.
- the inmate can be legally represented and can receive legal aid where eligible. The strengthening of the position of inmates in relation to the review process that this right has brought about is difficult to measure and will undoubtedly alter the way in which the procedure develops over the years.
- the inmate can question witnesses who have submitted evidence for the panel's consideration. Again, this matter has given increased power to inmates in being able to challenge what has been written about them in an open way with professional support. It will undoubtedly ensure that reports are written with this awareness in mind by those submitting evidence.

The legislation requires the Home Secretary to certify tariffs for all existing discretionary lifers who fell to be considered under the new arrangements; and certificates were issued after October 1992. There were some 330 discretionary lifers (some 70 per cent of the total numbers of them) who had passed their tariff by then—a considerable number whose expectations had to be met. The Parole Board aimed to complete all the 330 hearings by the end of December 1993 and a procedure was decided upon by them. Headquarters were anxious to ensure that lifers and staff working with them became aware of the procedures and the likely order in which cases were to be heard: see under *How DLPs work*.

Senior staff who were closely concerned with the arrangements held a series of seminars to be briefed about the arrangements and then communicated these to the staff at their establishments. Each prison that holds lifers has a Lifer Liaison Officer who is a governor grade. Their role is to co-ordinate the work that has to be arranged in the management of lifers and to provide a focal point for them to seek advice and counsel.

IV. HOW DLPs WORK

Section 34 Criminal Justice Act 1991 provides that when an offender is given a discretionary life sentence the court may order that after a specified part of the sentence the Parole Board shall have the power to order his or her release on licence—not simply to make a recommendation for release as in the past. The period specified by the court must take into account the seriousness of the offence and the fact that long-term prisoners given determinate sentences will now be released at a point between one-half and two-thirds of the sentence. (The period should, therefore, presumably be between one-half and two-thirds of the length which the court would have considered commensurate with the seriousness of the offence if it had not passed a life sentence).

In order to comply with the decision of the European Court of Human Rights in *Thynne, Wilson and Gunnell* above that such prisoners have the right to periodic reviews of their detention by 'a court', the Parole Board follows a judicial procedure, but the hearing procedures, which are modelled on those used by the Mental Health Review Tribunals, are, as far as possible, informal. The lifer is entitled to see all documentation put before the panel; to be present during the hearing; to be legally represented and to receive legal aid where eligible; and to question witnesses who have submitted evidence for the panel's consideration.

The Act required that the Home Secretary should certify tariffs for all existing discretionary lifers who fell to be considered under the arrangements. There were over 330 discretionary lifers in the system who had passed their tariff by October 1992. With the issue of these certificates some lifers found out for the first time what their tariff was.

The Parole Board aimed to hear the 330 cases as quickly as it could, hoping to hear all of them by the end of December 1993. Inevitably decisions had to be made about the order in which cases were to be heard. The basis of these decisions was made public. Those due for a review under the old arrangements before 1 June 1992 were offered the opportunity to defer their reviews so that they could benefit from the new procedures. Those who opted to defer were placed at the top of the list. Next listed were prisoners for whom the Parole Board had previously made a release recommendation which was not accepted. Thereafter, prisoners were ranked in order of their next scheduled review. Account was taken of any compassionate considerations indicating that an early hearing was appropriate.

Of major significance throughout the new procedures was the ruling of the Court of Appeal in the case of *Benjamin Wilson* by which all discretionary lifers are entitled to see all reports and information put before the Board. All reports prepared on discretionary lifers who had passed tariff had to be written with disclosure to the prisoner in mind. A summary of previous reports was compiled by Lifer Management Unit at Prison Service HQ and became part of the dossier that was made open.

The timing and scheduling of the panels which were a matter for the Parole Board were detailed in the communications from headquarters. Prisoners were to have four months notice of the date of their hearing and to have six weeks to study the papers and decide on their representations. The decisions of the Parole Board would be communicated to the prisoner with reasons within a week of the hearing. The view of the Home Office on those decisions and recommendations would be communicated very soon after. In the case of the decision being to release the prisoner arrangements had to proceed forthwith.

Procedural Rules governing the proceedings of the Parole Board when it considers discretionary lifer cases referred to it by the Home Secretary under Section 34 of the 1991 Act were made clear under the Parole Board Rules 1992 (now the Parole Board Rules 1997: see *Appendix B* to this work).

Results of hearings so far

From October 1992 to December 1997 the cases completed totalled 934 (207 dispersal, 242 category B, 315 C, 129 D, 11 female closed, 3 female open, 4 young offender institution (YOI), 14 PRES, 9 hospital. Decisions made by the panels resulted in the following outcomes:

- 174 directed for release (18.6%) (3 from dispersal, 15 from B, 37 C, 92 D, 3 female closed, 2 female open, 1 YOI (open), 14 PRES, 7 hospital (4 open, 3 closed));
- 2 recommended for release for deportation (0.2 per cent) (category C);
- 197 recommended for transfer to open conditions (21 per cent) 1 from dispersal, 31 B, 163 C and 2 female (closed);
- 16 recommended for transfer to PRES (1.7 per cent) (13 from D, 2 B, 1 C);
- 126 recommended for transfer to other prisons (13.5 per cent)
- 136 recommended for consideration for specialist treatment (14.6 per cent)
  —39 for hospital or for treatment of mental disorder;
  —6 for vulnerable prisoner units;
  —21 for Grendon;
  —56 for the Sex Offender Treatment Programme;
  —14 for psychological counselling or other treatment
- 283 no recommendation or remain in current location (30.3 per cent).

Updated figures show that between October 1992 and 1 October 1998 the Board conducted 1,091 hearings and directed the release of 186 (17%). Sixty-nine of these 186 inmates were from closed conditions. A further

224 were recommended for transfer to open prison. Of those released, 52 (28%) have subsequently been recalled to prison.

The rate of *recall* for those released by DLPs is higher than the rate of recall for those discharged through the more normal procedures. Forty-five prisoners released by DLPs have been recalled to prison (3 released from category B, 11 from C, one from a closed female prison, 28 from category D, and 2 from PRES). This rate of recall from October to December 1997 is 25.9% which compares with one of under 10% for those released through the previous systems. Particularly of concern were the numbers released from closed conditions who have been recalled—so much so that there are new guidelines to the Parole Board recommending that the normal place from which a lifer should be safely released is open conditions.

Problems associated with the changes
The speed with which the introduction of DLPs took place caused considerable *administrative* difficulties:

- there was uncertainty about the detailed knowledge of lifers and no centralised database from which the arrangements could be co-ordinated
- although there had been a structure of contact between the Headquarters' Lifer Management Unit and Prison Service establishments through the Lifer Liaison Officers the new arrangements called for a *co-ordination* between field and HQ that was not always present. Part of this difficulty arose from the complicated relationships between Ministers and the Parole Board and HM Prison Service HQ who were charged with implementing policy as it was being made
- the *communication* problem was considerable in that as well as ensuring that all prison establishments received, understood and acted upon the information in terms of preparing staff for the change in procedure, inmates involved had high expectations of the process speeding up the consideration of their review process and needed to have sound information upon which to act and consult their legal representatives
- the *training* implications for staff involved are immense and are being tackled over a period of time. Report writing skills will need to be improved as the scrutiny of evidence becomes a public matter and one in which the inmate has a central role. The roles of staff during the panel's hearing needed close support as it was a completely new position for them to present the case to an independent body and to be subject to cross examination
- there were sometimes conflicting pressures on those presenting cases when they did not personally agree with the line that the HQ

documents were directing. Often staff were advising a course of action for individual inmates that was in *conflict with official policy*—recommending the release of a lifer from category B or category C conditions without the necessity of going to an open prison, was the most frequent conflict.

There were *operational* problems in the implementation of the changes which were inevitable given the speed and the size of the adjustments:

- the *location* of panel hearings in prisons meant that suitable rooms and arrangements for the period of the work had to be made available. To achieve this within the security of the prison and to allow for the movement of prisoners and their representatives with safety and privacy has proved difficult in several places
- the *completion of the reports on time* was not an easy operation especially in those prisons that have had several panel hearings already. To work to the tight deadlines was a matter that took the working up of systems to ensure productivity as well as maintaining the high standard required
- the completion of the first round of *catching up panel hearings* identified many men who had been spending time without much purpose in inappropriate settings. The impetus of the panel hearings has given many men a focus on which to concentrate their efforts to prove their reliability. The reasons given by panels for not releasing men straight away and the recommendations for further work and different settings through which to proceed has resulted in an expectation that the Prison Service will be required to provide the facilities to ensure that the individual will be able to prove his or her suitability before the next panel hearing in two years.

The introduction of Discretionary Lifer Panels has focused on *intellectual* problems associated with the assessment of risk:

- the special opportunity of the discretionary life sentence has been discussed in that the sentence is often imposed in order to provide for an assessment of the dangerousness of the offender before they are released. It is in this assessment of dangerousness that skills have been developed over the years but this process has not always been subject to scrutiny nor cross examination
- the assessment process can never be an objective one in that the weight put to pieces of evidence and in fact the acceptance of certain behaviours as evidence are personal decisions. What can be achieved by a greater open assessment of the various factors is a

more explicit appraisal of the weight being put upon certain subjective judgements
- the assessment of risk of men who have very few decision-making opportunities when contained in prison increases the pressure to be cautious until men have had the opportunity to be in an open prison where there are many more dimensions to the decisions that have to be made in the organization of time. There has often been difficulty in getting men to open conditions in time for their tariff review and the timing of trust will continue to be a central concern.

The development of a more pro-active approach towards the assessment of development that men have made during their time in custody should enable the Prison Service to make better use of the resource of time that until now did not appear to be a commodity in short supply. The structured changes that have been brought about by the legislation introducing Discretionary Lifer Panels should enable us to confirm the culture emerging as lifers and staff compare their experience now with what existed earlier.

V. 'SECTION 2 DISCRETIONARY LIFERS'

With the introduction of the Section 2 discretionary life sentence under the Crime (Sentences) Act 1997 (see the end of *Chapter 1*) there is an expectation that around 200 cases will be received into prison each year from 1999. Already, the first prisoners sentenced under the 'two strikes' clause are arriving in prisons. The total population of such lifers is expected to be 1,000 by the year 2008.

The range of tariff length for these prisoners is expected to vary widely. The sentencing pattern for 1994 for second serious sexual or violent offences indicates that tariffs (based on one half of the determinate sentence passed) will range from as little as three months to ten years and over. Fifty-one per cent are likely to have tariffs of three years or less. Forty-nine per cent will have tariffs of three years and over. Only 16.5 per cent will have tariffs of six years or more.

Short tariff 'section twos' will need to be managed differently from lifers with longer tariffs because the statutory entitlement to a review by a Discretionary Lifer Panel of the Parole Board when tariff expires will, in many case, be triggered before it will have been possible to achieve much in the way of assessment or work on offending behaviour. As far as possible, however, section twos should be given preference on offending behaviour programmes (particularly cognitive skills and anger management courses) run in Main Centres.

The management of such lifers is likely to be arranged in the following way:

- *All cases* will be sent initially to one of the five lifer Main Centres (Brixton, Gartree, Wakefield, Wormwood Scrubs and Durham for females) which have expertise in dealing with lifers in the early stages of sentence. Those with very short tariffs will need to be given priority over those with longer tariffs (both section twos and all other lifers). Section twos with longer tariffs will be progressed through the lifer system in the usual way. The proposed arrangements for tariffs of between three months and up to seven years will be as described in the following paragraphs.

- *Tariffs of between three months and two years* will need special attention due to the remand time being on average nine months. As a result *tariffs of nine months and under* will have expired by the time of conviction/sentence and the lifers concerned will become immediately eligible for a DLP. It is anticipated that their cases will have to be referred to the Board immediately under an accelerated procedure which will considerably reduce the normal six month period between referral and hearing to, perhaps, three months. This matter is still to be reviewed by the Parole Board to establish a proper minimum period.

  Lifers in this category will be transferred to a Main Centre immediately after sentence for an accelerated assessment of about three months. The transfer for other lifers can take another nine months sometimes. Any reports prepared on the lifers while on remand will be sent with them. Parole Board papers relating to previous periods in custody will be obtained by LMU wherever possible and sent to the Main Centre. Following assessment the Main Centre will prepare a Life Sentence Plan, assess the appropriate security category required in the event that release is not directed at the first review and prepare reports for submission to LMU for inclusion in the DLP dossier.

- Those with tariffs of *between ten months and two years* will be treated in much the same way, except that where the tariff permits, the assessment period may stretch to six months (e.g. when the tariff is over 18 months). The DLP will be at the Main Centre. The result of the first review will in most cases be a two year 'knockback' because it is unlikely that the DLP will have been satisfied that the degree of potential risk is sufficiently low to justify release. In such cases lifers will be re-allocated (either to category B, Category C or, in exceptional cases, Category D) as soon as possible in the light of the Main Centre assessment of appropriate offending behaviour required.

- Those with *tariffs of over two but under five years* will be transferred to Main Centre immediately after sentence for an accelerated assessment period of six months, followed by transfer to a training prison where 12 months or more will be available before the first review, which will be by a DLP. In accordance with the DLP timetable, reports will be prepared after six months and submitted to LMU. Developments following submission of reports can be dealt with by way of update reports just before the hearing. In exceptional cases where a very early move to open conditions might be justified, consideration will be given to putting cases to the Board immediately after the six month assessment in Main Centre to increase the chances of release by a DLP on or shortly after tariff expiry.
- Those whose *tariff is over five years* will not be given priority places in Main Centre and so by the time they arrive they will have served around 18 months of their tariff. They will receive an 18 month period of assessment in Main Centre after which they will be re-allocated to training prisons. Those with a tariff of between five and seven years will have their first paper review by the Parole Board, as quickly as circumstances allow, which will be based on the reports prepared in Main Centre before transfer. Those with a tariff of seven years and over will have their first paper review by the Board at tariff minus three years in the normal way.

VI. CONCLUSIONS

Some critical work is being carried out as part of the process of greater openness and accountability on the issue of risk assessment. There is a clear need to identify the areas of risk which each lifer represents. Although each lifer is meant to have a career plan drawn up in the early part of their sentence, which informs succeeding prisons that they serve their sentence in—and this is regularly reviewed in the light of progress—the reality is that such work was patchy and not standardised. During the latter part of 1993 procedures were commenced to ensure that all lifers had such sentence plans, making clear the risk areas that should be worked upon and the means by which such sensitive and deep-seated matters could be remedied whilst a person is in custody. Identifying such matters will place a clear obligation on the Prison Service to offer programmes and procedures whereby the lifer can work on the issues with staff, and it will ensure that the motivation of the prisoner to tackle issues can be tested. Priority on offending behaviour courses has been requested for lifers and particularly those serving short tariffs. However the resource constraints in many prisons and the early state of some of the research into the effectiveness of such programmes as the cognitive skills and sex offender treatment programme in the cultural context of our prisons means that there remains a problem of ensuring that lifers will present themselves to a hearing with the identified issues of concern having been addressed or at least an attempt having been made to deal with them. The concern about those lifers who remain insistent about their innocence (see, generally, *Chapter 3*) remains a serious issue throughout this process, particularly in the light of recent cases of miscarriage of justice. The Parole Board and Prison Service staff are still faced with the legal responsibility to assess the risk to the public that the individual represents. More research needs to be done on the subject of risk assessment and although that assessment can never be objective and will always depend on the professional judgement of the report writer, there can be much movement towards a more explicit consideration of the risks involved in releasing a particular lifer. Report writers now have a structured report form that assists in addressing areas of risk in a systematic manner and training is taking place in all the prisons that hold lifers to develop awareness in this crucial matter.

For the Parole Board Rules 1997, see *Appendix B* to this work. The 1997 Rules reflect the earlier ones of 1992 which were in force (post-Criminal Justice Act 1991) at the time of earlier events described in this chapter. The only changes of substance in the 1997 Rules concern the extension of comparable procedures to young offenders detained at her majesty's pleasure ('HMPs') and to 'section 2 discretionary lifers' under the Crime (Sentences) Act 1997.

CHAPTER 6

Lifer Risk Assessment

We have used a meat axe to kill a spider. (Toby, 1974)

The assessment of risk relating to life sentence prisoners has always been an area which combines the polemic of politics and the argument of mental health professionals. On the one hand are the arguments regarding the moral right to detain people within the confines of an indeterminate sentence and, on the other, the arguments regarding how and if it is possible to assess accurately the risk that someone would pose if released from prison. In its 1995 statement regarding Life Imprisonment, the United Nations noted in regard to risk evaluation:

> Risk evaluation may be the most important factor in assessing the appropriateness of releasing a life sentence prisoner, if it can be assumed that the protection of society in a narrow sense is the main purpose of imprisonment. But the victim's human rights and interests may also have to be considered in making the assessment.

At this moment in time the group of people to whom the term 'life sentence prisoner' can be applied in England and Wales is growing due to the Crime (Sentences) Act 1997 which has introduce a 'three strikes and out'[1] element to the sentencing of some criminals. Prior to this Act, those who had committed murder received a mandatory life sentence and those who were viewed by the judiciary to warrant a life sentence due to the nature of their offence received discretionary life sentences. Due to the 1997 Act the life sentence group will now contain people who have received their life sentence on the basis of *frequency* rather than *severity* of offence. Furthermore the judiciary will have little if any discretion in the award of the life sentence. It is estimated that as many as 200 new life sentence prisoners will be added to the population each year in this way. The life sentence population is about to become more diverse, which will challenge the rationale for the way in which risk is assessed for this increasingly heterogeneous group.

The problem faced is that the form of risk assessment practised by the British Prison Service with life sentence prisoners is becoming increasingly less likely to be able to cope with the people to which it

---

[1] i.e. 'Three strikes' in the original USA scheme for enhanced punishment for repeat offending. The US concept of 'three strikes' became 'two strikes' in practice when it transferred to the UK via the 1997 Act: Editorial note and see the discussion of this provision at the end of *Chapter 1*.

will be applied. This chapter attempts to outline the major issues involved in risk assessment, to describe the current practices, and to explore the possible ways forward.

I. WHAT IS RISK ASSESSMENT? (BRIEFLY)

Towl and Crighton (1995) suggest that

> Broadly "risk" involves (1) the estimation of the likelihood that one or more undesirable behaviours will occur and (2) the influence of interventions aimed at reducing the likelihood of these behaviours occurring.

In the context of the life sentence prisoner, risk assessment is the estimation of the likelihood that a person, if released, will commit further offences the same or similar to those of which he or she was convicted. In the case of mandatory life sentence prisoners, who constitute 80% of the life sentence population, this means murder.[2] The range of possibilities for discretionary lifers is wider due to the range of offences that this will include, e.g. rape, arson and armed robbery. The discretionary lifer group used to make up the remaining 20% but they will now be joined by those sentenced pursuant to the 1997 Act bringing with them a yet wider range of offences such as burglary. In its broadest terms risk assessment has concentrated on the issues of dangerousness as related to the commission of further violent offences but that position is becoming increasingly difficult to maintain.

The term 'risk' will be used throughout this chapter as opposed to using the terms 'risk' and 'dangerousness' interchangeably. As Towl and Crighton (1995) point out, the term 'risk'

> . . . as a statement of probability, logically leads to an understanding of risk as a continuous variable. By contrast the term "dangerousness" more readily may be understood to imply a discrete variable. We would not wish to compound such possible confusion by imposing a discrete variable framework upon a continuous variable phenomenon.

I agree with this position and would therefore not want to produce such a confusion.

---

[2] Post-CJA 97 'two strikes' offenders also receive *mandatory* life sentences, albeit of a different species: see *Chapters 1* and *5*.

II. THE NEED FOR RISK ASSESSMENT

It seems at first glance that to ask the question 'Is risk assessment necessary?' is facile but within the context of the life sentence prisoner it is a relevant one. Kershaw, Dowdeswell and Goodman (1997) report that the reconviction rate of life sentence licensees released between 1983 and 1992 after two years of release was 9%. This compared to the almost 50% reconviction rate for a standard list offence by adult male prisoners discharged between 1983 and 1992. Because of the interaction between the age at which people are released and the effect that the number of previous convictions has on the figures the authors compared reconviction rates for those people over 30 years of age with and without previous convictions. The results showed that 5% of those who are on life licence with no previous convictions committed further offences within two years of release, while 10% of those with previous convictions committed further offences within the same time period. These figures compared to reconviction rates of 5% and 41% for the same population of general criminals. When the life licensee population was compared to those in the general criminal population who were reconvicted of violence against the person it was found that the reconviction rates were 10% for those without previous convictions and 33% for those with. In essence the life licence group with no previous convictions were no more likely to reoffend than other people with no previous convictions over the first two years of freedom, while those with previous convictions were four times less likely to be reconvicted than other released criminals with previous convictions. The life licensees with previous convictions were also three times less likely to commit violence against the person offences than their no life licence counterparts. The same pattern was found for those with previous convictions when comparisons were made for the conviction of grave offences. Once again, the life licensees with previous convictions were three times less likely to be reconvicted for violence against the person offences. Of the 1,691 people first released on life licence between 1972 and 1994, 28 have received a further life sentence, this is a rate of 1.66%.

It would appear clear from the study that released life sentence prisoners are no more likely to reoffend than other released prisoners and certainly those with previous convictions are far less likely to do so. Alter, Tsuei and Chein (1997) report that in Minnesota released homicide offenders had the lowest, 34%, reconviction rate of any offender group. In terms of risk of reoffending the life sentence group are a safe group compared with other offenders. If this is the case why is there such an emphasis on risk assessment? Clearly the public's fear of murderers killing a second or third time is not founded on statistical comparison but rooted firmly in the aversion to the severity of the crime. The comparative rarity of the crime has no effect on the general perception that the risk of repetition is an intolerable factor that must at all costs be made as minimal as possible. It is possible that this underlying attitude to the killing of another person is what fuels the continued capital punishment debate and the often grossly distorted portrayal of murderers in the media.

Another example which highlights the problem of knowing what the actual risks of releasing 'dangerous' people into society are is the outcome of the Steadman and Cocozza (1974) study of the *Bloxham* ruling by the United States Supreme Court. In 1966 the ruling was made that it was not constitutional to commit civilly a prisoner at the expiration of their prison sentence. Johnnie Bloxham had served his sentence in a prison hospital as a mentally ill inmate and on expiration of his sentence had been committed to a civil hospital. It was his challenge to the New York state that led to the court ruling and his subsequent release. The ruling led to a thousand similar patients being released and offered the opportunity to study the outcome of releasing such a group of supposedly 'dangerous' people back into the community. Steadman and Cocozza followed up a number of these patients and found that age and previous criminal history provided some predictive value of reconviction. However for the 17 people that they correctly identified as being at risk they identified 19 people for whom the prediction did not come true over a four and half year period. They concluded from their study that any prediction of outcome based on these factors would be less than 50% accurate. They also went on to calculate the accuracy with which further violence offences could be predicted. They found that for every case that was correctly predicted two other cases were falsely predicted. The study was later criticised by Stone (1985) for using only actuarial data and ignoring the clinical data available. This is a main issue to which I shall return.

Thornberry and Jacoby (1979) were able to replicate the work of Steadman and Cocozza when a similar court ruling allowed 586 patients to be moved from a hospital for the criminally insane to a civil setting which led to release into the community. Of the 414 who had an opportunity to reoffend during an average follow up period of three years, 24% were arrested at least once. This rate of recidivism was close to the Bloxham study rate of 20.4%. Thornberry and Jacoby also looked at the ability to predict which people would be arrested for violence. They were unable to find either singly or combinations of variables that would predict violence with any high degree of success. Age was found to be the single most predictive variable. Using this variable alone provided a positive predictive power of only 18%. When the researchers added to age the criteria used in the Bloxham study to predict violence there was no appreciable effect. If the simple prediction that no member of the group being studied was going to be violent had been made, it would have been accurate in 86% of cases.

It would thus seem that there *is* sense in asking the question regarding whether or not risk assessment is necessary. On the face of it the 'dangerous' populations are not the violently predisposed populations that they are assumed to be, they are however still more violent than the general population (Webster *et al*, 1994).

One point that is worthy of note is that made by Lawrence (1998) that in 1994 the 8,819 prisoners incarcerated for murder in the Texas prisons were 11% of the total population. In 1994 there were three murders in Texas prisons, all of which were gang related. This rate of murder within the population of Texas prisoners falls well below the 9.5 per 100,000 of the national murder rate of the United States of America. It would appear on these figures that a population of incarcerated murders is a population at less risk of committing murder than the general population.

If there was no attempt to assess the risk posed by the release of any individual who has demonstrated that violence was an active part of their behavioural repertoire, on what basis could a decision for release be made? It is inconceivable that those people with the responsibility for releasing past killers, arsonists, rapists and attempted murderers will not ask the question 'What is the likelihood that this person will not do the same thing again?' If they are advised that statistically they are going to be right in predicting that a person will not get another life licence 98.34% of the time will they still not ask 'How do I know which are the 1.66% who will?' Furthermore what would we think of them if they did not? It is obvious that there is a responsibility to make decisions on the best possible basis when dealing with people's lives; not only for the prisoners but on behalf of everyone in the general community, who are the potential victims.

The mechanisms within the British Prison System, the guidelines within which the Parole Board operates and the constraints of the Criminal Justice Act 1991 and Crime (Sentences) Act 1997 all dictate that the determination of risk is a major factor in the decision-making process of the life sentence prisoner. As Munro and Macpherson (1998) note in their discussion of risk assessment

> ... the demands by Criminal Justice Services for psychological assessments are unlikely to cease and such assessments are now a required professional ability for psychologists working within the forensic setting.

While this is the case there is a responsibility for all concerned to ensure that the methods and procedures for that risk assessment process is the most appropriate and efficient that can be produced.

III. HOW IS RISK ASSESSMENT DONE?

Risk assessment of violent behaviour has a history, which starts approximately in the early 1970s when workers began to investigate whether or not the predictions regarding risk by psychiatrists, psychologists and others involved in the forensic field were accurate. The Baxstrom and Dixon studies already referred to demonstrated that the predictions being made were not reliable and over inclusive. From this point a lot of work was generated in trying to analyse what processes provided the best outcomes and which variables provided the best predictors. The early work on reconviction which was more actuarial in nature is dealt with below. Traditionally there have been two ways of making a risk assessment—clinical prediction and actuarial prediction.

Clinical prediction (first generation assessments)

This form of prediction is dependant on the professional's, clinician's and key worker's judgement of the prisoner's risk of re-offending. The data considered in this process will range from records of contact, previous reports by other professionals, psychometric data, self-report data, structured interview records and some behavioural observations or recorded events. The literature on risk assessment is very clear that those people called upon to make such assessments are notoriously poor at doing so. The major inaccuracy is that of over inclusion, or put another way the creation of too many false positives (Dershowitz, 1969; APA, 1974; Cocozza and Steadman, 1978; Greenland, 1980; Megargee, 1981; Cooper and Werner, 1990). A false positive, in this context, is where it is predicted that an individual will in fact commit another violent offence but in reality does not do so. The false positives constitute the over prediction cases. Poor performance at this task is in large part due to the inherent difficulties involved in human decision-making (Kahnemann and Tversky, 1973). They pointed out the common practice of making clinical judgements based on interviews with offenders was open to a wide range of cognitive and personal biases. One of the most difficult to deal with is that people are poor at judging relative probabilities. Kahnemann and Tversky illustrated, e.g. that in probabilistic judgements people systematically employ the use of the 'representativeness heuristic'. In essence people apply beliefs or knowledge about a small sample to a whole population but in doing so make unwarranted assumptions. The result is that errors of judgement are made. This can be seen as an adaptive tool, as it allows a useful shortcut in decisions of extreme complexity, but it leads to an insensitivity to base rate considerations. Such base rate considerations are highly pertinent to life sentence prisoners, due to the relative rarity of excessive violence in the general population (Meehl and Rosen, 1955; Monahan, 1981).

Personal biases, which can influence clinical judgement, are inherent in our individuality. For example, our personal value systems and our prior experience will in part determine judgements of risk. Therefore, the reliability of this method is highly questionable (Blackburn, 1984). A study by Montandon and Harding (1984) looked at data from six countries to try and assess the inter-rater reliability of clinical assessments. They found that not only agreement between psychiatrists was low, but also that it was no better than that of other professionals or lay people. These findings have been substantiated in the literature (Menzies and Webster, 1995).

Actuarial (statistical) prediction (second generation assessments)

The roots of this type of prediction lie in the work of Professor Burgess of the University of Chicago who in the 1920s studied the factors that seemed to determine the success or failure of prisoners paroled in Illinois. At about the same time Glueck and Glueck (1930) carried out a long-term follow up study of 500 prisoners who were released from the Massachusetts Reformatory. Their findings that age of first delinquency, previous criminal history, previous custodial experience, 'mental condition' and previous work history were the important factors in predicting success or failure remain true today. Many of the Gleuck's factors remain amongst the most important variables in current prediction.

In essence the actuarial system of prediction relies on the collection of data relating to events in peoples lives and comparing the frequency with which an event occurs for those groups of people that you are interested in. In the case of criminals they can be divided into those who are reconvicted within two years of release and those who are not. By comparing the frequency with which a particular event occurs in the lives of the people in either group it becomes possible to identify whether it is statistically more likely to appear in the life of a reconvicted or non-reconvicted person. If an event, e.g. being arrested for the first time before the age 16, occurs significantly more often in the reconvicted group then that event becomes one of the possible predictive factors of reconviction. Of course no one single life event is going to unfailingly predict reconviction but as a constellation of such factors begins to emerge then the more factors from the constellation that are in a person's profile the more likely they are to be reconvicted. As Munro and Macpherson (1998) note:

Static predictors have much greater empirical support than dynamic variables and many studies are available to demonstrate the power of actuarial variables in the prediction of recidivism. Using a six-variable actuarial model, Cooke and Mitchie (1996a) were able to achieve a "hit" rate of 83% accuracy in predicting reconviction of a prisoner population within two years, stressing the value of simple, readily accessible actuarial variables over complex clinical ones.

There are of course some obvious drawbacks to this form of assessment. It is clear that the factors used in actuarial prediction tend to be crude. The data used is usually easily accessible and tends to provide simplistic measures of complex behaviour. An example of this cited by Towl and Crighton (1995) is the number of previous convictions. A further drawback is that the evaluation of risk is fixed as none of the data can change. The vast majority of data used is pre-custodial and therefore takes no account of anything that may have happened during imprisonment. The process is unaffected by changes that may occur over time. Yet another problem is that the technique works best with a diverse population. As the sample becomes more homogeneous the method becomes less effective and the powers of discrimination decrease. This is particularly pertinent to the life sentence population. The last issue to come out of this is that it lacks focus on change. There is little in the method that can be directed towards those programmes that are designed to impact upon reconviction.

The dynamic factors
Andrew and Bonta (1994) classified risk factors into two categories: *static* and *dynamic*. As explored above the static factors form the basis of actuarial assessment and reflect the offender's past. Dynamic risk factors or needs reflect the present circumstances of the offender, and as such, are mutable. There appear to be two types of offender needs: *criminogenic* and *non-criminogenic*. Criminogenic needs would include offenders' attitudes, cognition, and behaviours related to employment, education, authority, drug use and interpersonal relationships that lead to conflict with the law. If there is to be a hope of reducing the risk of future risk behaviour then it is within these factors that programmes and treatments need to be focused. If the criminogenic needs are focused upon then it is reasonable to expect a reduction in offenders' criminal behaviour.

Gendreau, Gogin and Little (1996) undertook a meta-analysis of recidivism prediction research and noted three reasons why the dynamic factors had been progressively ignored over the last 20 years. They suggest that within the criminological literature the notion, and importance of, individual differences had been derided. They saw this as a result of ideological concerns and professional self-interest of sections of the professions of criminology and sociology. The second reason for the decline of the dynamic factors is put down to the perception that dynamic factors are unreliable. Because they change measurement is required and this is seen as inevitably bringing subjective bias into the process. This in turn would suggest that they are weak predictors of criminal behaviour. Finally it is suggested that criminal justice professionals have been oblivious to the possibility that assessment of criminogenic needs might enhance the prediction of criminal behaviour. This blindness may have been reinforced by the philosophy of incarceration that relates to a preventive economic model. Crudely put, it suggests that it is cheaper to keep a person in prison for a longer period of time than to attempt to alter the risk of reoffending by resourcing intervention programmes. Gendreau *et al* conclude:

> This denial of the utility of dynamic risk factors, obviously, has serious ramifications for corrections professionals who are routinely required to reclassify offenders for prison transfer, parole/probation supervision, and treatment services. Simply put, reclassification is devalued if the measurement of change has little validity.

Actuarial plus dynamic risk assessment (third generation assessments)
Bonta (1996) suggested that there were assessment instruments available that utilised the dynamic factors. In the first instance he suggests that some of the instruments encompass prediction measures that include dynamic factors. He cites Motiuk (1993), development of the Community Risk/Needs Management Scale and the Level of Service Inventory (LSI-R) from the work of Andrews and Bonta (1995). These inventories also include the assessment of criminogenic need. The second type of assessment instrument that is available is the personality tests that include scales in the antisocial personality/sociopathy/psychopathy content area. Although some of these scales contain static items they also contain dynamic ones. He cites the Psychopathy Checklist (PCL-R), Hare, 1991, and the Socialisation Scale of the California Personality Inventory (CPI), Gough, 1957.

In order to assess what works in terms of prediction of adult recidivism Gendreau *et al* (1996) conducted a meta-analysis of 114 risk prediction studies. Within the group of studies used were representatives of all types of prediction, i.e. first, second and third generation methodologies (see above) were included. The results demonstrated that the static factors continued to predict recidivism, but it was found that the dynamic factors also produced good predictive power. Gendreau *et al* state:

> The time is long past when those offender risk factors that are dynamic in nature can be cavalierly ignored. Indeed, criminogenic needs produced higher correlations with recidivism a much higher percentage of the time

than did several other predictor domains. When considering all predictor domains, as statistically significant difference was found in favour of the dynamic risk factors.

The authors of this study conclude from their reading of the studies available that the strongest predictors found in the results of their meta-analysis also applied to violent offenders. They draw attention to the high correlation between the composite measures of general recidivism such as the Level of Service Inventory (LSI) and the measures intended to predict violence such as the Psychopathy Checklist—Revised, as suggestive evidence for this conclusion.

Given that the analyses available suggest that there is now a possibility that the dynamic and the static factors can be utilised to predict risk the question remains as to whether the risk assessment employed with life sentence prisoners in England and Wales is the most efficient. Does it consider both the static and the dynamic factors required for prediction.

IV. THE ASSESSMENT OF RISK IN LIFE SENTENCE PRISONERS AS PRACTISED IN ENGLAND AND WALES

The Risk Assessment model currently used in the Prison Service was derived from a local initiative which took place at HM Prison Wakefield. Initially there was a need for staff to be able to handle the information they gathered about life sentence prisoners in a useful and logical framework. Staff wished to be able to make sound judgements on the information that they had but had no overall schemata to fit the information into. Because HMP Wakefield received life sentence prisoners at the start of their sentence there was a need to provide a baseline against which future behaviour could be compared. There was also a need to make judgements about reallocation and recommendations for future work, this involved making some assessment of the likelihood of future poor adaptive behaviour. The Risk Assessment model developed by Clark, Fisher and McDougall (1993) aimed to provide a framework in which to place the work being done and to provide risk factors for an individual. Clark *et al* state that the purpose of the model was to

> identify the consistent behaviour patterns associated with risk of offending and monitor these as a more objective method of assessing level of risk. They would also focus more clearly on behaviours which should be targeted for treatment intervention and behaviour change.

In essence the model functions on two basic principles:

1. That past behaviour is the best predictor of future behaviour. This is clearly borne out by the predictive power of the actuarial method of prediction of recidivism (Gendreau *et al*, 1996).
2. That behaviour remains consistent across a number of different situations.

The second assertion has been the subject of intense debate. Mischel (1968:77) conducted an empirical evaluation of studies and found a high level of situation specificity across a number of different situations. For example, attributes such as 'attitude towards authority' were shown to be specific to certain situations. This would suggest that prison behaviours might not relate with non-institutional behaviours. Cooke (1997) places this in context when pointing to the differences in the levels of violent behaviour by the residents of the Barlinnie Special Unit. He suggests that the lowered levels of violent behaviour indicate the ability of prisoners to alter their behaviour in response to a new environment. He states that

It is unlikely, therefore, that the substantial changes in behaviour noted can be attributed to an experimental artefact; the BSU appears to have been successful in containing violent offenders in a manner that avoided further violence.

There is also strong empirical evidence for the counter-proposal. Olweus (1980) reviewed studies on aggression and found that there was a high level of cross-situational consistency. This was supported by Farrington's study (1978), which found that teachers of 13-year-old boys were able to predict future violent behaviour. Zamble and Porporino (1990) found that prisoners responded similarly to a range of prison situations as they would to situations outside the custodial setting. Further their evidence suggested that the longer someone remained in custody the more likely they were to repeat outside behaviour patterns. As well as present offending behaviours they also found that behavioural and attitudinal measures were predictors of re-offending. More recently, Briggs (1995) using data from the Clark model of Risk Assessment found strong correlations between risk factors and predicted behaviours and actual behaviours. When she split her sample into those men who had previous custodial experience and those who had none there was evidence to support behaviour generality in that both groups displayed the predicted behaviours generated from their risk factors.

As that work was being put into place the Criminal Justice Act 1991 was being enacted by Parliament. In that Act the Home Secretary was directed to pay particular attention to: (a) the need to protect the public from serious harm from offenders; (b) the desirability of preventing the commission by them of further serious offences and of securing their rehabilitation (Jason-Lloyd, 1992). In view of this a new form of Life Sentence Plan was devised to enable the more effective identification of risk factors and the greater specification of individual needs from the beginning of sentence. Thus the Risk Assessment process of Clarke *et al* became built into the new Life Sentence Plan documentation (McDougall, Clark and Woodward, 1995).

McDougall and Clark (1991) suggested an approach that enabled prison staff to develop observational skills and provided guidance on what should be observed in order to obtain information regarding risk. This approach combines knowledge regarding behaviour, characteristics and situational aspects that contributed to the index offence with institutional monitoring. There is a clear assumption that an offender's behaviour will then be monitored through sentence to observe whether behaviour patterns associated with the offence are repeated.

Zamble and Porporino (1988) point out that there is a lack of methodologically sound psychological research on the effects of imprisonment, however they claimed that behavioural measures can successfully predict disciplinary offences during imprisonment. Zamble and Porporino (1990) found that most specific behaviours are amenable to change. They argue that if measures of behaviour in prison predict recidivism then it is possible that they include some of the patterns of behaviour that lead to reoffending. If these behaviours can be changed the recidivism can be reduced. Gendreau and Ross (1987) also found that the appropriate application of behavioural and cognitive treatments could change offender's behaviour.

There are five steps to Clark's risk assessment model as follows:

- *Analysis:* The offending behaviour of an individual is analysed by completing a standardised proforma. This directs the attention of the completing staff member to the relevant areas of offending behaviour. It provides a description of the actions of the offender at the time of the offence. Information about the index offence is derived from pre-sentence information: police reports, trial summaries, pre-sentence (formerly social inquiry) reports, psychiatric reports and depositions.

- *Identification of risk factors:* From the first analysis a set of possible risk factors is generated. These are defined as stable characteristics which contribute to the offending behaviour.

- *Examination of past history for supportive evidence:* The third stage involves an analysis of the available information about the prisoner to see whether the risk factors generated are detectable in the prisoner's previous lifestyle.

- *Prediction of how risk factors may be displayed in prison:* A series of predicted behaviours that would be expected to be observed in the prison environment if the risk factors are stable patterns of behaviour for the prisoner is generated.

- *Monitoring:* The final stage involves monitoring the behaviour of the prisoner over time within the prison system, and then comparing actual behaviour with the predicted behaviours to see whether they remain part of the person's repertoire.

To date there are few studies that have examined Clark's Risk Assessment model in operation. Clark (1993) conducted a pilot study of the reliability of the system. He examined the implementation of the system in five prisons. The results were encouraging on a wide range of criteria, including correct initial analysis. Predicted behaviours had a high utility in that they were observable and measurable in the prison environment. Clark drew the conclusion that

> All establishments were fully competent in completing documentation to a high standard. There was no evidence that psychologists produced better, more concise or more appropriate risk factors than other members of staff.

He did however suggest that as the process became routine the integrity of the process could be challenged. In recent studies at HMP Gartree the integrity of the process has been investigated and found wanting. Kelly (1994) compared the risk assessments carried out at three prisons receiving newly sentenced life sentenced prisoners. He discovered a number of implementation difficulties including a low number of Predicted Behaviours, poor utility of Predicted Behaviours, cited evidence for the Risk Factors generated was rare. Similarly Robertson (1994) found low numbers of Risk Factors and Predicted Behaviour generated at one of the Life Sentence prisoner Main Centres. These findings have been substantiated in the research to date. (Whatton, 1994; Briggs, 1995). Working in the same establishment Doherr (1996) found that the generation of risk factors was a strength within the model but she too found that the number and utility of the Predicted Behaviours was a major weakness. These findings are a major concern as the research reflects the stage of the process where the first Risk Assessment is made and in due course is used in the process of writing the first official assessment of a life sentence prisoner. It is this risk assessment that sets the 'baseline' for a particular individual and as such needs to be as full and comprehensive as possible. Without sufficient Predicted Behaviours based on well evidenced Risk Factors the process of meaningful monitoring cannot take place.

More recently, two studies have been undertaken that relate to characteristics of recalled lifers. Bailey (1998) has shown that a sample of recalled lifers are more likely to have previous convictions for violence, have previous parole/probation failures, have been released with additional licence conditions, to be unemployed on release and to change the community based probation officer. This finding appears to add weight to the dictum that previous behaviour is more likely to be repeated but Bailey notes that 'Recall was only directly linked to the original offending behaviour in four out of the 15 recall cases, a finding which also warrants further research'.

Young (1998) tested the hypothesis that there would be a significant difference between the recalled and non-recalled groups of life licensees in the behaviour displayed in the prison environment in relation to identified 'risk' areas. She suggested that the recalled lifers would show more consistency in their behavioural repertoire from the offence through custody, than the non-recall group. Conversely Young suggested that non-recalled lifers would show more change in their behavioural repertoires from the offence through custody. By conducting Risk Assessments and analysing the prison behaviour of the recalled and non-recalled mandatory and discretionary lifer groups she was able to demonstrate that, as hypothesised, non-recall lifers did in fact demonstrate significantly greater change in their 'risk' behaviours than recalled lifers. This finding suggests that it is possible to demonstrate that the process of risk assessment and the focusing on offence-related behaviour within the prison setting can predict life licence failure. The author suggests that what is required is further analysis of the constellations of behaviours that relate to particular offence related risk behaviours in order to produce more accurate predictions of success or failure.

V. MAJOR CRITICISMS AND WAYS FORWARD

Towl and Crighton (1995) suggest that each of the stages of the Clark model has problems attached to it. The information used in the initial analysis of the index offence is adversarial in nature and therefore biased towards the view that the defendant committed the offence. This slant on the information renders it less than objective, and there is no way of knowing what information has been omitted. Of graver consequence is the criticism that there is no evidence that the risk factors derived are actually related to reoffending. Towl and Crighton suggest that even if the risk factors were related it is 'actuarially unacceptable' to give them equal weight. This it is argued may lead to risk factors being erroneously summated in some sort of additive process. Further problems are related to the cognitive processes involved with the prediction of the 'manifestation of "risk factors" within prison'. It is suggested that people are insensitive to predictability. When Kahnenman and Tversky (1973) asked people to predict performance in five years of people for whom they had current data they provided predictions of performance as extreme as those rating current performance despite knowing that such a time distant sample would have little predictive value. This is clearly pertinent when it is remembered that risk assessment for life sentence prisoners begins on average eleven to 12 years before they can be released. There is also an illusion of validity in which observers show an unwarranted confidence in the relationship between predicted outcomes and input information. This continues to hold true even when they are made aware of the factors that limit the accuracy of the process. Finally there is the 'illusory correlation'. In general people appear to form illusory correlations between unrelated and non-causal events. It would appear that these are persistent, as people are resistant to changing something that appears to explain, make sense of, experience. Also in this section of critique is the challenge that the model does not, and perhaps cannot, take account of the powerful processes of fantasy and the cognitive structures in which they take place.

Apart from these criticisms are the difficulties of monitoring the behaviour of prisoners. This is compounded if the behaviours are stereotypic prison behaviours that are viewed by prison staff in a particular way. If the behaviours are not specified in enough detail to be objectively observed then the over inclusion of behaviours in larger, cruder categories such as 'anti-authority' will occur.

The critique by Towl and Crighton has had some support from the work of Kelly (1994), Whatton (1994), Briggs (1995) and Doherr (1996). All of these workers found that the problems related to the initial information and the generation of predictive behaviours were playing an active role in reducing the effectiveness of the process. It is also clear that in the prison setting it is difficult to produce regular collections of behavioural data that are related to individual prisoners.

Munro and Macpherson (1998) have attempted to deal with the problem of collecting behavioural information on prisoners. They agree with Hollin (1996) in calling for observed accounts of prisoners' behaviour within institutional settings to be gathered in a systematic way, rather than informally communicated, to ensure accuracy of reporting. To this end they have developed an Observable Behaviour Scale which takes the form of a semi-structured interview that is administered to prison staff by a psychologist. The results of this are then reviewed alongside psychopathy ratings based on the Hare Psychopath Checklist—Revised. The authors suggest that this provides a more objective method of collecting behavioural data and relating it to other predictive measures.

Needs and Towl (1997) have suggested a model for the clinical risk assessment of life sentence prisoners: CLASP. In this model they argue that the personal experience of the offender needs to be taken into account. For them the *context* in which the offence takes place needs to be known and understood. Importantly, there is a need to know what role the offender played in the development of the circumstances in which he or she committed the offence. *Life history* is seen as providing the necessary information regarding the key influences in the offender's life which have created the themes and issues of importance in the offender's life. It is these that were brought to the offence situation and may have had a role to play. The *agenda* of the individual includes the reasons why that person was in the situation and what 'intentions, expectations, planning, preoccupations and any fantasies, issues for resolution, or emotional priming' the person harboured. Sequence is the fourth factor in the model, the narrative of the offence and the moving into the consequences of the offence. Here the important process is the developing sequence of actions. Within this narrative are likely to be the cues that will alert workers to the points in the sequence at which situational factors shaped the next behaviours, if in fact they did. Finally *personal meaning* needs to be considered. The way in which an individual makes sense of the world, their place in it and their behaviour along with that of others is a major influence on the behaviour of people. In essence this model is a plea that the individual's own characteristics and experience of the world are taken into account when risk assessment is undertaken. What this model does not offer is a procedure that can be easily applied in a standardised way, nor is there any indication of how this information could be related to other forms of risk assessment.

Webster *et al* (1994) published the Violence Prediction Scheme based on the Harris, Rice and Quinsey 1993 study of secure hospital patients at the Oak Ridge Division of the Penetanguishene Mental Health Centre. This scheme attempts to draw together both actuarial and dynamic factors. It uses an actuarial estimate Risk Assessment Guide (RAG) comprising 12 variables one of which is the Psychopathy Checklist Score. The scores from this assessment are laid alongside those obtained by using the ASSESS—LIST which is a rating scale for ten clinical areas such as self-presentation and institutional management. The scores are used to make a judgement about the level of risk that a patient poses but it is worth noting that in the notes for integrating the clinical and actuarial judgements Webster *et al* write the following:

It must be stressed that there is, by definition, no scientific method of deciding upon a final risk score through combining the clinical and actuarial scores. Because there is, however, much more evidence for the actuarial than clinical predictors, we advocate that the actuarial score be modified only slightly by the clinical judgements. It is our recommendation that the actuarial judgement be altered by no more than 10% in either direction, and that only in very unusual cases should it be altered by that much.

There is of course here the paradox that this comprehensive scheme which ultimately has at its heart an actuarial bias has, as demonstrated by Harris *et al* (1993), as its most powerful variable the Psychopathy Checklist—Revised. This same instrument is seen by others as a third generation instrument which embodies dynamic factors as well as static ones and would not strictly come under the rubric of being actuarial.

IV. CONCLUSIONS

At this moment in time life sentence prisoners are recommended for release on the basis of the risk they are perceived to pose to the public. If it is considered that there is sufficient risk that they will behave in the same or similar way to that in which they committed their offence they will remain in prison. Although the prison system has in place a Risk Assessment model it is one that is applied unevenly across the Prison Service, suffers from methodology in terms of generating meaningful predictive behaviours and faces severe problems in monitoring institutional behaviour in a way that relates to risk behaviours. The Prison Service faces the same problems that every organization and agency faces when trying to estimate the risk of an individual behaving in a particular way in the distant future. As Farrington and Tarling (1985) point out 'In the interests of justice, those predictions should be made as accurately as possible'. It is still too early to know whether the Clark model of risk assessment has value in the prediction of reconviction; only recently has research begun to assess this, the first report of this work being expected in the autumn of 1998.

Risk assessment will continue, not because the expectation is that we will quickly find an efficient system that will be applicable to all life sentence prisoners, but because there is a need to ensure that we do not go on imprisoning men for years beyond the point at which they are an acceptable risk to society. We also need to become capable of focusing on that relatively small percentage of people whose untimely release creates further victims.

It is possible that Walker (1996) has come close to the mark when he says

With these reservations, previous violence is the best predictor of future violence which we are ever likely to have. It may be possible to increase its accuracy a little by adding information about the abuse of intoxicants, the use of weapons, or assessments of personality or mental disorder, but the prediction of violence will never become an exact science.

I would like to add to this my own comment that it would be unwise to underestimate the ability of a man to change once he has decided to live his life differently.

*This chapter was contributed by **Roland Woodward** who is a Chartered Forensic Psychologist and at the time of publication head of Psychological services at HM Prison Gartree. Gartree is currently the only all life sentence prisoner prison in Britain and specialises in working with men who are in the early stages of a life sentence. Within this setting, Roland Woodward is the Therapy Manager for the Gartree Therapeutic Community (again, the only one of its kind, in that it is comprised solely of lifers). He is the Director of Therapy designate for the new 200 place Therapeutic Community at HM Prison Marchington which is due to open in the year 2000.*

© Roland Woodward

CHAPTER 7

Beyond Criminal Justice

Any attempt to understand how a country deals with the most serious and challenging offenders stops indefensibly short if it does not consider the widest implications for both that society and the offender. Policies and treatment will always risk being short-sighted or, worse, ill-judged if they are not founded upon sound ethical principles. This chapter addresses some of the key perspectives in this regard including the ethics of life imprisonment and the extent to which there is a political dynamic to their release. Another section explores the influence of the traditional religious and cultural view that some men are evil; that their crimes are a manifestation of this. Finally, we look at the recent introduction of yet another variation of the more punitive American penal influences, where second serious offences may now serve to imprison some people for life and the equally vindictive policy of detaining some prisoners until they themselves die.

I. THE ETHICS OF LIFE IMPRISONMENT

In one of the most closely and rigorously reasoned tracts, Honderich (1976) considers the arguments and 'supposed justifications' for punishment. In this, his principle conclusion is that a state is justified in punishing offenders to the extent that it satisfies two essential conditions. The first is that of *utilitarian values*; the second is of *equality*. We apply these principles to the question of the extent to which it is ethically defensible to imprison our fellow citizens for life.

Utilitarian values
Honderich argues that a state is justified in punishing individuals against their will when they have:

(a) endangered someone else against their will; and (b) whatever punishment is determined appropriate is "economically deterrent".

A finding of guilt in a recognised court of law presumably satisfies (a). However (b) is rather more difficult in some sense to satisfy, particularly in the case of life imprisonment. How may we determine what constitutes deterrence and, more especially, to whom should fall the question of the economic sufficiency of that deterrence? When the case in question is one of murder, we presume in one sense that this principle is satisfied *a priori*, i.e. that such an extreme offence pre-empts economic considerations. Yet, as we have seen, lifers are the least risk category of re-offending in kind of all (*Chapter 1*). Honderich refers rather to deterrence in the sense that, for our purposes, it 'must prevent certain possible distress'. If we interpret this to mean the potential distress to the survivors of the murder or other serious crime, then the principle takes on a completely new meaning and one which might give greater credence to Michael Howard's pronouncements on the need to maintain the respect of the public by never releasing some lifers.

The position across the Atlantic in many influential quarters is less philosophical. The primary motivation behind the phenomenally high rates of incarceration, and of the execution, of murderers seems to be retribution. Witness an opinion from Balzer (1997) in the *Prison Service Journal* letters section. In explaining (and defending) the increasingly punitive approach to crime taken over the past decade, he argues that:

> Capital punishment is seen by most Americans as a form of community self-defence. Because of entrenched legal practices in most states, a true 'life' sentence is not possible; even the most dangerous criminals are eventually turned loose. Change this, and public executions could well stop.

The author had asserted earlier in his letter that 'Coincident with the increase in incarceration during the period 1980 to 1994, serious crime rates, as measured by both official reports . . . and victimisation surveys, declined steadily for all categories except murder'. There are, of course, at least two problems with this argument. The first is that, if the decline in crime rates is *coincidental*, rather than cause and effect, then the increase in rates of incarceration are not proven to be related. It would follow that, with over 1.7 million Americans imprisoned at a cost in excess of 35 billion dollars a year, there is a not insignificant flaw in the punitive argument. The principle of utilitarian values does not get a 'look-in' in this equation.

The second problem with Balzar's assertions is that the rates of murders did not decline but, in fact, increased. Given that the majority of American states have the death penalty, and most have had it for the same period referred to in the article, there seems scant evidence that this is having any deterrent effect if murder rates continue to increase. Perhaps it is more to do with a society which is fragmenting socially and racially divided, increasingly devoted to immediate self-gratification and which protects and enshrines the personal possession of so many weapons of mass destruction—from small handguns to the most sophisticated automatic 'machine guns'—and which believes that the 'solution' to record crime and imprisonment rates is to increase the sentence lengths to ever more ludicrous extremes and kill more prisoners. When the most materialistic nation on earth has an underclass based primarily on race, and no federal, national policies towards a coherent criminal justice system but rather 50 different prison systems, then we are expecting too much for the American public to be aware that many criminologists, using meta-analyses of hundreds of reconviction studies, have proven that, in fact, *quite a lot works* in terms of reducing recidivism. We would refer Balzar to, e.g. Andrews *et al* (1990), Garret (1985), Gendreau and Ross (1980), Gottschalk *et al* (1987), Lipsey (1992), Losel (1993), Lipton (1998), McGuire (1995) and Thornton (1987).

In any event, the huge, and hugely expensive, American prison business hardly meets Honderich's utilitarian value condition of being 'economically deterrent'. Balzar does, however, raise the classic utilitarian argument first raised by its creator, Jeremy Bentham:

> General prevention ought to be the chief end of punishment as it is its real justification . . . But when we consider that an unpunished crime leaves the path open, not only to the same delinquent but also to all those who may have the same motives . . . we perceive that punishment inflicted on the individual becomes a source of security to all. That punishment which considered in itself appeared base and repugnant to all generous sentiments is elevated to the first rank of benefits . . . as an indispensable sacrifice to the common safety.

Thus the deterrence argument is born.

The second of Honderich's two conditions is called *equality*. As we understand this, the penalty given must in some sense be *equivalent* to the grievance, or distress, caused by the crime. Now here is 'the rub'. In a darker sense, this is more to do with the retribution 'drive' or 'instinct' and can only be satisfied in its purest meaning by an eye for an eye, i.e. capital punishment. If the state retained the death penalty, it might be obliged to do as some countries do and offer the family of the victim (of murder) the option of requesting the death penalty. This would certainly satisfy the equality principle of justification in the eyes of some. If not, then we are left with the concern to satisfy the offender's 'debt to Society'. If the arbiter of this is in the person of the Executive or Home Secretary, it is natural to assume that the determination as to when the penalty is equivalent to the crime will be inevitably

(a) influenced by the individual differences of the incumbent; and
(b) even more influenced by that person's perception of the public will.

In the United Kingdom, the public will is, and has been for some time, along the punitive end of the punishment continuum. If, alternatively, the judiciary were to assume this responsibility, the public's perception is that the length of sentences would shorten. What evidence there is to support this is more presumed than apparent. In 1979, the year the

Conservative party came to power, the average sentence length for lifers was nine years, a term which had remained static with no contrary manifestation of the public will since before the Abolition of the Death Penalty Act in 1965. In the years since then, the average has climbed steadily to over 13 years in 1991 and over 14 years in 1995. It seems destined to continue to rise. Data collected by the Psychology Unit at Wormwood Scrubs in 1990 and submitted to the then Home Secretary indicated that the average *tariff* given to a sample of 106 lifers was 13.1 years and 13.6 for murderers. With the addition of the risk element of at least 3 years for the majority, lifers are apparently destined to serve, on average, over 16 years in the next decades.

Why is this? Has the principle of *equality*, or just deserts, been redefined? Are those sentenced to life committing more terrible crimes? Not according to a comparison of the male lifers of 1977 analysed in Home Office Research Unit Report No. 51 (1979) compared with the murderers of the 1989 Home Office submission to the House of Lords sub-committee. Perhaps the single most significant factor to appreciate in this rise is the power of the Home Secretary and Ministers to increase the tariff which the trial judge had recommended in court. The Home Office figures to the Select Committee confirm that, of 106 cases considered between April and September 1988, the Home Secretary set a tariff higher than the trial judge in 63 (60%) of cases. There were no reductions. The prison Governor was told by way of explanation by a representative of the Secretary of State that

> this reflects the policy of Ministers and the judiciary on the question of sentencing for violent crimes; and it is an important element in the maintenance of public confidence in the life sentence system.

This explanation overlooks the inherent contradiction in that it is the Ministers overturning the decisions of the judiciary which provoked the question. Is it possible, rather, that these decisions, in maintaining 'public confidence', are shaped more by political pressure than judicial judgement? Lord Campbell of Alloway, in the record of the House of Lords Committee, said that

> There is a problem . . . that we have had over and over again where the Home Secretary in England bumps up the sentence, over half the sentences, in fact the convicted person served longer than was intended because the Home Secretary bumped it up. What do we do about this? *It is contrary to the European Convention On Human Rights; it is not a judicial act.* (Authors' emphasis)

The Prison Reform Trust submitted that:

Similarly, the procedures governing the length of time life sentence prisoners serve are unsatisfactory. The degree to which politicians can over-ride the judicial view, and the lack of clear and openly stated criteria are *an affront to the cannons of natural justice* . . . It is astonishing that a junior Minister should, in effect, be making the sentencing policy. (Again, authors' emphasis).

Not only are the Ministers more punitive than the judiciary in the setting of tariffs at the beginning of life sentences, they are consistent in their pattern regarding accepting or rejecting the recommendations of the Parole Board for the release of lifers as well. In Written Reply No. 118, House of Commons (22 May 1991) evidence was presented that in 1980, of the 102 lifers recommended for parole, only 6 (5.8%) were not accepted. The rate declined briefly in the next two years but then increased steadily until in 1990, of 138 recommendations, 35 (25%) were not accepted. There is no way to determine whether the cases considered varied significantly in some substantive element, as all arguments put to the Parole Board and all decision by Ministers are secret, even to Prison Service staff who are involved in the cases. When questioned by one author over a specific lifer case, the relevant member of the Prisons Board opined that the Home Secretary has to be 'entirely unfettered when [he takes] a decision on individual cases'.

It is difficult to discern how, at the beginning of the criminal justice system, the courts are not constrained in reaching decisions, in open court, having heard the evidence and arguments both for and against, and then determining a man's custody or freedom, but at the other end, when he is considered again, the same principles do not apply. There is an ethical inconsistency. The imposition of Discretionary Lifer Panel procedures on the English Prison Service by the European Court in 1991 has accentuated the injustice for mandatory lifers whose release is still at the discretion of the 'unfettered' Secretary of State or Minister.

Lord Campbell of Alloway, questioning an Under-Secretary of State's opinion that lifer release is 'probably a political judgement in the last resort' asked:

> But is it really such a political decision and if it were would that not be almost disastrous? . . . Is that not rather a shattering thought that there should be a political element in this at all?

Dr Roger Sapsford of the Open University, giving evidence, stated:

> The conclusion must be that although lifers may have been sent to prison justly, how they are treated inside and the procedures used to determine their release are not just. Justice implies the application of rules known to both sides, for reasons which are available to both sides, on the basis of evidence which is available to both sides and can be contested. This is not

how day-to-day decisions are taken in prison, and it is not how our highest authorities treat prisoners when their possible release on licence comes up for consideration . . .

According to *The Times*, 3 July 1991:

Under the law as it stands, mercy killers have to receive the same sentence as IRA bombers: life. Judges have no discretion in sentencing for murder . . . Under the present law, the term "mandatory life sentence" is a misnomer. It is an unquantified sentence rather than a lifelong one, the quantity being determined by politicians, usually of later generations, for reasons which are not open and judicial. The proper people to decide such questions are judges, whose decisions can be openly challenged on appeal if they are wrong. Thus the issue between the Lords and the Commons is a consititutional one; the role of politicians versus the role of judges.

There is apparently some room for interpretation on the principle of retribution. There is no measure of equivalent suffering; of being able to say that so many years imprisonment is equal to taking another's life. The element of *equality* is difficult to apply in the case of murderers. If we, as a society, wish the lifers to suffer in their imprisonment as well as their being imprisoned, research suggests this is satisfied (see, e.g. Walker, 1983; Toch, 1977; and Sapsford, 1983). If, on the other hand, we wish the law to reflect principles of justice, reason and compassion, then it is past time for the mandatory nature of a life sentence for murder regardless of the circumstances to be abolished, as has recently been recommended by Lord Bingham, Lord Chief Justice. Speaking in *The Guardian* newspaper in March 1998, Lord Bingham addressed the impasse between the Home Secretary and the judges over the related powers of the Home Secretary and Ministers to determine the length of mandatory life sentences and to abolish the law dictating the mandatory nature of the sentence. He referred as well to the secrecy of the process whereby the release decisions are made, even going so far as to say that 'If such a system had been operated in Stalin's Soviet Union, Hitler's Germany or Amin's Uganda, we should have been very quick to condemn it as a glaring violation of democratic principal'.

He cited the inherent inequity whereby 'The law required the same sentence to be passed on the wife who had been maltreated for years by a brutal husband and eventually killed him . . . as on a person who tortured, abused and killed children for sadistic or sexual satisfaction'. This is only the most recent in an ever increasing group of informed voices in Parliamentary, judicial and criminological fields which have been calling for a change in this most fundamental of issues for over two decades. The Parliamentary All-party Penal Affairs Group (1986), the House of Lords Select Committee on Murder and Life Imprisonment (1989), NACRO (1991), the independent Committee on the Penalty for

Homicide (1993) and the Penal Affairs Consortium representations to the House of Commons Home Affairs Committee Inquiry into the Mandatory Life Sentence (1995) have all recommended that the life sentence should no longer be mandatory in murder cases. The point is not that life imprisonment is not the right sentence for the majority of those so sentenced, it is that there is no element of discretion to reflect the huge range of circumstances which lead to, and in some cases substantially mitigate culpability for, taking human life.

II. DO LIFERS HAVE HUMAN RIGHTS?

Fowles (1985) recorded that, in addition to judicial intervention in prison life being required to reduce the amount of human suffering caused by poor or overly secure conditions:

> There is a second and perhaps more important reason why prison administrators should obey the constitution and protect prisoners' rights: those who have been convicted of breaking the law are most in need of having respect for the law demonstrated to them.

The response of the Prison Service to recent accusations from prisoners in Wormwood Scrubs of having been physically assaulted by prison officers (most of the prisoners were also black) is particularly important to the public perception of a fair, law-abiding and racially impartial treatment for *all* those who find themselves in custody. It is also perhaps a simple additional step to advocate that, in order for prisoners to have any real rights, they must not only have due process demonstrated to them but they should actually be party to those processes themselves i.e. they must become re-enfranchised, re-empowered. If we accept that the deprivations of imprisonment are inevitable consequences of living in such secure and complex institutions as prisons, or that through their crimes they have forfeited these rights, then offenders have no say, should remain passive subjects to the will of their captors and do as they are told.

If we don't allow the prisoners' voice to be heard in some degree of self-determination and to ensure access to independent legal advice, then we are not blameless for his or her reactions to those conditions imposed upon him or her or when he or she may feel most grievous injustices about either the fact or conditions of that imprisonment. Yet advocating greater rights through greater involvement for prisoners in the actual processes of decision-making is heresy to some insiders. There is a strong school of thought that holds to increase the rights of prisoners is to increase their power and thus reduce the power of staff, making them more vulnerable. The experience however of those prisons which practice this enfranchisement, such as Grendon where elected inmate representatives meet with senior staff to discuss, and sometimes alter, prison policies which affect the daily lives of all the prisoners, is that staff are given greater respect and become a far more influential force on prisoners' attitudes and behaviour. The Prison Service has moved towards this perspective in the 1990s, beginning with the White Paper *Custody, Care and Justice: the Way Ahead for the Prison Service in England and Wales* (HMSO, 1991). In this, the Prison Department expressed its

> duty as part of the criminal justice system to ensure that prisoners are treated with justice, humanity, dignity and respect.

However, in the ten chapters and 108 pages of that report, there are only a few lines specifically relevant to lifers:

> Introduce and improve sentence plans for all life sentence prisoners. The Government is considering introducing a more structured plan centred on offending behaviour and setting programme objectives which will determine progress towards release.

To their credit, the Prison Service has achieved this. We are left however, with a mentality of control, security as paramount and a perception on the part of most prison staff that most prisoners are to be restrained from empowerment and that, if prisoners were to acquire greater rights and responsibilities, there would be an inevitable tendency for the majority to abuse them. The evidence of the authors' combined experience of over 80 years as Governors and psychologists in British prisons is that this fear is largely unfounded.

III. THE NATURE OF EVIL

Why people commit crime is one of the oldest, and most enduring of questions posed by criminologists. Debate about this question has dominated criminology from its inception in the Victorian period, and continues today. Much of this debate centres on the question of whether or not people have free will, or responsibility for their actions; or whether, alternatively, the environment in which they are brought up—unemployment, education, housing and so forth—influences their behaviour either to conform, or to commit crime. This type of debate is sometimes described as 'nature' versus 'nurture ', and has now expanded, as scientific knowledge has increased, to include issues such as genetics, diet, and DNA.

Even this very brief description of the liveliest field of enquiry within criminology should indicate that there has, as yet, been no definitive answer to the question why people commit crime. Perhaps there never will be, although some geneticists are now busy trying to locate a 'criminal gene', which in one very obvious sense echoes the Victorian certainty that there was a 'criminal type', recognisable by the shape of the forehead, the earlobes, and the nose. On the other hand some criminologists would argue that this type of investigation rarely includes proper control groups, and stereotypically concentrates upon those people who have anyway ended up in prison, making the very nature of the research tautological. Other criminologists would argue that the problem with all of this is that we also tend to concentrate on a rather narrow definition of what 'crime' actually is, and rarely do we see the person who defrauds a bank or pension fund as 'a criminal'.

With those people who commit murder there has been a tendency, especially amongst the UK media, to grasp a motivation which ignores the dynamism of the nature of the crime, and the more generic debate as to why people commit crime at all. In short, they are 'evil', or 'monsters'. This label is thereafter used to justify policies which ensure that such prisoners are locked up and 'the key thrown away'. The UK tabloid press is filled with examples of campaigns to keep this or that prisoner locked up forever.

The use of the label 'evil' is at best unhelpful, and at worst deliberately misleading. Notions of evil are usually associated with our Christian tradition of good and bad, which are seen as separate and divisible, or with a patchwork of political events, or movements either historically, or from our own time. In relation to this latter description, Hitler's Third Reich, e.g. is commonly seen as an 'evil' regime, during which time six million Jewish people were sent to their deaths, and more recently the Provisional Irish Republican Army (PIRA), along with other terrorist groups, has been described as 'evil', and thus outside of the 'normal' boundaries of society.

Of course one group's 'terrorist' is another's 'freedom fighter', and it is interesting to note how the peace process in Northern Ireland has gradually had to accommodate people who only a few years ago were commonly labelled as 'evil' or 'monsters'. More courageously, Hannah Arendt,[1] writing about the trial of the Nazi leader Adolf Eichmann in 1963, described him as 'ordinary', and that 'despite all the efforts of the prosecution, everybody could see that this man was not a "monster"'. Indeed she subtitled her book *A Report on the Banality of Evil*. What was of interest to Arendt was how everyday, and commonplace Eichmann was, rather than how odd, and unusual.

---

[1] H Arendt (1994), *Eichmann in Jerusalem: A Report on the Banality of Evil*, Harmondsworth: Penguin Books, p.54

This insight allows us to understand a little more clearly the issue of 'good' or 'bad'. Rather than seeing these concepts as separate and mutually exclusive, perhaps we have to accept that within one person are the desires and motivation to both do good or bad, depending on the circumstances in which that person finds himself or herself. If the circumstances are exceptional—whether through alcohol or peer pressure or during a war etc.—then even the most 'ordinary' person might be provoked to behave differently, and to murder. Indeed, with no sense of irony, the serial killer Dennis Nilsen described himself as 'an ordinary man come to an extraordinary conclusion'.[2]

The experiments of Stanley Milgram on obedience to authority showed that people far removed from the world of serial killers can be induced to administer extremely painful, and life-threatening electric shocks, if they believe that their individual responsibility has been surrendered to some greater authority, on whose behalf they are acting.[3] Such greater authorities might include governments, or dictators, or political or social movements of many colours. We easily accept the horror of Hitler's Germany, for example, but of late the torture and abuse of people at a time of war has been a problem faced by the Americans during the Vietnam War, and more recently by the Canadians during their so-called 'peace-keeping' mission in Somalia in 1994, on behalf of the United Nations. This mission ended with the killing of a 16 year-old Somali boy who had entered the Canadian compound, and who over a period of a few hours was punched, kicked, and burned, and had his shins broken with a metal bar before he eventually died. The death only came to light as several of the soldiers involved took photographs of their victim being tortured.[4]

Removing ourselves from the battlefield, it is important to remember that it is children under one year of age who are most at risk of being murdered in our society, with a homicide rate of 44 per million of the population, compared to an overall risk of 12 per million of the general population. Indeed people who kill children are most commonly seen as those deserving of our greatest condemnation, and editorials abound of the kind 'How on Earth Can They Do Such A Thing?'. Yet, the vast majority of children who are murdered are not murdered by strangers, but by their parents, or step-parents. Rather than warning our children about 'stranger-danger', we should instead concentrate on eradicating the circumstances which encourage parents to take the lives of their own offspring.

---

[2] See B Masters (1985), *Killing for Company: The Case of Dennis Nilsen*, London: Jonathan Cape

[3] S Milgram (1974), *Obedience to Authority: An Experimental View*, New York: Harper and Row

[4] See the report in *The Independent On Sunday*, 13 November 1994

IV. NATURAL LIFE

The emphasis of the management of lifers is on preparing them to be considered for release and then enabling that to happen in the most effective way to provide a quality of life on release. A dimension which has been growing in the recent past is the phenomenon of lifers who are not considered to be ever suitable for release. Some of these are very high profile murderers and those who have killed inside prison. There are thus a small number, about 20 at present (although the service would not disclose any 'official' policy and figures to us) of life sentence prisoners for whom a 'whole life tariff' is considered necessary. Under the review arrangements announced by the then Home Secretary, Michael Howard, on 7 December 1994 these prisoners will not be eligible for a Parole Board review. All those with whole life tariffs will be reviewed by Ministers after 25 years, and every five years thereafter. In such cases, Ministers will be deciding whether or not to change the tariff from whole life to a tariff of a fixed period. This Ministerial review will not be concerned with risk. The Parole Board is therefore not involved. In the Home Secretary's words:

> I have decided that for those life sentence prisoners for whom it is decided that the requirements of retribution and deterrence can be satisfied only by their remaining in prison for the whole of their life, there will in future be an additional Ministerial review when the prisoner has been in custody for 25 years. The purpose of this review will be solely to consider whether the whole life tariff should be converted to a tariff of a determinate period.

The emergence of this explicit group of lifers who are not to be considered for release under the normal criteria and who are therefore unlikely ever to be released poses considerable problems for the lifers and for those managing them. The risks of hopelessness, already a strong likelihood amongst lifers, is exacerbated by this dynamic once the representations and appeals to Europe have been exhausted.

Although there have been many lifers in the past who have not been released and have died in prison there has never been the explicit statement of this likelihood and thus this labelling of lifers. The fact that there is now a growing group in this category poses a new dynamic in the management of the life sentence. The implications have not yet fully been considered by the Prison Service and policies and protocols are being worked on at the time of writing. The 'no hope' lifers may represent an increased danger to themselves and possibly to other prisoners and staff as a result of this dimension to their imprisonment. For many lifers with long tariffs the dynamics may well be the same at the start of their sentence, but the time structure of the tariff does place their self-management in some context which begins to make sense. For

164 Beyond Criminal Justice

the natural life tariff prisoners, however, prison could well be all they have to experience. Coming to terms with this will call for new skills and sensitivities from staff and new structures within prisons. As the number of such lifers grows there will be an urgency to ensure that those skills are in place.

V. CONCLUSION

There seems an instinct in man to create a distance between those of us who live (relatively) law-abiding lives and those who commit terrible crimes, particularly those who kill. We, most of us, seem to draw some comfort and reassurance from demonising killers, as if to affirm that there must be some inherent difference so fundamental, and therefore possibly attributable to evil or badness, that we can sustain a belief that *we* are incapable of such horrible acts. Such people are reduced to the word describing the worst thing they ever did. Imagine using this logic on yourself. What if you were judged by that which you are most ashamed of. If you were not allowed to be considered as anything other than that act, that deed. The current hysteria to track down, brand and demonise every sex offender, every paedophile, is a variation on this mentality. With these labels we can dehumanise the criminal, rob him or her of their individuality and capacity to change and to return to society. They are stripped of what may have been a good, even exemplary life for many decades and reduced to a word derived from their crime.

The current imperatives in society towards crime is to get tough with it (and its causes!). The current twin imperative in the Prison System of England and Wales (and it is only a whisper compared to the American roar) is *Security and Control*. It pervades every aspect of imprisonment and threatens every positive initiative which calls for the slightest degree of trust in prisoners. The language of containment starves basic human contact of the freedom to relax and treat someone as another person first and a prisoner second. This is a direct consequence of a handful of prisoners escaping from two prisons. These people were subsequently caught and returned to prison without having committed further offences. The other 60,000 prisoners (and the 40,000 staff who look after them) have as a consequence been victimised by an overreaction of seismic magnitude. Yet the truth is that the overwhelming majority of those people serving life sentences are more compliant to prison rules than are the determinate prisoners. The truth is that the overwhelming majority of these same life sentence prisoners will, when eventually released, not reoffend—again unlike their fixed sentence counterparts. In truth, the overwhelming majority of lifers, if treated with dignity, courtesy and respect, return these in full measure.

CHAPTER 8

Proposals

This book has highlighted the related issues of murder and life imprisonment. We hope it has illuminated a number of vital areas of concern regarding both the interaction between a culture and an individual's violent destructive behaviour. Rather than leave general impressions, we want to focus the reader's attention finally on what we feel are the areas which represent the greatest risks and opportunities for constructive, creative solutions.

I. CONTAINMENT

The use of indeterminate sentences, i.e. life imprisonment, in England and Wales has increased in the 1990s beyond either that purpose for which such sentences were originally intended or, as the authors argue, that which the safety of society requires. The prediction of the doubling of the size of the lifer population over the next ten years presents us with a prospect of grave concern.

The life sentence appears to have become a political shorthand tool to signal the toughness of the government of the day, responding to the seemingly media-induced stridency for the punishment of crime to match—even exceed—the severity of the crime. We have argued that this cultural 'press' driven expedient is an inappropriate way to determine sentencing policy. Equally, the authors express their concern regarding the influences of American judicial and criminological 'innovations'—almost entirely more punitive even than their British equivalents—on our decision-making and offer instead the European model of liberal empiricism as a more humane, prudently-based alternative.

As the population of lifers increases the issues of containment and management will become more critical. The number of prisons in which they are held will increase, they will dominate the long-term population of prisons and the resourcing of the programmes to meet their needs will preoccupy local management. So we propose:

- a life sentence should be the maximum, rather than the mandatory sentence for murder
- the tariff element of the life sentence should be set in open court and be fixed by the judiciary. Home Office Ministers should have no part in the tariff setting

- all life sentenced prisoners should have a legal right to be informed of the tariff and of appeal
- the sentence and release stages of all life sentences should be open and judicial, rather than secret and executive; and
- procedures for reviewing the claims of lifers concerning the wrongness of their conviction should be reviewed with greater research into the phenomenon and linked to the experience of the CCRC.

II. TREATMENT

The variety and complexity of murderers and lifers defeats most people who approach the subject, but it is this variety which we must first accept. There is no good in demonising those who kill, it only serves to inflame public opinion, confuses attempts to understand and prevent offences and creates an artificial sense of security for those of us who feel we could never do something like that.

Strategies for intervention in the lives of these prisoners—both in prison and in the community—must start from a principle of valuing all human life and from the realisation that we all benefit most by helping to make all life sentence prisoners as safe as possible. This can only be done through programmes of proven efficacy informed by people of genuine goodwill. The current debate about whether severe personality disordered offenders are 'treatable' or can only be 'managed' over time does not excuse those with the responsibility of care to do all in their power to offer opportunities for the most recalcitrant to begin to review their life within a context of therapeutic safety. So we propose that:

- the management and location of lifers within prisons should be based on the issues of their Life Sentence Plan in order to offer developing opportunities towards consideration for release. The Lifer Management Unit should have responsibility for all treatment interventions in liaison with the Offending Behaviour Programmes Unit.
- HM Prison Service staff's aim should be to prepare lifers for release on tariff
- the range and availability of evidence-based effective treatment programmes should be increased so that the expectation that all lifers can progress through such work towards consideration for release can be realised. Priority should be given to lifers to have access to therapeutic community places as well as other accredited offending behaviour programmes.

- Prison Service Training Services training in lifers management should be developed to include the psychology of murder, the nature and dynamics of life imprisonment and strategies for help after release. The dependence on the *Lifer Manual* as a procedural guide can miss the dynamics of working with people.
- staff skills required to manage lifers should form part of the training experience. The task of managing lifers should be considered within the work profile of each prison and be given due weight as numbers of lifers increase and the quality of work with them improves.

III. PUBLIC SAFETY

The price paid for the current apparent emphasis on public safety we have shown is too high and need not remain as damaging to the lives of so many offenders and their families. It is possible to develop systems for improving the testing of lifers whilst in custody to help them become safer when released. The range of evidence-based interventions has increased and provides us with a more focused approach to treatment than the current dependence on length of time in custody and ageing. It is only with a more public approach to discussing such issues that there emerges a consensus against our current dependence on life sentences. Thus we propose:

- there should be a review of comparative European experience in managing serious offenders without dependence on life sentences and holding such offenders in custody for shorter periods than in England and Wales
- the Prison Service Directorate of Healthcare should initiate a review of unmet psychiatric need within the life sentenced population
- the work of the review of severe personality disordered offenders undertaken by the National Health Service and the Home Office should be made more widely known to inform the discussion about the 'treatability' or not of those serious offenders with mental disorders.

IV. RISK

The accurate prediction of behaviour after release for life sentence prisoners is one of the most challenging problems in the criminal justice process. The current inevitable burden of collective responsibility which falls, perhaps disproportionately, on Parole Board members tends to oblige excessive caution, i.e. 'If in doubt, don't release'. While most of us would regard this as entirely appropriate, more accurate methods of prediction would ease the skewed, onerous task and reduce the rates of re-offending for the gravest of crimes. So we propose:

• the Prison Service should apply the current Risk Assessment model consistently and accurately across all cases in order to properly assess predictive validity for prison-based behaviour.

And we would advocate:

• the use of the Violence Scheme of Webster *et al* on English and Welsh prison populations alongside existing procedures used by the Parole Board to help determine the most potent techniques.

With the level of attention currently being paid to the lifer system the time is right to re-assess our dependence on such a sentence which provides dynamics for the creation of maximum dependence in a group which is being assessed for their ability to survive in independent freedom. There are many ways of countering these forces, retaining a sense of justice for victims and their families and providing opportunities for damaged and damaging people to become citizen contributors to society, rather than remaining alienated and excluded. We have offered ways in which this could be achieved.

Appendix A: Alex's Story. Secret Justice. An Extreme Illustration of Why Discretionary Lifer Panels Were Needed

The description which follows underscores many of the underlying themes of this book, including the problem which occurs when a lifer insists on maintaining innocence in the face of Prison Service policies which, notwithstanding a proliferation of miscarriage of justice cases, do not acknowledge or cater for this eventuality. The case involves a discretionary life sentence where the hope of the sentencing judge (as expressed at the time) that a short period in custody would be served—perhaps 'a couple of years'—was patently not honoured. As will be seen, Alex finally served 24 years in custody: for no apparent good reason and certainly, due to its secretive nature, on no basis which was open to challenge. This serves to emphasise why there was such a need for the open justice provided by the still relatively novel Discretionary Lifer Panels outlined in *Chapter 5* (as well as raising fundamental questions about whether there may be a case for retrospective compensation for discretionary lifers whose terms of imprisonment may, in the past, have been unacceptably prolonged beyond the requirements of the law or of preventive justice).

Alex was born in 1953 in Lancashire of an English mother and a Ukrainian father. He was frequently punished, sometimes severely and physically, by his father who he remembers as domineering and aggressive and first ran away from home aged ten. By 12, he was placed in local authority care and regularly absconded from homes. When he was 15, Alex was convicted of theft and sent to approved school, followed by the familiar graduation through borstal and prison, so that he was almost continuously inside for the next five years. Late in 1970, he was convicted of entering a house and threatening a young girl with a knife. He was sentenced to 18 months imprisonment. He was 18 on release and was only free for two weeks before he was apprehended and charged with the offences for which he has served two discretionary life sentences.

Life sentence
Alex was found guilty of aggravated burglary and wounding with intent to do grievous bodily harm (GBH) in the course of a house-breaking. He pleaded guilty after, he alleges, he had been mistreated by the police. Two psychiatrists who eventually interviewed him some weeks after arrest recommended to the judge that he be treated in hospital for severe depression and risk of suicide. The judge, concluding that although he knew Alex was sick and was sorry for him, felt his greater responsibility was to protect others from Alexandrowicz and sentenced him to life times two in December 1971. Alex's security category was determined as A.

He was transferred to HMP Wakefield to begin his term of imprisonment. His passage over the next few years was uneven and, at times, disruptive. He was obliged to associate with some prisoners who were violent and others who felt strong political alienation from the Government, including IRA members. Even before his twenty-first birthday, i.e. while still a young prisoner (YP). Alex got a reputation as an unstable and troublesome prisoner although he was rarely on report for bad behaviour. He was forcibly raped by four prisoners and took his revenge on one of his attacker with an iron bar. Although it could not be proved, Alex was assumed to have carried out the attack and was transferred to another prison. He was regularly placed on Rule 43 ('own protection'), a Prison Service procedure of separating vulnerable prisoners from the mainstream which is initiated at their request, due to various pressures of being an inadequate, depressive young man made to associate with violent people in a maximum security prison on the highest security classification. He got into debt and, through his political ideas and having had a father of Ukrainian descent asked to become a Soviet citizen. Although the trial judge had recommended that Alex's future '. . . will now depend upon the view that the doctors take of his recovery and parole in the future will depend largely upon their view' there is scant evidence in his official record of having ever seen psychiatrists during his first ten years inside. He was, however, labelled as 'a very disturbed personality of the inadequate psychopathic type' by a medical officer who had not actually interviewed him. By the end of the first decade, his survival strategy was fixed, moving from prison to prison and within days getting himself placed on Rule 43 for his own protection and psychological survival, often spending months trying to avoid the main prison wings and landings.

Life in prison
From 1981 to 1985, Alex was transferred between six different prisons and had spent most of his time in segregation units and on Rule 43. In spite of this, the Governor in charge of his latest prison went on record in an act of rare candour and some courage, saying:

> Much has been written about this prisoner in the past 15 years and numerous labels have been applied in an effort to describe his personality and behaviour. With the invaluable tool of hindsight firmly in my grasp, I feel that I must take issue with much that has been written . . . to set the matter straight, to establish the facts as they really are, and to make positive suggestions for the future.

> When evaluating Alex's behaviour, we need to be clear about the foundations from which that behaviour emanates. As an example, an individual whose whole life experience has consisted of cold, impersonal relationships can hardly be expected to have developed the same personality traits, character strengths, and human values as a person from a more favourable background.

He continued:

> It is therefore essential that we remind ourselves of the facts. This man is reported to have had an unhappy childhood and to have been deprived of parental care from the age of 12 years. Since that time – for a total of 21 years – he has virtually spent his life in custody. He has experienced children's homes, approved schools, detention centres, borstals, and a previous prison sentence. I wonder if anyone really expects that a person with such a background, and who began his life sentence as an 18 year old youth, should be exhibiting what we like to regard as "normal" behaviour? For myself, I prefer to adopt a more realistic approach and to accept that A is the product of the criminal justice system . . . Let us remember that A, like the rest of us, consists of

his experiences . . . he is very aware that life is passing him by . . . and he now realises that he will probably have completed half of his expected life-span by the time he is released from prison.

It is worth pausing to reflect on Clarke's (1980) observations regarding situational determinants of crime:

. . . regarding the offender as a rational decision-maker also provides a useful alternative way of conceptualising motivation: the motives for misconduct in the institution . . . are seen to rest not in basic features of personality, but in the benefits that the offender thinks he will obtain Thus the approved school boy absconds not because he is impulsive . . . but because he wants to escape a bully.

Perhaps Alex chose to live segregated from 'normal' prison life as a form of escape from a life too brutalising to endure. Equally, when his repertoire of interpersonal skills were so limited, his choice of options were commensurate. The Governor's report continued:

Whilst he committed a serious crime, he sees murderers being released after less time than he has served and this adds to his confusion . . . (and bitterness?) . . . we are left with the question of this man's future. Alex's behaviour . . . in prison shows clearly that he is a somewhat solitary individual, who does not make friends easily . . . his relationships with the less "official" members of staff have been reasonable and potentially positive, but his interpersonal skills, perhaps understandably, are not of a high order. As a result, and as his record shows, he seems happiest when serving his sentence as a series of short-stay "blocks" of imprisonment interspersed with regular changes of environment. I regard this as reasonable behaviour and I see no need to condemn him for it.

The Governor concluded by outlining his recommendations for Alex's progression through Category C, open prison and a pre-release hostel leading to release. He envisaged this taking about three years, giving Alex freedom in mid-1989, concluding:

By that time, he will have served some 18 years for this offence. If we equate this to a fixed term of imprisonment, then his sentence, with full remission, would have been 27 years. I think this may be regarded, by even the most extremist members of society, as a sufficiently long sentence to be served by a juvenile for unlawful wounding.

In spite of this eloquent argument, and the support of the Local Review Committee (charged with making parole decisions and recommendations), Alex's provisional release was not granted. He was moved again, this time to Grendon, the therapeutic prison. At Grendon, Alex's progress was outstanding. He accepted his previous anxieties, withdrawal and failure to cope in conventional prisons. He discussed in detail the damage caused by his parenting and early years but continued to deny the index offences for which he was imprisoned. On his Community wing, Alex was elected Vice-Chairman, made a 'Red Band' trustee—positions of greatest responsibility and trust within the inmates—became an Inter-wing Committee representative for the entire prison and was responsible for organizing a Wing Social for 60 guests and for giving the 'thank you speech'.

Views of the people closest to the events

As a result of the positive progress he made during his two years in therapy, including a remarkable period of nine months when the prison was closed for major electrical repairs and Alex and the prisoners were 'housed' in three other prisons, Alex's F75 Reports (preparatory to formal Release review) were brought forward a year. The *Wing Therapist* reported:

> This man's imprisonment is . . . the most appalling example of injustice I have experienced . . . Natural justice and human compassion, as well as the long-since paid tariff and the minimal risk, demand this man's release at the earliest possible date.

The *Psychiatrist* responsible said: 'I do not see his imprisonment being of great value or of help'.

The *Governor* of the prison said:

> Alex has been under close scrutiny from highly skilled staff and his fellow inmates . . . and his attitude has been tested and is considered genuine. He does not present a risk to the outside public and further incarceration would not only be of no benefit to society and to him but would merely enhance the process of prisonisation . . . we would recommend . . . to prepare him for release as expeditiously as is considered Ministerially possible.

The *Local Review Committee Chairman* said:

> He has committed no offences of assault for 13 years. He has consistently matured despite all the odds against him . . . A provisional date given quickly could undo some of the damage that has been caused to this man through this prolonged period of imprisonment.
> He has made excellent progress since coming back to Grendon.
> It is our view that he should be released from Grendon . . . It was quite clear from the reports since 1980 that nothing other than damage can be done to this man by prolonged imprisonment. We ask for a speedy decision to be made please. We are appalled at the length of time that this man has served in prison.

The reports went into the Lifer Section and Parole Board for consideration. Eight months later, when Alex had still not had an answer, further reports became due for the internal six monthly Review Board standard then for all lifers.

The *Lifer Governor* concluded:

> What can one add to this case? He was reviewed in September and is awaiting an answer. The general and overwhelming feeling here is that he is ready for release.

The *Chaplain* said:

> All I can say at this stage is that those in authority need to be told yet again that he should be released from his long, long prison sentence as quickly as possible.

The *Probation Officer* said:

> He can now see and value a stable future life, but feels powerless as to reaching it and so I feel he needs to be given hope as soon as possible.

The *Psychiatrist* now responsible said:

He has, by all accounts, made quite significant progress in therapy and is perhaps the most respected member of the community, whose impartial criticism, relevant observations and constructive advice are much appreciated by his peers and staff alike. He is very articulate and expresses his strong views without fear or favour. He is also very polite, respectful of authority and exercises a strong stabilising influence on the community by his example. There is no evidence of any disorder of the processes of thought or any aberration of perception. There is no evidence of a depressive illness or an organic cerebral lesion. He has re-established a relationship with his mother and a very close one with his girl-friend who appear to look forward to the day of his eventual release. They jointly provide him with all the encouragement and support he needs.

There does not appear to be any further benefit which could accrue to him by prolonging his stay in the penal system.

We are aware of no more categorical a set of recommendations for release. Yet, in spite of this overwhelming support from every grade and profession of staff possible, and a recommendation from the Parole Board, Alex was not given a Provisional Release Date. He was given a transfer to a Cat D prison and a recommended review in two years, which would mean that he would serve another three years *at least* before being released, bringing his total term of imprisonment to 24 years. Alex said that he would run away from the Cat D prison if transferred there because he did not need it and because he was ready to be released and wanted to be released from Grendon. He was transferred anyway and absconded a few weeks later, surrendering himself voluntarily, and after having publicised his case in the newspapers, to Grendon. He was immediately transferred to a Category C prison. About a year later, the European Court ruled that the Prison Service was obliged to introduce Discretionary Lifer Panels (see *Chapter 5*). Alex's case was one of the first considered and, following the DLP sitting and hearing the case for and against release, Alex was ordered to be released immediately.

The Chair of the Panel apologised to Alex, stating that his was the worst case he had heard to date. Since that date, 4 July 1993, Alex has been free but has struggled to live an independent life after having been so completely institutionalised. In his own words:

When I was being sentenced to two discretionary life sentences the judge said: "You will go to prison until the doctors are confident about you and then you will be released". He went on to add: "This sentence is not as savage as it may sound to you". At that time, I was 18 years old and I had been convicted of GBH and aggravated burglary. This was in December 1971. It was emphasised by the prison authorities that a murderer could expect to serve around 11 years but, as a "discretionary lifer", I would serve much less. I was not prescribed any course of psychiatric treatment whilst I was in prison and after six years there was not shown to be any "medical" reasons for me to have to remain locked up. Although prison doctors had stopped recommending any further detention by 1981, I was turned down for release by the Parole Board. In 1992, I was shown a letter from . . . a Home Office Minister, which stated clearly the reason why the Parole Board had not recommended my release from prison: ". . . Mr Alexandrowicz's behaviour whilst in prison, particularly his assaults on staff, has not generated confidence (for a successful release application)". I was able to prove immediately, by open reference to my disciplinary record, that I had *never* assaulted a member of staff. A year later, in July 1993, I was granted immediate release by a Discretionary Lifer Panel. I had served 22 years and I was 40 years old.

What is evident is that I was tried twice—by the judiciary and then by the Home Office. After the judicial criteria had been fulfilled the second trial, based on what was proven to be false evidence, took place at the Home Office and, as a result, I was made to serve a sentence, savagely distorted and out of all proportion to the charges I was convicted of; an abrogation of justice. I have not been compensated by the Home Office for the trauma and distress caused to myself and my family. Nor have I been offered one word of apology.

Throughout his 22 years of imprisonment and five years of subsequent life licence, Alex has maintained his innocence. His case has recently been accepted by the Criminal Cases Review Committee, which considers possible miscarriage of justice cases.

It must be said that most life sentence prisoners experience nothing like this kind of treatment, but there are a not insignificant number who are either serving terms significantly longer than what both their crime and their prison behaviour might justify and who may very well be innocent. *Chapter 3* addresses the latter of these two groups and the implications for all in the criminal justice system.

Alex's story is told in full in *The Longest Injustice* by Alexander Alexandrowicz (with additional materials by Professor David Wilson) scheduled for publication by Waterside Press in 1999

Appendix B The Parole Board Rules 1997[1]

PART I: INTRODUCTION
1. *Title, commencement, etc.*

Application and interpretation
2. (1) Subject to rule 19, these Rules apply where a prisoner's case is referred to the Board by the Secretary of State under section 28(6)(a), section 28(7) or section 32(4) of the Act.
   (2) In these Rules, unless a contrary intention appears -
"Board" means the Parole Board, continued by section 32(1) Criminal Justice Act 1991,
"Chairman" means the chairman of the Board appointed under paragraph 2 of Schedule 5 to the Criminal Justice Act 1991,
"governor" includes a director of a contracted out prison,
"panel" means those members of the Board constituted in accordance with rule 3,
"parties" means the prisoner and the Secretary of State,
"prison" includes a young offender institution or any other institution where the prisoner is or has been detained,
"prisoner" means a person to whom section 28 of the Act applies,
"the Act" means the Crime (Sentences) Act 1997.

PART II: GENERAL

Appointment of the panel
3. (1) The Chairman shall appoint three members of the Board to form a panel for the purpose of conducting proceedings in relation to a prisoner's case.
the Board. The chairman of each panel must hold judicial office (Rule 3).
   (2) The members of the panel appointed under paragraph (1) shall include a person who holds or who has held judicial office and who shall act as chairman of the panel.

Listing the case for hearing
4. The Board shall list the case for hearing and, as soon as practicable thereafter, notify the parties of the date when the case was so listed.

Information and reports by the Secretary of State
5. (1) Within eight weeks of the case being listed, the Secretary of State shall serve on the Board and, subject to paragraph (2), the prisoner or his representative -
   (a) the information specified in Part A of Schedule 1 to these Rules.
   (b) the reports specified in Part B of that Schedule, and
   (c) such further information that the Secretary of State considers to be relevant to the case.
   (2) Any part of the information or reports referred to in paragraph (1) which in the opinion of the Secretary of State should be withheld from the prisoner on the ground that its disclosure would adversely affect the health or welfare of the prisoner or others shall be recorded in a separate document and served only on the Board together with the reasons for believing that its disclosure would have that effect.
   (3) Where a document is withheld from the prisoner in accordance with paragraph (2), it shall nevertheless be served as soon as practicable on the prisoner's representative if he is -
   (a) a barrister or solicitor,

---

[1] The 1997 Rules supersede the Parole Board Rules 1992, the only material changes being their extension to the analogous situation of young offenders detained at Her Majesty's pleasure and to 'section 2 discretionary lifers' pursuant to the Crime (Sentences) Act 1997. This aspect apart, the procedures, requirements and substance of the 1997 Rules remain broadly the same as under the original 1992 version of the Rules.

(b) a registered medical practitioner, or

(c) a person whom the chairman of the panel directs is suitable by virtue of his experience or professional qualification;

provided that no information disclosed in accordance with this paragraph shall be disclosed either directly or indirectly to the prisoner or to any other person without the authority of the chairman of the panel.

Representation, etc.

6. (1) Subject to paragraph (2), a party may be represented by any person who he has authorised for that purpose.

(2) The following are ineligible to act as a representative before the Board -

(a) any person liable to be detained under the Mental Health Act 1983,

(b) any person serving a sentence of imprisonment,

(c) any person who is on licence having been released under Part III of the Criminal Justice Act 1967 or under Part II of the Criminal Justice 1991 or Part II of the Act.

(d) any person with a previous conviction for an imprisonable offence which remains unspent under the Rehabilitation of Offenders Act 1974.

(3) Within five weeks of the case being listed, a party shall notify the Board and the other party of the name, address and occupation of any person authorised in accordance with paragraph (1).

(4) Where a prisoner does not authorise a person to act as his representative, the Board may, with his agreement, appoint someone to act on his behalf.

(5) A party may apply, in accordance with the procedure set out in rule 7(1) and (2), to be accompanied at the hearing by such other person or persons as he wishes, in addition to any representative he may have authorised; but before granting any such application the Board shall obtain the agreement of -

(a) in the case where the hearing is to be held at a prison, the governor, and

(b) in any other case, the person in whom is vested the authority to agree.

Witnesses

7. (1) Where a party wishes to call witnesses at the hearing, he shall make a written application to the Board, a copy of which he shall serve on the other party, within 12 weeks of the case being listed, giving the name, address and occupation of the witness he wishes to call and the substance of the evidence he proposes to adduce.

(2) The chairman of the panel may grant or refuse an application under paragraph (1) and shall communicate his decision to both parties, giving reasons in writing, in the case of a refusal, for his decision.

Evidence of the prisoner

8. (1) Where the prisoner wishes to make representations about his case, he shall serve them on the Board and the Secretary of State within 15 weeks of the case being listed.

(2) Any other documentary evidence that the prisoner wishes to adduce shall be served on the Board and the Secretary of State at least 14 days before the date of the hearing.

Directions

9. (1) Subject to paragraph (3), the chairman of the panel may give, vary or revoke directions for the conduct of the case, including directions in respect of -

(a) the timetable for the proceedings,

(b) the varying of the time within which or by which an act is required, by these Rules, to be done,

(c) the service of documents,

(d) as regards any documents which have been received by the Board but which have been withheld from the prisoner in accordance with rule 5(2), whether the disclosure of such documents would adversely affect the health or welfare of the prisoner or others, and

(e) the submission of evidence;

and following his appointment under rule 3, the chairman of the panel shall consider whether such directions need to be given at any time.

(2) Within 14 days of being notified of a direction under paragraph (1)(d), either party may appeal against it to the Chairman, who shall notify the other party of the appeal; the other party may make representations on the appeal to the Chairman whose decision shall be final.

(3) Directions under paragraph (1) may be given, varied or revoked either -

(a) of the chairman of the panel's own motion, or

(b) on the written application of a party to the Board which has been served on the other party and which specifies the direction which is sought;

but in either case, both parties shall be given an opportunity to make written representations or, where the chairman of the panel thinks it necessary, and subject to paragraph (6)(b), to make oral submissions at a preliminary hearing fixed in accordance with paragraph (4).

(4) Where the chairman of the panel decides to hold a preliminary hearing, he shall give the parties at least 14 days' notice of the date, time and place which has been fixed in respect thereof

(5) A preliminary hearing shall be held in private and information about the proceedings and the names of any persons concerned in the proceedings shall not be made public.

(6) Except insofar as the chairman of the panel otherwise directs, at a preliminary hearing -

(a) the chairman of the panel shall sit alone, and

(b) the prisoner shall not attend save where he is unrepresented.

(7) The chairman of the panel shall take a note of the giving, variation or revocation of a direction under this rule and serve a copy on the parties as soon as practicable thereafter.

PART III: THE HEARING

Oral hearing
10. (1) Except in so far as both parties and the chairman of the panel agree otherwise, there shall be an oral hearing of the prisoner's case.

(2) The prisoner shall, within five weeks of the case being listed, notify the Board and the Secretary of State whether he wishes to attend the hearing.

Notice of hearing
11. (1) When fixing the date of the hearing the Board shall consult the parties.

(2) The Board shall give the parties at least three weeks notice of the date, time and place scheduled for the hearing or such shorter notice to which the parties may consent.

Location, privacy of proceedings
12. (1) The hearing shall be held at the prison or other institution where the prisoner is detained.

(2) The hearing shall be held in private and, except in so far as the chairman of the panel otherwise directs, information about the proceedings and the names of any persons concerned in the proceedings shall not be made public.

(3) The chairman of the panel may admit to the hearing such persons on such terms and conditions as he considers appropriate.

Hearing procedure
13. (1) At the beginning of the hearing the chairman of the panel shall explain the order of proceeding which the panel proposes to adopt.

(2) Subject to this rule, the panel shall conduct the hearing in such manner as it considers most suitable to the clarification of the issues before it and generally to the just handling of the proceedings; it shall so far as appears to it appropriate, seek to avoid formality in the proceedings.

(3) The parties shall be entitled to appear and be heard at the hearing and take such part in the proceedings as the panel thinks proper; and the parties may hear each other's evidence, put questions to each other, call any witnesses who the Board has authorised to give evidence in accordance with rule 7, and put questions to any witness or other person appearing before the panel.

(4) The chairman of the panel may require any person present at the hearing who is, in his opinion, behaving in a disruptive manner to leave and may permit him to return, if at all, only on such conditions as he may specify.

(5) The panel may receive in evidence any document or information notwithstanding that such document or information would be inadmissible in a court of law but no person shall be compelled to give any evidence or produce any document which he could not be compelled to give or produce on the trial of an action.

(6) The chairman of the panel may require the prisoner, or any witness appearing for the prisoner, to leave the hearing where evidence is being examined which the chairman of the panel, in accordance with rule 9(1)(d) (subject to any successful appeal under rule 9(2)) previously directed should be withheld from the prisoner as being injurious to the health or welfare of the prisoner or another person.

(7) After all the evidence has been given, the prisoner shall be given a further opportunity to address the panel.

Adjournment
14. (1) The panel may at any time adjourn a hearing for the purpose of obtaining further information or for such other purposes as it may think appropriate.

(2) Before adjourning any hearing, the panel may give such directions as it thinks fit for ensuring the prompt consideration of the application at a resumed hearing.

(3) Before the panel resumes any hearing which was adjourned without a further hearing date being fixed it shall give the parties not less that 14 days' notice, or such shorter notice to which all parties may consent, of the date, time and place of the resumed hearing.

The decision
15. (1) Any decision of the majority of the members of the panel shall be the decision of the panel.

(2) The decision by which the panel determines a case shall be recorded in writing with reasons, signed by the chairman of the panel, and communicated in writing to the parties not more than seven days after the end of the hearing.

PART IV: MISCELLANEOUS

Time
16. Where the time prescribed by or under these Rules for doing any act expires on a Saturday, Sunday or public holiday, the act shall be in time if done on the next working day.

Transmission of documents etc.
17. Any document required or authorised by these Rules to be served or otherwise transmitted to any person may be sent by pre-paid post or delivered -
(a) in the case of a document directed to the Board or the chairman of the panel, to the office of the Board;
(b) in any other case, to the last known address of the person to whom the document is directed.

Irregularities
18. Any irregularity resulting from failure to comply with these Rules before the panel has determined a case shall not of itself render the proceedings void, but the panel may, and shall, if it considers that any person may have been prejudiced, take such steps as it thinks fit, before determining the case, to cure the irregularity, whether by the amendment of any document, the giving of any notice, the taking of any step or otherwise.

References to the Board following recall
19. Where the Secretary of State refers a prisoner's case to the Board under section 32(4) of the Act, these Rules shall only apply where the prisoner has made representations under section 32(3) of the Act, and shall apply subject to the following modifications -
(a) rules 5(1), 6(3), 7(1), 8(1) and (2), 9(2) and (4), 10(2), 11(2), 14(3) and 15(2) shall apply as if for references to the periods of time specified therein there were

substituted a reference to such period of time as the chairman of the panel shall in each case determine, taking account of both the desirability of the Board reaching an early decision in the prisoner's case and the need to ensure fairness to the prisoner;
(b) rule 5 shall apply as if for the references in paragraph (l)(a) and (b) of that rule to the information and reports specified in Schedule 1 there were substituted a reference to the information and reports specified in Schedule 2.

Parole Board Rules 1997

SCHEDULE 1   Rule 5(1)

INFORMATION AND REPORTS FOR SUBMISSION TO THE BOARD BY THE SECRETARY OF STATE ON A REFERENCE TO THE BOARD UNDER SECTION 28(6)(a) OR 28(7) OF THE ACT

PART A: INFORMATION RELATING TO THE PRISONER

1. The full name of the prisoner.
2. The age of the prisoner.
3. The prison in which the prisoner is detained and details of other prisons in which the prisoner has been detained, the date and reasons for any transfer.
4. The date the prisoner was sentenced and the details of the offence.
5. The previous convictions and parole history, if any, of the prisoner.
6. The comments, if available, of the trial judge in passing sentence.
7. Where applicable, the conclusions of the Court of Appeal in respect of any appeal by the prisoner against conviction or sentence.
8. The details of any life sentence plan prepared for the prisoner which have previously been disclosed to him.

PART B: REPORTS RELATING TO THE PRISONER

1. Any pre-trial and pre-sentence reports examined by the sentencing court and any post-trial police report on the circumstances of the offence(s)
2. Any report on a prisoner while he was subject to a transfer direction under section 47 of the Mental Health Act 1983
3. Any current reports on the prisoner's performance and behaviour in prison and, where relevant, on his health including any opinions on his suitability for release on licence (reports previously examined by the Board need only be summarised) as well as his compliance with any sentence plan
4. An up-to-date home circumstances report prepared for the Board by a probation officer, including reports on the following:
   (a) details of the home address, family circumstances, and family attitudes towards the prisoner;
   (b) alternative options if the offender cannot return home;
   (c) the opportunity for employment on release;
   (d) the local community's attitude towards the prisoner (if known), including the attitudes and concerns of the victim(s) of the offence(s);
   (e) the prisoner's response to previous periods of suspension;
   (f) the prisoner's behaviour during any temporary leave during the current sentence;
   (g) the prisoner's response to discussions of the objectives of supervision where applicable;
   (h) an assessment of the risk of reoffending;
   (i) a programme of supervision;
   (j) a recommendation for release; and
   (k) recommendations regarding any special licence conditions.

Parole Board Rules 1997

SCHEDULE 2   Rules 5(1) and 19(b)

INFORMATION AND REPORTS FOR SUBMISSION TO THE BOARD BY THE SECRETARY OF STATE ON A REFERENCE TO THE BOARD UNDER SECTION 32(4) OF THE ACT

PART A: INFORMATION RELATING TO THE PRISONER

1. The full name of the prisoner.
2. The age of the prisoner.
3. The prison in which the prisoner is detained and details of other prisons in which the prisoner has been detained, the date and reasons for any transfer.
4. The date the prisoner was sentenced and the details of the offence.
5. The previous convictions and parole history, if any, of the prisoner.
6. The details of any life sentence plan prepared for the prisoner which have previously been disclosed to him.
7. The details of any previous recalls of the prisoner including the reasons for such recalls and subsequent re-release on licence.
8. The statement of reasons for the most recent recall which was given to the prisoner under section 32(3)(b) of the Act.
9. The details of any memorandum which the Board considered prior to making its recommendation for recall under section 32(1) of the Act or confirming the Secretary of State's decision to recall under section 32(2) of the Act, including the reasons why the Secretary of State considered it expedient in the public interest to recall that person before it was practicable to obtain a recommendation from the Board.

PART B: REPORTS RELATING TO THE PRISONER

1. The reports considered by the Board prior to making its recommendation for recall under section 32(1) of the Act or its confirmation of the Secretary of State's decision to recall under section 32(2) of the Act.
2. Any other relevant reports.

Appendix C: Comparisons Between the Mandatory and Discretionary Life Sentence Systems

Tariff/Relevant Part	*Mandatory*	*Discretionary*
Setting	Known as 'tariff'. Set by Home Office Minister after consultation with trial judge or Lord Chief Justice. Prisoner given opportunity to make representations.	Known as 'relevant part'. Set by trial judge in open court. Length of relevant part can be appealed or referred by the Attorney General.
Timing of reviews	First review three years before expiry of tariff. Subsequent reviews as set by Secretary of State taking into account Parole Board's recommendation.	First review three years before expiry of relevant part. Second review by DLP usually after expiry of tariff (or in exceptional cases before). Subsequent reviews at two yearly intervals or earlier if Home Secretary so decides.
Review Procedures	Review by Parole Board panel. Dossier disclosed to prisoner. Interviewed by Parole Board member before panel considers case.	Review by DLP. Dossier disclosed to prisoner.
	Prisoner given opportunity to make written representations, but does not attend panel. Outcome conveyed to prisoner in writing.	Prisoner can attend DLP hearing, be legally represented and call witnesses. Written decision within seven days of hearing.
Recommendations for Transfer to Open Conditions	Decision taken at Ministerial level.	Decision taken at Ministerial level.
Recommendations for Release	Decision taken personally by Home Secretary, following consultation with judiciary.	DLP have power to release.
Recall	Decision taken at Ministerial level following a Parole Board recommendation. If not possible to consult Board, then case referred to them as soon as possible after recall.	Decision taken at Ministerial level following a Parole Board recommendation. If not possible to consult Board, then case referred to them as soon as possible after recall.
Representations Following Recall	Prisoner has right to make representations against recall. Case referred to Parole Board who may recommend immediate release. Such a recommendation is binding on the Home Secretary.	Prisoner has right to make representations against recall. Where he or she does so, case referred to DLP who may direct immediate release.
Review Following Recall	Set by Secretary of State in light of Board's recommendation	Statutory review two years after recall to prison unless Home Secretary decides earlier review appropriate.

Bibliography

Aarvold, Sir C (Chairman) (1993), *Report on the Review of Procedures for the Discharge and Supervision of Psychiatric Patients Subject to Special Restrictions*, Cmnd. 5191, London, HMSO

Advisory Council on the Penal System (1968), *The Regime for Long-Term Prisoners in Conditions of Maximum Security*, London: HMSO

Advisory Council on the Penal System (1978), *Sentences of Imprisonment: A Review of Maximum Penalties*, London: HMSO

Alter, J, Tsuei, C and Chein, D (1997), *Recidivism of Adult Felons*, Office of the Legislative Auditor: St. Paul, Minnesota (658 Cedar Street, MN 55155)

American Psychiatric Association (1974), *Clinical Aspects of the Violent Individual*, APA: Washington, DC

American Psychiatric Association (1994), *Diagnostic and Statistical Manual of Mental Disorders – DSM-IV*, APA: Washington DC

Andrews, D A *et al* (1990), 'Does Correctional Treatment Work? A Clinically Relevant and Psychologically Informed Meta-analysis', *Criminology*, 28, 369-404

Andrew, D A and Bonta, J (1994), *The Psychology of Criminal Conduct*, Cincinnati, Ohio: Anderson

Andrew, D A and Bonta, J (1995), *LSI-R: The Level of Service Inventory-Revised*, Toronto: Multi-Health Systems Inc.

Argyle, M (1978), *The Psychology of Interpersonal Behaviour*, Third Edn., London: Pelican Books

Aust, A (1996), 'A Practitioner View of Risk: A Case Study for Life Licence' in Kempshall H and Pritchard J (Eds.), *Good Practice and Risk Management*, Jessica Kingsley

Baker, K (1993), *The Turbulent Years: My Life in Politics*, London: Faber and Faber

Balzer, A J (1997), Letter to the *Prison Service Journal*, No. 113, September 1997

Blackburn, R (1984), 'The Person and Dangerousness' in Miller, D J, Backman, D F and Chapman, A J (Eds), *Psychology and Law*, Chichester: J Wiley and Sons

Boswell, G (1996), *Young and Dangerous: The Background and Careers of Section 53 Offenders*, Avebury: Aldershot

Bonta, J (1996), 'Risk-Needs Assessment and Treatment' in Harland, A (Ed), *Choosing Correctional Options That Work: Defining the Demand and Evaluating the Supply* (pp. 18-32), Thousand Oaks, Ca: Sage

Boswell G (1996), *Young and Dangerous: The Background and Careers of Section 53 Offenders*, Aldershot: Avebury

Bottomley A K (1986), 'Blueprints for Criminal Justice', *Howard Journal*, 25, 199-215

Bottoms, A E and Brownsword R (1982), 'The Dangerousness Debate After the Foud Report', *British Journal of Criminology*, 22(3), 229-254

Bottoms A E and Brownsword R (1983), 'Dangerousness and Rights' in J W Hinton (Ed.), *Dangerousness: Problems of Assessment and Prediction*, London: Allen and Unwin

Bottoms, A G and Light, R (1986), *Problems of Long-Term Imprisonment*, Cambridge Studies in Criminology, No LVIII

Briggs, E (1995), *Is Risk Assessment a Valid Method of Pedicting Violence in the Lifer Population?*, MSc thesis, Loughborough University, unpublished

Brody S R (1976), *The Effectiveness of Sentencing: A Review of the Literature*, Home Office Research Studies No. 64, London: HMSO

Brody S R and Tarling R (1980), *Taking Offenders Out of Circulation*, Home Office Research Studies No. 64, London: HMSO

Bruce, A, Burgess, E W and Harno, A J (1928), *The Workings of the Indeterminate Sentence: Law and the Parole System in Illinois*

Casey, M, 'Lifers and the SOTP', *Prison Report*, 34, 24

Christoph, J B (1962), *Capital Punishment and British Politics*, London: Allen and Unwin

Clark, D A (1993), 'Risk Assessment: Pilot Study Evaluation', *Inside Psychology: the Journal of Prison Service Psychology*, 1 (2), 16-21

Clark, D A, Fisher, MJ and McDougall, C (1993), 'A New Methodology for Assessing the Level of Risk in Incarcerated Offenders', *British Journal of Criminology*, 33, 436-448

Clark, R V G (1980), 'Situational Crime Prevention: Theory and Practice', *British Journal of Criminology*, 20, 136-147

Clemmer, D (1940), *The Prison Community*, New York: Holt Rhinehart and Winston

Cocozza, J J and Steadman, H J (1978), 'Prediction in Psychiatry: An Example of Misplaced Confidence in Experts', *Social Problems*, 25: 265-276

Cohen, S and Taylor, L (1981), *Psychological Survival: the Experience of Long-Term Imprisonment*, Penguin: London

Coker, J B and Martin, J P (1985), *Licensed to Live*, Oxford: Blackwell

Conlin, G (1990), *Proved Innocent*, London: Hamilton

Cooke, D J and Michie, C (1996), *Recidivism of a Scottish Prison Sample*, SHHD

Cooke, D J (1997), 'Barlinnie Special Unit: The Rise and Fall of a Therapeutic Experiment' in *Therapeutic Communities for Offenders*, Cullen, J E, Jones, L E and Woodward, R, Chichester: John Wiley and Sons

Cooper, R and Werner, P D (1990), 'Predicting Violence in Newly Admitted Inmates', *Criminal Justice and Behaviour*, 17, 431-447

Council of Europe (1984), *Results of the Enquiry into Policy and Practice Concerning Life Sentences*, Council of Europe

Cressey, D (1961), *The Prison: Studies in Institutional Organization and Change*, New York: Holt, Rhinehart and Winston

Cullen, J E (1993), *Life Imprisonment and Prison Regime Stability*, doctorate thesis, The Open University: Milton Keynes, unpublished

Cullen, J E, Jones, L J and Woodward, R (Eds.) (1997), *Therapeutic Communities for Offenders*, Chichester: John Wiley and Sons

Currie, E (1998), *Crime and Punishment in America*, New York: Metropolitan Books/Henry Holt and Company

Dershowitz, A (1969), 'The Psychiatrist's Power In Civil Commitment: A Knife That Cuts Both Ways', *Psychology Today*, February, 47

Ditchfield, J (1997), 'Actuarial Prediction and Risk Assessment', *Prison Service Journal*, No. 113, September 1997

Doherr, E (1996), *Ensuring the Integrity of the Risk Assessment Process at HMP Gartree: Threats, Explanations and Recommendations*, MSc Thesis, Leicester University, unpublished

Farrington, D P (1978), 'The Family Backgrounds of Aggressive Youths' in Henor, L, Berger, M and Schaffet, D (Eds.), *Aggression and Antisocial Disorder in Children*, Oxford: Pergamon

Farrington, D P and Tarling, R (1985), 'Criminological Prediction: An Introduction' in *Predictions in Criminology*, Farrington and Tarling (Eds.), State University of New York Press

Flanagan, T J (1980), 'The Pains of Long-term Imprisonment: A Comparison of British and American Perspectives', *British Journal of Criminology*, 20, 148-156

Flanagan, T J (1995) *Long-Term Imprisonment: Policy, Science and Correctional Practice*, London: Allen Lane

Foot, P (1986), *Murder at the Farm: Who Killed Carl Bridgewater?*, Harmondsworth: Penguin

Foucault, M (1977), *Discipline and Punish: The Birth of the Prison*

Garrett, C J (1986), Effects of Residential Treatment on Adjudicated Delinquents: A Meta-Analysis, *Journal of Research in Crime and Delinquency*, 22, 287-308

Genders, E and Player, E (1988), 'Women Lifers: Assessing the Experience' in Morris A and Wilkinson C (Eds.), *Women and the Penal System*, Cropwood Conference Series No 19, University of Cambridge Institute of Criminology

Gendreau, P and Ross, R R (1987), 'Revivification of Rehabilitation: Evidence from the 80s', *Justice Quarterly*, 4, 349-407

Gendreau, P and Ross, R R (1990), Effective Correctional Treatment: Bibliography for Cynics in Gendreau, P and Ross, R R (Eds), *Effective Correctional Treatment*, Toronto: Buterfields

Gendreau, P, Goggin, C and Little, T (1996), *Predicting Adult Offender Recidivism: What Works*, Public Works and Government Services, Canada

Gleuck, S. and Gleuck, E T (1930), *Five Hundred Criminal Careers*, New York: Alfred Knopf

Goffman, E (1961), Asylums, Harmondsworth: Penguin

Gottschalk, R, Davidson, W S, Mayer, J P and Gensheimer, L K (1987), 'Behavioural Approaches With Juvenile Offenders: A Meta-Analysis of Long-Term Treatment Efficacy' in E K Morris and C J Braukmann (Eds.), *Behavioural Approaches to Crime and Delinquency: A Handbook of Application, Research and Concepts*, New York: Plenum Press

Greenland, C (1980), 'Psychiatry and the Prediction of Dangerousness', *Psychatric Treatment and Evaluation*, 2: 97-103

Gunn, J et al (1991), *Mentally Disordered Prisoners*, Home Office

Guy, E (1992), 'The Prison Service's Strategy', in *The Penal Response to Sex Offending*, London: Prison Reform Trust

Harris, G T, Rice, M E and Cormier, C A (1991), 'Psychopathy and Violent Recidivism', *Law and Human Behaviour*, 15, 625-637

Harris, G T; Rice, M E and Quincey, V L (1993), 'Violent Recidivism of Mentally Disordered Offenders: The Development of a Statistical Prediction Instrument', *Criminal Justice and Behaviour*, 20, 315-335

Hawkins, G (1976), *The Prison: Policy and Practice*, Chicago University Press

Holmes, R M and Holmes, S T (1994), *Murder in America*, Sage: Thousand Oaks, London, New Delhi

Home Office (1973), *Report of the Working Party on Dispersal and Control*

Home Office (1982), Circular Instruction No 1, 'Prisoners Serving Life Sentences'

Home Office (1984), Circular Instruction No 55, 'Throughcare and Supervision of Life Sentenced Prisoners'

Home Office (1989), Circular Instruction No 2, 'Life Sentence Prisoners: Procedures for the Management, Documentation and Review, and for the Eventual Release of Life Sentenced Prisoners'

Honderich, T (1976), *Punishment: The Supposed Justifications*, Harmondsworth: Penguin Books

Jason-Lloyd, L (1992), *Criminal Justice Act 1991*, Huntingdon: ELM Publications

Jones, K and Fowles A J (1984), Ideas on Institutions: Analysing the Literature on Long-term Care and Custody, London: Routledge and Keegan Paul

Kahnemann, D and Tversky, A (1973), 'On the Psychology of Prediction', *Psychological Review*, 80: 223-251

Kelly, C (1994) 'A Comparison of the Risk Assessment Process at the Three Main Lifer Centres', MSc Thesis, Birkbeck College, London University, unpublished

Kershaw, C, Dowdeswell, P and Goodman, J (1997), 'Life Licensees – Reconvictions and Recalls by the end of 1995: England and Wales', *Home Office Statistical Bulletin*, 29 January 1997

King, R and Elliott D (1978), *Albany: Birth of a Prison – End of and Era*, London: Routledge, and Keegan Paul

Lane, Lord (Chair) (1993), *Report of a Committee on the Penalty for Homicide*, Prison Reform Trust

Lawrence, P G (1998), 'The Prediction of Future Dangerousness in Prison For Capital Murder Defendants', Internet communication, Skyview Psychiatric Facility, Rusk, Texas: Texas Department of Criminal Justice-Institutional Division

Laycock, G (1979), 'Bahaviour Modification in Prisons', *British Journal of Criminology*, 19, 400-415

Lewis, D E (1986), 'The General Detterent Effect of Longer Sentences', *British Journal of Criminology*, 26, 47-61

Lipsey, M W (1992), 'Juvenile Delinquency Treatment: A Meta-analytic Inquiry into the Variability of Effects' in T Cook *et al* (Eds), *Meta-analysis for Explanation: A Casebook*, Russell Sage Foundation: New York

Losel, F (1993), 'The Effectiveness of Treatment in Institutional and Community Settings', *Criminal Behaviour and Mental Health*, 3, 416-437

Lipton, D (1998), Paper presented to a conference on Psychology and Law, York University

Luckenbill, D F and Doyle, D P (1989) 'Structural Position and Violence: Developing a Cultural Explanation', *Criminology*. 27, 3

Maguire, M, Vagg, J and Morgan R (1985), *Accountability in Prisons: Opening Up a Closed World*, London: Tavistock Press

McConville, S (1981), *A History of English Prison Administration*, Vol. 1, London: Routledge and Kegan Paul

McDougall, C, Clark, D A and Woodward, R (1995), 'Application of Operational Psychology to Assessment of Inmates', *Psychology, Crime and Law*, Vol. 2, 85-99

McGeorge, N (1990), *A Fair Deal for Lifers*, Quaker Council for European Affairs

McGeorge, N (1995), 'Lifer Imprisonment', *Criminal Justice*, Vol. 13, 2

McGuire, J (1995), *What Works: Reducing Reoffending: Guidelines for Research and Practice*, Chichester: J Wiley and Sons

McGurk, J J (1978), 'Personality Types Among 'Normal' Homicides', *British Journal of Criminology*, 18, 146-161

Meehl, P and Rosen, A (1955), 'Antecedent Probability and the Efficacy of Psychometric Signs, Pattern or Cutting Scores', *Psychological Bulletin*, 52: 194-246

Megargee, E I (1981), 'Methodological Problems in the Prediction of Violence' in Hays, J R, Roberts, T K and Solway, K S (Eds.), *Violence and the Violent Individual*, New York: Spectrum

Menzies, R and Webster, C D (1995), 'Construction and Validation of Risk Assessments in a Six-year Follow-up of Forensic Patients: A Longitudinal Analysis', *Journal of Consulting and Clinical Psychology*, 63(5), 766-778

Miscel, W (1968), *Personality and Assessment*, New York: John Wiley and Sons

Miscel, W (1977), 'The Interaction of Person and Situation' in Magnossan, D and Endler, N S (Eds.), *Personality at a Crossroads*, Hillsdale, New Jersey: Lawrence Erlbaum

Monahan, J (1981), *Predicting Violent Behavior: An Assessment of Clinical Techniques*, Beverley Hills, Ca: Sage

Monahan, J and Steadman, H J (1994), *Violence and Mental Disorder*, University of Chicago Press: Chicago

Montano, G and Harding, T (1984), 'The Reliability of Dangerousness Assessments: A Decision-Making Exercise', *British Journal of Psychiatry*, 144: 149-155

Morris, T (1976), *Deviance and Control: The Secular Heresy*, London: Hutchinson and Co

Morris T (1977), 'Unprecedented Ferocity: The Lessons of Hull', *New Society*, July 28

Morrissey, C (1994), 'Groupwork with Life Sentence Prisoners', Occasional Paper No. 23, Division of Criminological and Legal Psychology, The British Psychological Society

Mowbray, A (1993), 'Life Prisoners and Parole: The Home Secretary's Duty, *Journal of Forensic Psychiatry*, Vol. 4, No. 1, 132-134

Mullin, C (1990), *Error of Judgment*, London: Chatto and Windus

Munro, M and Macpherson, G J (1998), 'Risk Assessment: Development of the OBS', *Forensic Update*, Issue 53, Division of Criminological Psychology, British Psychological Society, April, 1998

NACRO (1991), 'The Penalty for Murder, The Case for Amending the Criminal Justice Bill to Make the Life Sentence the Maximum, Rather than the Mandatory Sentence for Murder', London: NACRO

NACRO (1991), 'Life Sentence Prisoners', NACRO Briefing

NACRO (1995), 'Life Sentence Prisoners', NACRO Briefing

Needs, A and Towl, G (1997), 'Reflections on Clinical Assessments with Lifers', *Prison Service Journal*, No 117

Olweus, D (1980), 'The Consistency Issue in Personality Psychology Revisited With Special Reference to Aggression', *British Journal of Social and Clinical Psychology*, Vol. 119: 377-390

Parker, T (1995), *The Violence of Our Lives: Interviews with Life Sentence Prisoners in America*, Harper Collins: London

Parliamentary All-Party Penal Affairs Group (1986), *Life-sentence Prisoners*, Chichester: Barry Rose

Penal Affairs Consortium (1994), *The Mandatory Life Sentence*, PAC: London

Prins, H (1986), *Dangerous Behaviour: The Law and Mental Disorder*, London: Tavistock Press

Prison Disturbances April 1990: Report of An Inquiry (1991), London: HMSO

Prison Reform Trust (1993), *Report of the Committee on the Penalty for Homicide* Prison Reform Trust: London

Prisoners Information Handbook: Questions and Answers About Your Time In Prison (1996), London: HM Prison Service/ Prison Reform Trust

Radzinowicz L and Hood R G (1986), *A History of English Criminal Law, Volume 5, The Emergence of Penal Policy*, London: Stevens

Reiner, R (1988), *British Criminology and the State*, British Journal of Criminology, 28, 138-157

Restorative Justice Group (1995), *Repairing the Harm: Friends and Restorative Justice*, Religious Society of Friends (Quakers)

Richars, B (1978), 'The Experience of Long-term Imprisonment', *British Journal of Criminology*, 18, 162-169

Rock, P (1988), *A View from the Shadows*, Oxford: Clarendon Press

Rose, D (1996), *In The Name of the Law: The Collapse of Criminal Justice*, London: Vintage

Rose, J, Panter, S and Wilkinson, T (1997), *Innocents: How Justice Failed Stefan Kisko and Lesley Molseed*, London: Fourth Estate

Sapsford, R (1993), *Life-sentence Prisoners: Reaction, Response and Change*, The Open University Press: Milton Keynes

Sapsford, R (1983), 'Indeterminacy: Memorandum to the House of Lords Committee on Murder and Life Imprisonment'

Sepejak, D S, Menzies, R J, Webster, C D and Jenkins, F A S (1983), 'Clinical Predictions of Dangerousness: Two-Year Follow-Up of 408 Pre-Trial Forensic Cases', *Bulletin of the American Academy of Psychiatry and the Law*, 11, 171-181

Shapland, J, Wilmore, J and Duff P (1985), *Victims of the Criminal Justice System*, Aldershot: Gower

Smart, C (1977), *Women, Crime and Criminology*, London: Routledge and Keegan Paul

Smith, D (Ed.) (1979), 'Life Sentence Prisoners', *Home Office Research Study No. 51*, HMSO: London

Staples, J (1981), 'The Management of Life Sentence Prisoners', *Prison Service Journal*, 42, 4-8

Steadman, J J and Cocozza, J J (1984), *Careers of the Criminally Insane: Excessive Social Control of Deviance*, Lexington, Mass: Lexington Medical and Scientific Books

Stern, V (1987), *Bricks of Shame: Britain's Prisons*, Harmondsworth: Penguin Books

Stone, A A (1984), 'The New Legal Standard of Dangerousness: Fair in Theory, Unfair in Practice' in Webster, C D, Ben-Aron, M H and Hucker, S J (Eds.), *Dangerousness: Probability and Prediction, Psychiatry and Public Policy*, New York: Cambridge University Press

Stone, N (1997), *A Comparian Guide to Life Sentences*, Ilkley, West Yorks: Owen Wells

Swinton, M, Maden, A and Gunn, J (1994), Psychiatric Disorder in Life-Sentence Prisoners, *Criminal Behaviour and Mental Health*, 4, 10-20

Sykes, G (1958), *The Society of Captives*, Princeton N J: Princeton University Press

Taylor I, Walton P and Young J (1973), *The New Criminology*, London: Routledge and Keegan Paul

Taylor, M A (1982), *Community, Anarchy and Liberty*, Cambridge: Cambridge University Press

Taylor, P J (1986), 'Psychiatric Disorder in London's Life Sentence Offenders, *British Journal of Criminology*, 26, 63-69

Thomas J E and Pooley R (1980), *The Exploding Prison*, London: Junction Books

Toch, H (1977), *Living in Prison: The Ecology of Survival*, MacMillan Press: New York

Thornton, D (1987), 'Treatment Effects on Recidivism: A Reappraisal of the "Nothing Works" Doctrine' in B J McGurk, D M Thornton and M Williams (Eds.), *Applying Psychology to Imprisonment*, HMSO: London

Thornberry, T P and Jacoby, J E (1979), *The Criminally Insane: A Community Follow-Up of Mentally Ill Offenders*, Chicago, Ill: University of Chicago Press

Toby (1974), Foreword to Steadman, H J and Cocozza, JJ, *Careers of the Criminally Insane: Excessive Social Control of Deviance*, Lexington, Mass: Lexington Medical and Scientific Books

Towl, G, and Crighton D (1995), 'Risk Assessment in Prisons: A Psychological Critique', *Forensic Update*, Issue 40 Division of Criminological and Legal Psychology, British Psychological Society, January

Trasler, G (1962), *The Explanation of Criminality*, London: Routledge and Keegan Paul

United Nations (1995), *Life Imprisonment*, New York: United Nations

Walker, C and Starmer, K (1993), *Justice in Error*, London: Blackstone

Walker, N (1980), *Punishment, Danger and Stigma: The Morality of Criminal Justice*, Oxford: Basil Blackwell

Walker, N (1993), 'Side-effects of Incarceration', *British Journal of Criminology*, 23, 1, 71-73

Walker, N (Ed.) (1996), *Dangerous People*, London: Blackstone

Walker, N (1996), 'Ethical and Other Problems' in *Dangerous People*, Walker, N (Ed), London: Blackstone Press

Webster, C D, Harris, G T, Rice, M E, Cormier, C and Quinsey, V L (1994), *The Violence Prediction Scheme: Assessing Dangerousness in High Risk Men*, Centre of Criminology: Toronto

West, D J (1982), *Delinquency: It's Roots, Careers and Prospects*, London: Heineman

Whatton, H (1994), 'The Practice of Risk Assessment at HMP Gartree', Applied Psychology Division, Aston University, unpublished

Wheatley, P (1981), 'Riots and Serious Mass Disorder', *Prison Service Journal*

Wilson, A V (Ed.) (1993), *Homicide: The Victim/Offender Connection*, Cincinatti: Anderson Publishing Co.

Wilson, D and Bryans, S (1998), *The Prison Governor: Theory and Practice*, Leyhill: Prison Service Journal

Wolfgang, M (1958), *Patterns of Criminal Homicide*, Philadelphia: University of Pennsylvania Press

Wolfgang, M E and Ferracutti, F (1967), *The Subculture of Violence*, Tavistock: London

Wormith, J S (1984), 'The Controversy Over the Effects of Long-term Incarceration', *Criminology*, 22, 423-437

Wright, J (1991), *Journal of Forensic Psychiatry*, Vol. 2, No. 1, 8-9

Zamble, E and Porporino, F (1988), *Coping, Behavior and Adaptation in Prison Inmates*, New York: Springer

Zamble, E and Porporino, F (1990), 'Coping, Imprisonment and Rehabilitation', *Criminal Justice and Behaviour*, 17(1), 53-70.

Subject Index

Murder (continued)
numbers, UK and US, 11-12
Murderers
descriptions, 12, 14
the psychology of, 32-41
relationship to victim, 13-14

'Natural life', 163-164
Novaco assessment model for
violent behaviour, 39

Parole Board, 20-21, 124
Pre-Release Employment Scheme (PRES), 26
Prison Reform Trust, 56
Prison Service, HM
attitude to innocence or guilt, 60-64
management of lifers, 95-96
Offending Behaviour Programme Unit, 99-102
policies for lifers, 18-19
Probation,
role and responsibilities, 96-98
Psychopathy, 34
checklist, 151
Public safety, proposals 167

Quaker Council for European Affairs,
survey, 19-20

Retribution, 157-158
Risk Assessment,
actuarial, 141
clinical, 140
description, 136-137
need for, 137-140
static and dynamic factors, 142
Prison Service model, 144-150
CLASP (model for lifers), 150
Risk, proposals, 167-168
Royal Commission, 1959, 17-18
Rule 43, 75
good order and discipline, 75
own protection, 75

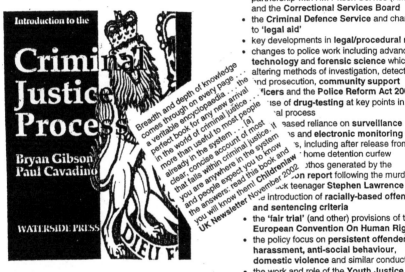

Also from Waterside Press

Grendon Tales

STORIES FROM A THERAPEUTIC COMMUNITY

Ursula Smartt

For anyone wishing to understand what 'drives' some people to commit serious and sometimes unspeakable crimes – and what is achievable through therapy - the first-hand 'tales' in this book merit close study.

For over 40 years Grendon Prison and its therapuetic communities of high security 'residents' has remained unique among Britain's prisons. Researcher Ursula Smartt was given extensive access to interview residents and prison staff – governors, prison officers, therapists and probation officers – and to observe their day-to-day routines. The result is *Grendon Tales,* a fascinating, perceptive and at times shocking account of life inside this unique and world famous establishment. Grendon houses many dangerous, disturbed and disruptive criminals (from armed robbers to paedophiles, to rapists and murderers). For many it is 'the last chance saloon' – a final opportunity to alter their thinking patterns and behaviour and maybe to convince the authorities that their security category should be downgraded with a view to future safe release back into the community.

Even now, the approach remains unique - as can be seen from comparisons in the book with Europe and another therapeutic regime which started in 2001 at the privately managed prison, HMP Dovegate.

With a Foreword by Lord Avebury

From the reviews:

'A breathless personal slide through her year talking to some of Britain's most dangerous prisoners': *Community Care.* 'A work of intimacy and frankness . . . Concrete evidence that therapy does help expose the failures of the past whilst offering hope for the future': *Prison Service News.* 'As readable as a novel . . . I could not put it down until finished': *The Magistrate.* 'The tales are recounted in a style which allows the reader to read in colour . . . A tale well told and worth reading': *RPGA Newsletter.* 'Indispensible reading . . . for practitioners and policy-makers alike': *Scolag Legal Journal.* 'Several books have already been published about Grendon but none with the depth of understanding that this author brings to Grendon Tales . . . Uplifting . . . A book that deserves a wide readership': *New Law Journal.* As featured on BBC Radio 4

ISBN 1 872 870 96 1 **£18** (plus £2.50 p&p).

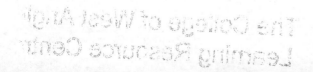